Perspectives on E. M. Forster's *A Passage to India*

A Collection of Critical Essays

Professor Shahane has also written

E. M. Forster—A Reassessment (1962)

Perspectives on E. M. Forster's *A Passage to India*

A Collection of Critical Essays

Edited and with an introduction
by V. A. Shahane

Barnes & Noble, Inc. New York
Booksellers & Publishers Since 1873

L. C. Catalogue Card Number: 68–20661

Printed in the United States of America

TO

THE MEMORY OF MY FATHER

Acknowledgments

The Editor and Publisher make grateful acknowledgment to the following for permission to reproduce copyright material:

Glen O. Allen, *Structure, Symbol, and Theme in E. M. Forster's* A Passage to India (New York, *PMLA,* December 1955), LXX, pp. 934–954. Copyright © 1955 by The Modern Language Association of America.

Ted E. Boyle, *Adela Quested's Delusion: The Failure of Rationalism in* A Passage to India (Champaign, Ill., *College English,* March 1965), XXVI, 6, pp. 478–480. Copyright © by The National Council of Teachers of English.

Nirad C. Chaudhuri, *Passage to and from India* (London, *Encounter,* June 1954), pp. 19–24. Copyright © 1954 by Encounter, Ltd.

Louise Dauner, *What Happened in the Cave? Reflections on* A Passage to India (Lafayette, Ind., *Modern Fiction Studies,* Autumn 1961), VII, 3, pp. 258–270. Copyright © 1961 by Purdue Research Foundation.

K. W. Gransden, "The Last Movement of the Symphony," *E. M. Forster,* Writers and Critics Ser. (Edinburgh, 1962), pp. 101–106. Copyright © 1962 by Oliver and Boyd Ltd.

Keith Hollingsworth, A Passage to India: *The Echoes in the Marabar Caves* (Detroit, Mich., *Criticism: A Quarterly,* Summer 1962), IV, 3, pp. 210–224. Copyright © 1962 by Wayne State University Press.

Hugh Maclean, *The Structure of* A Passage to India (Toronto, *University of Toronto Quarterly,* January 1953), XXII, 2, pp. 157–171. Copyright © 1953 by the University of Toronto Press.

James McConkey, "The Prophetic Novel: *A Passage to India,*" *The Novels of E. M. Forster* (Ithaca, N.Y., 1957), pp. 80–93. Copyright © 1957 by Cornell University Press.

Edwin Nierenberg, *The Withered Priestess: Mrs. Moore's Incomplete Passage to India* (New York, *Modern Language Quarterly,* 1964), XXV, 2, pp. 198–204. Copyright © 1964 by the *Modern Language Quarterly.*

Benita Parry, "Passage to More Than India," *Forster: A Collection of Critical Essays,* ed. Malcolm Bradbury (Englewood Cliffs, N.J., Prentice-Hall, Inc., 1966), pp. 160–174. Copyright © 1966 by Benita Parry.

V. A. Shahane, *Symbolism in* A Passage to India: *'Temple'* (Groningen (Holland), *English Studies,* December 1963), XLIV, 6, pp. 423–431. Copyright © 1963 by *English Studies.*

David Shusterman, *The Curious Case of Professor Godbole:* A Passage to India *Re-Examined* (New York, *PMLA,* September 1961), LXXVI, 4(1), pp. 426–435. Copyright © 1961 by The Modern Language Association of America.

George Thomson, *Thematic Symbol in* A Passage to India (Denver, Colo., *Twentieth Century Literature,* July 1961), 7(2), pp. 51–63; reprinted in *The Fiction of E. M. Forster* (Detroit, Mich., Wayne State University Press, 1967). Copyright © 1961 by *Twentieth Century Literature;* copyright © 1967 by Wayne State University Press.

Gertrude White, A Passage to India: *Analysis and Revaluation* (New York, *PMLA,* September 1953), LXVIII, 4, pp. 641–657. Copyright © 1953 by The Modern Language Association of America.

Contents

Introduction

Since its publication in 1924 *A Passage to India* has earned the admiration of the intelligentsia and attracted the attention of a very wide reading public in the English-speaking world and also become an object of considerable critical comment. In view of this widespread response and recognition, a critic may confidently claim that *A Passage to India* has now become a modern classic. But this position of acknowledged greatness, achieved in a little over four decades, should not lead anyone to complacently assume that the novel has not passed through radical differences of critical judgment and changes in the climate of political opinion in England and elsewhere.

A Passage to India, like many other great novels, strikes a variety of chords in the readers' minds and evokes responses at different and varying levels of sensibility. As a human document, a great work of art, an artistic testament of the liberal creed, a metaphysical novel, a western agnostic's passage to the unfamiliar East, it creates a variety of response and encourages multi-faceted approaches which themselves emerge from different types and kinds of sensibility and sense of values. Academic critics and casual commentators, Liberals and Tories, traditionalists and innovators quite often wrote admiringly, but sometimes adversely, about Forster's *A Passage to India,* its intriguing involvement with religion and race relations and its complicated levels of meaning.

I

In its critical phase, soon after its publication, *A Passage to India* was primarily considered a sociological expression of contrasted cultural relations and, consequently, its political and social implications were particularly emphasized. Whereas the initial liberal reaction to this great novel was one of enthusiastic admiration, Tory and Anglo-Indian responses were of protest, anger, and sometimes even of indifference verging on scorn. The contemporary controversies and reviews in newspapers and periodicals reflect these attitudes amply and even sharply. The novel was considered by some as an expression of British liberalism in its approach to the problems of dependent India and race relations. A then contemporary reviewer, Isabel Paterson observed:

> Mr. Forster turns an X-ray on the thick complacent inert mind of British Officialdom and the result is truly a devastating novel, a complete exposure of the super-Babbittry of Imperialism.[1]

Whereas Isabel Paterson concentrated on Forster's exposure of British or Anglo-Indian Officialdom in India, Nihal Singh, an Indian commentator, wrote on the novelist's exposure of the Indians, suggesting Forster's equipoise in choosing his objects of irony:

> Not that it refrains from showing up the weak traits in the Indian character. On the contrary, it gives the impression that there is no such thing as an Indian, for the Muslim disdains the Hindu and is in turn hated by the Hindu and Hindus and Muslims alike are slack, prevaricating, not quite honest, unreliable, sexually loose—in a word, inefficient from every point of view. The author is, however, not content with such an exposure but mercilessly tears away the gaudy vestments and gew-gaws which Anglo-Indians or "Europeans" as they prefer to call themselves have draped about themselves and displays a sight which will revolt some persons, shame others and enrage still others.[2]

Forster criticism has advanced greatly from the position Nihal Singh assumed in his remarks, yet Singh clearly reflected the mood of his time and his remarks are interesting in a historical context. One of his contemporaries, Ralph Wright, approached the novel from a sociological point of view as an expression of the problem of race relations:

> In *A Passage to India* he has chosen a subject of enormous difficulty. Race feeling or the violent reaction from what seems like intolerable race feeling of our own fellows, is strong in everyone of us. It is almost impossible to start a conversation on India, at dinner or in a railway carriage, even in this country, without producing a heated quarrel. For in the case of India there is much more than even race feeling, which is strong enough to disturb us. There is our behaviour to a conquered country. There is a ticklish question of conscience.[3]

However, Ralph Wright's liberal approval of the portrayal of Anglo-Indians in *A Passage to India* brought forth a sharp rejoinder from E. A. Horne who wished to convey "how the book strikes an Anglo-Indian—a task for which I claim to possess qualifications, having spent the last fourteen years of my life in Chandrapore (Patna) itself." E. A. Horne, with his credentials thus secure, entered the fray with a strong note of protest against Forster's depiction of Anglo-Indians:

[1] Isabel Paterson, Review of *A Passage to India, The Bookman* (New York, December 1924), p. 495.

[2] Nihal Singh, "Indians and Anglo-Indians as portrayed to Britons by British Novelists," *The Modern Review* (Calcutta, September 1924), p. 251.

[3] Ralph Wright, *The New Statesman and Nation* (London, June 21, 1924), p. 317.

> . . . But the Anglo-Indians? Where have they come from? What planet do they inhabit? One rubs one's eyes. They are not even good caricatures, for an artist must see his original clearly before he can successfully caricature it. They are puppets.[4]

E. A. Horne's anger was shared by the British bureaucracy in India. Forster, too, was deeply conscious of such attitudes as is revealed in his description of a meeting between the Viceroy of India, Lord Reading and H.H. the Maharajah of Dewas State Senior in Delhi:

> Another time he [H.H.] got some amusement out of *A Passage to India*. He dined at the Viceregal Lodge at Delhi soon after it had been published, and found that it was ill thought of there. Lady Reading did not care for it at all, and the newly appointed Indian member of Council expressed himself severely.[5]

It is clear that the British ruling class in India disapproved of the novel for the very reasons which made it such an important document of liberalism at home in England. It is in this context that Nirad C. Chaudhuri's comments in "Passage to and from India" assume special significance and represent the conservative Indian view of the novel. However the idealistic British intellectual, on his way to India, continued to read and to like the novel as an admirable introduction to that mysterious subcontinent.

With Lionel Trilling's *E. M. Forster—A Study* (1943), critical emphasis shifted from political liberalism to a literary and thematic interpretation, and the artistic as well as the moral aspects of Forster's art were presented in a balanced perspective. This view was an expression of critical equilibrium since Trilling knew that Forster was within the liberal sphere as well as outside it. "For he stands," wrote Trilling "in a peculiar relation to what, for want of a better word, we may call the liberal tradition, that loose body of middle class opinion which includes such ideas as progress, collectivism and humanitarianism. To this tradition Forster has long been committed—all his novels are politically and morally tendentious and always in the liberal direction. Yet he is deeply at odds with the liberal mind, and while liberal readers can go a long way with Forster, they can seldom go all the way." It is true that liberalism cannot come to terms with good-and-evil, which is an essential element in Forster's fiction. Yet Trilling's criticisms, though brilliant in their own way, were still only the beginnings of the major concentrated analyses which came in the wake of two Forster revivals. The first of these revivals started around 1945, but did not strike the philosophical and metaphysical depths reached by the

[4] Letter from E. A. Horne, I.E.S. (Patna, India), *The New Statesman and Nation* (London, August 16, 1924), p. 543.

[5] E. M. Forster, *The Hill of Devi* (London, 1953), p. 160.

second Forster revival which has commenced and grown in the last decade and which is still in progress, traversing unexplored fields. Both these revivals point up the many intangibles in Forster's artistic cosmos and moral universe which appeal to war-torn generations and excite and mystify the intellectual today.

II

"There is something baffling and evasive in the very nature of Forster's gifts" wrote Virginia Woolf in 1942. Whereas many critics in earlier years found Forster "baffling" (I. A. Richards), the later critics found him "difficult to pin down in words" (Arnold Kettle). It is precisely this "elusive" and "exciting" quality of Forster's mind and art which elicits the growing amplitude of concentrated criticism. Every new reading of Forster, wrote Trilling in 1943, gives new sensations, fresh insights, and a novel nuance to an earlier experience of having come to terms with the novelist.

This is perhaps more true of *A Passage to India* than Forster's other works since most readers and almost all critics have come to think of it as the apex of Forster's literary achievement: thus it is in *A Passage to India* that Forster has found his own path from the finite to the infinite, from the real to the visionary, from England and Europe—the locales of his earlier novels—to India and the East—these unfamiliar horizons which challenged his imagination and sensibility; and it is in this truly great work that he has offered his considered comment on the complexities of life.

Although Forster was respected even at the outset of his career as a cultured humanist, a keen, sensitive, and subtle artist and although his mature poise was acknowledged (his "maturity was innate" wrote Elizabeth Bowen in an essay subsequently included in her *Collected Impressions*), yet there seems to me a clear and substantial difference between the quality of Forster's earlier achievement and that of a later masterpiece like *A Passage to India.* Forster's earlier novels present the English and the Italian scene and revolve round a central pattern of theme and symbol. The themes of the earlier novels, Sawston-Italy, Sawston-Cambridge are undoubtedly treated with penetrating skill and great charm but their canvas is limited, whereas, in *A Passage to India* Forster's themes find greater amplitude and a subtler depth.

The rising curve of Forster's literary reputation is truly remarkable. I. A. Richards wrote in 1927 that the English intellectuals, quite impressed by Forster's subtle portrayal of the moral dilemmas of the British middle class, complacently assumed that they alone had real access to the genuine understanding of Forster's work and his special "assumptions," and it was precisely for this reason that his reputation in the earlier years was limited to a rather small sophisticated, academic, and exclusive circle. I. A. Richards wrote:

> When with *A Passage to India* he burst into public notice, many of his admirers undoubtedly felt an obscure grievance. Unconsciously they had allowed their admiration to take on a snobbish tinge.[6]

The publication of *A Passage to India* changed the complexion of the intellectuals' response to E. M. Forster. They believed that the work gave a new dimension to the personality of this "essentially Edwardian" novelist, and that it marked a new beginning and an almost abrupt "end" in Forster's literary career. It surely broke new ground since Forster's men and women, creations of the Edwardian ethos, enter a strange land, are exposed to an unfamiliar tropical sky and, while seeking fulfillment and fruition, are confronted with new facets of the mystery and muddle of life.

A Passage to India, though different in many ways from Forster's first four novels, is a continuation in a new setting of the theme and values which sustain his earlier work. *Howards End* lacks the mature artistry of *A Passage to India* partly because of its weak symbolic framework. Though Trilling believed that *Howards End* was a work of "full responsibility and maturity," its weaknesses have been observed by other critics and perceptively analyzed. *Howards End,* it must be said, is free from Forster's later skepticism which hangs like a shadow over *A Passage to India.* Yet there is a close relationship between *Howards End* and *A Passage to India,* though the Wilcoxes abroad are very different from the Wilcoxes at home. Forster aimed at connecting, through the interaction of the Wilcoxes and Schlegels, the "outer life" of "telegrams and anger" with the "inner life" of personal relations. Forster while showing the adequacy as well as the inadequacy of the Schlegels points out that despite their strength the world entirely peopled by the Schlegels would be "a bloodless, grey place" and that the values they represent are complementary to those embodied in the Wilcoxes. Whereas the Wilcoxes realize the value of the material life and lack spiritual insight, the Schlegels concentrate on the life of the spirit without comprehending the truth that the spirit cannot grow in a vacuum, devoid of the value of the material. To connect the Wilcoxian valuation with the Schlegelian outlook on life is the essence of Forster's search for a synthesis. "To connect" are the two key words which are at the very heart of Forster's portrayal of this world and the world beyond. It is a magic phrase (one might call it a *mantra*) which animates and penetrates all the layers of Forster's presentation of character and incident; "people" and "prophecy"; down-to-earth worldliness and visionary other worldliness.

[6] I. A. Richards, "A Passage to Forster—Reflections on a Novelist," *The Forum* (New York, December 1927), p. 915.

III

There is a distinct change in the critical assessment of Forster's fiction since the twenties and thirties. The criticism of Forster in the thirties was focused mostly on his art, technique, treatment of the social comedy, irony, and skill of presentation. Elizabeth Drew in 1926 paid a tribute to Forster's "most acute observation of the conversational inanities, the emotional delusions of these human creatures . . . in *A Passage to India*." Catholics like Montgomery Belgion (1934), and J. D. C. Pellow (1940) acknowledged Forster's rich talent, yet felt that his constant mockery of bishops and the clergy "leaves a smell of brimstone behind it." To Marxists like D. S. Savage the very subject matter of Forster's fiction, the moneyed middle class, appears an agglomeration of false social values and therefore "no stable system of moral symbolism can be erected upon it." The Marxist criticism of the 'thirties, reflected in the writings of Ralph Fox (1937), and Christopher Caudwell (1938), appeared to regard Forster as a mere "loiterer" by the paths of "psychological subtlety."

However, the shift from a purely artistic or sociological angle of criticism to an understanding of the philosophical aspect of Forster's achievement took place only gradually, although I. A. Richards had, even as early as 1927, emphasized Forster's "half-mystical pre-occupation" with the survival theme. Rex Warner too called Forster a philosophical novelist. In Forster's novels, wrote G. S. Fraser, "we feel as we do not feel in Galsworthy's or Bennett's or in Kipling's or in Conrad's either that a philosophical mind is at work." The moral approach to Forster so persuasively presented by F. R. Leavis in England and Lionel Trilling in America has, in recent years, been overshadowed first by philosophical and metaphysical scrutinies of the novel and then, more recently, by the new psychological approaches. These new approaches, along with newer ramifications of old attitudes and changes in modes of critical analyses and judgments, are in some measure related to different aspects of modern criticism and the application to prose fiction of critical techniques previously associated with poetry. This critical emphasis on a very close reading of the text, and its interpretative analysis, is reflected in criticism on *A Passage to India* in recent years. There is an ever-growing body of Forster critics: R. A. Brower, George H. Thomson, Arnold Kettle, J. B. Beer, Cyrus Hoy, Frederick C. Crews, K. W. Gransden, Hugh Maclean, Gertrude White, Glen O. Allen, Keith Hollingsworth, Edwin Nierenberg, Frederick C. McDowell, Alan Wilde, David Shusterman, Wilfred Stone, James McConkey. Among recent critics John Colmer, Louise Dauner, Benita Parry, Norman Kelvin, and Malcolm Bradbury have illuminated one or more aspects of Forster's art. Whereas Lionel Trilling considered *Howards End,* a novel about England's destiny, to be Forster's masterpiece, an opinion shared by I. A.

Richards, almost all the modern critics appear to regard *A Passage to India* as the novelist's greatest work. A few of these critics have made a very close and deep study of Forster's fiction.

Thus, the conventional approach to Forster which had emphasized his civilizing intellect, liberalism, social comedy, and irony now found new nuances and subtler interpretations by way of the methods of contextual criticism. The difference, for instance, between Lionel Trilling, Frederick C. Crews, and C. B. Cox in relation to the analysis and interpretation of Forster's liberalism and the mythological element of the short stories indicates this process of critical development. The recent analyses of Forster's short stories and earlier fiction by John V. Hagopian and Frederick McDowell continue this critical trend.

An important dimension of Forster's achievement in *A Passage to India* is its alluring but elusive metaphysical and philosophical implications. Gertrude White's evaluation of *A Passage to India,* Glen O. Allen's analysis of structure, symbol, and theme in the novel, Cyrus Hoy's critical assessment of *Howards End,* James McConkey's perceptive analysis of the "physical reality," the "transcendent reality," and the "Forsterian voice" amply indicate the newly developed philosophical and metaphysical overtones of Forster criticism. Gertrude White in expounding her ideas on the theme in *A Passage to India* of "fission and fusion," of separation and desired union interprets it in the context not merely of India and Anglo-India but of the universe itself. *A Passage to India* thus becomes a drama of division and union on the cosmic scale. She envisages the three sections of the novel: Mosque, Caves, and Temple as representing the thesis, antithesis, and synthesis of the Hegelian philosophy. This is a new and primarily philosophical view of the structure of *A Passage to India* and differs from Hugh Maclean's analysis which reflects the earlier aesthetic view of Forster's achievement. Hugh Maclean's sensitive essay on the structure of the novel is a fine summation of the critical approach dominated by the idea of the aesthetic form of Forster's fiction. Making lesser use of the avowed philosophical positions, R. A. Brower's excellent essay on the vision and design of *A Passage to India* expounds the three sections Mosque, Caves, and Temple as a group of three symbolic metaphors, a concept which is essentially structural and yet becomes another source of subsequent philosophical interpretations. I have in my own essay "Symbolism in E. M. Forster's *A Passage to India: 'Temple,'*" accepted Brower's premises but moved to different conclusions, bringing out the central importance of the "Temple" section in *A Passage to India.*

Glen O. Allen is probably the first American critic to probe deeply into Forster's portrayal of what is termed the "controlling cosmos" and to examine its relationship with theme and symbol. His interpretation of the cosmic significance of the novel, the three contexts of the wasp, the analysis of Atman and Brahman, the Self and the Not-Self, its mystical relation and the light and sun imagery is most penetrating and perceptive. His idea that the "undying worm" indirectly alludes to Schopenhauer's blind striving will needs close scrutiny. Although it is true that Allen leans rather heavily on philosophical interpretations, yet, his presentation of the parallel between "OM" and Forster's "oh-boum" is very engaging and meaningful.

The question of the Marabar Caves is part of the philosophical complexity of the novel. "What happened in the Caves" is a never-ceasing enigma of the story and plot of *A Passage to India.* Austin Warren writes that "Lowes Dickinson, as well as others, asked Forster what really happened in the caves?" and then declares, "the author does not say." The question has not yet been answered adequately and in this context the essays of Louise Dauner, Keith Hollingsworth, and Edwin Nierenberg are of special value. "The echoes" writes Keith Hollingsworth, "continue to tantalize"; they seem to suggest different meanings to readers and critics who find them baffling indeed. He draws attention to communication as the main theme of Forster's fiction and interprets the Marabar echo as "a mockery of communication." Mrs. Moore is "the Western religious believer, in the midst of a rationalistic scientific culture, posing ultimate questions of value." She represents the slow decline of Christian belief in the West in an environment dominated by science and rationalism. And this English rationalism is embodied in Adela Quested. Whereas Mrs. Moore is up against the value of science in the nineteenth-century context—Darwinian biology—Adela Quested encounters more caves and more echoes. She believes in the "supremacy of the conscious mind" and the efficacy of reason. "If Christianity is a delusion, so is the self" for her. And her echo, a physical phenomenon, is a denial of values for her. Keith Hollingsworth too has traced the recurrent contexts and meanings of "the echo" in *A Passage to India.*

In commenting on Mrs. Moore's "incomplete passage to India" Edwin Nierenberg interprets the character and the role of this "withered Priestess." She is, he observes, "neither a saint nor a devil, neither an altogether redemptive nor yet a fallen character, but a figure with concurrent attributes of sincerity and self-deception." He has skillfully pointed out Mrs. Moore's strengths and limitations.

Whereas the earlier philosophical interpretation of *A Passage to India* revolves round "the twilight of the double vision" which Mrs. Moore experiences in the caves, many of the newer interpretations center on the personality of Professor Narayan Godbole and his part in the festival of the birth of Lord Krishna. This is a complex, and even baffling, element in

A Passage to India and strikes various chords. For this book I have therefore chosen a variety of critical essays which deal with both Mrs. Moore and Professor Godbole from different points of view. The Marabar Caves and their function and meaning were hitherto regarded as central to an understanding of *A Passage to India.* Whereas even such a perceptive critic as F. R. Leavis found the third (Temple) section of the novel weak and an evidence of failing in Forster's "poise," later critics have elevated it to a dominant position in the steadily evolving meaning and significance of the novel. In fact the center of critical concentration has shifted from the "Caves" to the "Temple," and it marks a radical change in our understanding and interpretation of *A Passage to India.*

This shift in critical focus is quite significant inasmuch as it reveals a new facet of Forster's philosophical predicament: the complex confrontation of an agnostic (Fielding) with the mystical experience of someone dear to his heart (Godbole). The predicament is all the greater because the agnostic in Forster is confronted with two mutually opposite kinds of experience: the nullity or the negation of the Marabar echo and the sacred syllables and bewilderment associated with Professor Godbole and the Temple ceremony. The Edwardian phase of Forster's literary development reveals (and rightly, one may assume) his dominant agnostic trend, though this is in some measure modified by his subtle response to true religious experience. Forster's agnosticism was part of the credo of Bloomsbury, an Edwardian extension of the nineteenth-century strands of unbelief. Virginia Woolf and the eminent Cambridge men who met at her home in Bloomsbury had nurtured the Victorian unbelief subscribed to earlier by her father Leslie Stephen. Leslie Stephen's confessions of an agnostic [7] might have struck a sympathetic chord in Forster's youthful personality. Forster's agnosticism had already been shaped by an earlier confrontation with the evangelical beliefs of the Clapham Sect. Yet the essential agnostic base of Forster's credo, which Evangelicalism could not alter, was in great measure altered by his chance confrontation with Hinduism.

This development is quite extraordinary and offers new nuances of meaning to what has all along been a baffling question, the centrality of Hinduism in *A Passage to India* and its real significance, which brings us to a consideration of the most enigmatic character in the novel, Professor Narayan Godbole.

Professor Narayan Godbole is as controversial a personage as Mrs. Moore, and the shift in critical emphasis from "Caves" to "Temple," just pointed out, has sharpened the edge of this controversy. Whereas we find the experience of Mrs. Moore in the caves curious—either a mystery or a muddle—we are equally uncertain about the exact meaning and value of

[7] *An Agnostic's Apology and Other Essays,* Putnam's (New York, 1893).

Godbole's words and actions and their true significance in the total pattern of Forster's novel. Forster, the agnostic, is perhaps in the same position as is Fielding, the cultured humanist, in relation to the enigmatic Godbole. Aziz is arrested on the fantastic charge of having assaulted Adela Quested. Fielding is deeply grieved and shocked by this painful and tragic event and in this state he meets Godbole in the college. Fielding asks him: "Is Aziz innocent or guilty?" And the answers of Godbole, showing his detachment and involving the somewhat tedious philosophical exposition of the operative forces of good and evil, baffle Fielding completely. The evil action, says Godbole, was performed by "Dr. Aziz . . . by the guide . . . by you . . . by me . . . by my students . . . by the lady herself. . . ." "When evil occurs," continues Godbole, "it expresses the whole of the universe. Similarly when good occurs." The fact that in the face of the grave, nerve-racking tragic event Godbole should ask Fielding for an appropriate name for his projected English medium school at Mau is significant in two ways: Fielding is appalled by Godbole's philosophical detachment "for no eye could see what lay at the bottom of the Brahman's mind" and secondly because Godbole's subtle approach to the action of an individual is complex. Yet it seemed to Fielding that "he [Godbole] had a mind and a heart too, and all his friends trusted him, without knowing why." It is in this context that the views of James McConkey, Benita Parry, and David Shusterman assume special significance. Shusterman's point of view is the very opposite of that of Benita Parry and James McConkey. He writes: "The essence of Godbole, like the cave a lump of God's universe (remember his name), comes almost ultimately to 'ou-boum,' the hollow, dull echo which makes everything appear to be identical, entirely devoid of distinction." In any assessment of Godbole, this is one philosophical extreme and therefore valuable. James McConkey's excellent analysis of Godbole's part in *A Passage to India* in addition to Shusterman's essay which, in essence, is a rejoinder, are studies in contrast.

Cyril Fielding's dilemma in responding to Godbole is partly Forster's own and it seems to be the dilemma of his critics too. The sensitive, rational, liberal, cultured Fielding is baffled by Godbole's curious ways and words. And yet Fielding's rationalism gives way to the overpowering waters of the Mau tank. He wonders whether there are worlds beyond this world which neither his intellect nor his imaginative faculty can perceive or fathom. He also realizes that his wife Stella is in some imperceptible way influenced by Hinduism and that the unseen world may hold within itself mysteries which no rational agnostic can ever understand, much less realize.

It is this realization of the unknowable, intangible, and complex mysteries of the unseen and the instinctive desire to accord it the value and validity it demands, that marks Forster's approach to the enigmatic character of Professor Godbole, who is so unmistakably modeled on the personality and character of Sir Tukoji III, the Maharajah of Dewas State Senior. [Forster's charming portrait of Sir Tukoji in *The Hill of Devi* (1953) and several incidents described in it make it an excellent sourcebook for *A Passage to India.*[8]] For some, Professor Godbole may be a charming person, an embodiment of the harmony between East and West, and of the peace that passeth understanding, but for others he is just a "curious case." He seems to some the best representative of the Hindu way of life and to others, such as Nirad Chaudhuri, the very travesty of Hinduism. All these points of view are represented in this book in the hope that the earnest reader will himself formulate his own response to this highly enigmatic character.

Aziz, Fielding, and Adela are the other important characters, but they are not quite as controversial or challenging as Godbole and Mrs. Moore. Yet Nirad C. Chaudhuri's comments on Aziz and Ted E. Boyle's analysis of Adela's rationalism (included in this volume) are provocative and absorbing and represent a significant angle of vision. Ted E. Boyle's interpretation of Adela's actions as a "subconscious recognition of her unsatisfactory relationship with Ronny" and the visit to the caves as a "subconscious search for the adventure which she senses she has missed" is most interesting and valuable.

IV

Criticisms of Forster's work, and specially of *A Passage to India,* are in some measure affected by Forster's methods as an artist. James McConkey's sensitive analysis of Forster even follows the terms Foster used

[8] Surely there is a close connection. *A Passage to India* expresses in a subtle way Forster's responses to Christianity, Islam, and Hinduism, though these responses are highly contextual. Many critics have made much of Forster's statement in *The Hill of Devi* unmindful of the date of its writing and the period of composition of *A Passage to India.* While on a visit to Hyderabad from Dewas Forster wrote on 12th November 1921: "I have passed abruptly from Hinduism to Islam and the change is a relief. . . ." Again Forster's statement that he came to Islam through Hinduism has to be understood in the context of the date of composition of *A Passage to India.* He began this novel before his 1921 visit but could not complete it in India because "the gap between India remembered and India experienced was too wide" (*The Hill of Devi*). It seems to me that the letters collected in *The Hill of Devi,* which were written in 1921, three years before the completion of the novel only show "India experienced" in all its immediacy. The novel is an artistic expression of "India remembered"—in England—and therefore the attempt to relate the letters to the visionary quality of *A Passage to India* is clearly illogical.

in his *Aspects of the Novel* (1927) such as People, Fantasy, Rhythm, and Prophecy. E. K. Brown has made a specially interesting contribution to the analysis of rhythm in Forster's work. McConkey expounds his notion of both the human and transcendent realities in Forster's novels and the "double vision" which is so central to his art. His interpretation of the tonal quality and the "Forsterian Voice" touches on one of the most subtle aspects of Forster's art as a novelist. McConkey's essay is valuable because he shows how the major mythological element in the novel—Hinduism—is presented to us primarily through recurrent symbolism and, more importantly, how this myth enables Forster to utilize a framework in keeping with the implications of his "voice" and that the prophecy of the novel results from such a relationship.

"The backbone of a novel has to be a story" writes Forster in *Aspects of the Novel* and his adherence to tradition in the technique of fiction has impelled some of his critics to explain and exploit plot, character, and theme and even to summarize the sequence of stories in relation to the idea, though it is true that "to summarise any good, developed idea is to betray it."

Another significant aspect of the modern criticism of Forster is a concentrated study of the symbolism of his short stories and novels. In "Thematic Symbol in *A Passage to India*" (included in this volume) George H. Thomson shows that *A Passage to India* is a study like Eliot's *The Wasteland* (1922) "in the spiritual condition of twentieth century man." He analyzes the two aspects of Forster's symbols: their connection with the outer life and the realistic narrative and also their inward suggestive quality and meaning. And the inward and outward meanings of symbols or symbolical action have been perceptively analyzed by him as well. His recently published study *The Fiction of E. M. Forster* (1967) offers excellent analyses of Forster's symbols.

The studies of Forster's symbols have assumed new dimensions of philosophical and psychological significance. Louise Dauner's excellent essay touches on an entirely fresh aspect of Forster's symbolism associated with the cave episode. This essentially Jungian approach, based on the belief that Forster's insights are derived from "what Jung calls the Collective Unconscious"—the source of creative art—attempts to interpret Forster's fiction in terms of the value of "primordial experience common to humanity." Equating the Marabar Caves with Plato's Cave of Illusion, Louise Dauner describes Adela's experience as a variation of the realization of *Māyā,* which is illusion. This *Māyā,* or illusion, is superimposed on reality and gets hold of her mind, partly because of her lack of knowledge of truth, her high and dry rationalism, and her confrontation with the "real

India." The Caves are archetypal and therefore a "constituent of the collective unconscious." They provide an appropriate setting for Adela's experience, which is described on two levels: first as surrender to *Māyā* and secondly as a subsequent confrontation with the unrelenting process of reality. She runs away from the Marabar and this flight represents a rejection, says Dauner, of "the value-implications which the cave symbolically carries." This Jungian approach to the cave episode interprets Adela's experience in a new light.

In Wilfred Stone's comprehensive study of E. M. Forster, *The Cave and the Mountain* (1966) the cave is presented as one aspect of Forster's vision and the mountain as another, and these two aspects are shown as achieving an excellent synthesis in *A Passage to India.* All the unrealized conflicts of Forster's earlier fiction, of matter and spirit, the seen and the unseen, human and divine, says Stone, are forged into a single unity in *A Passage to India.* Fundamental to Stone's attitude is his assertion that circular symbols are central to Forster's novel. The Cave which is circular in fact and in episode, and the Temple, which symbolizes the world-mountain, are both important in conveying meaning in Forster's classic.

V

Forster's social comedy is Meredethian in many respects and yet it depicts a clash of motivation which may be interpreted in terms of time-honored metaphysical opposites: the real and the ideal, the body and the soul, the human and the divine, the seen and the unseen, the rational and the mystical, the many and the one, the intellect and the spirit, the dual and the non-dual, the abstract and the concrete, the illusory and the real. These opposites sustain and nourish the movement of thought and feeling in *A Passage to India* and they are implicit in the progress of events and development of plot and character in the novel. And the ultimate question, the basic problem in Forster is the one that inevitably arises out of the clash of these opposites in this supremely contemplative novel: where then does the reality lie and what precisely are its attributes in terms of the experiences depicted in *A Passage to India?* What is the reality in *A Passage to India?* He who finds an adequate answer to this central problem has truly traversed the Forsterian passage to India and has negotiated the odd turns on this road to reality; he has at last come to terms simultaneously with the artist and the thinker in Forster.

The final meaning of *A Passage to India* hinges on Forster's attitude toward Christianity, Islam, and Hinduism and this has to be distilled from the three sections of the novel and their artistic and philosophical cohesion and harmony. In this context K. W. Gransden's ideas are specially valuable since he finds "between the second and third parts of the novel" a Kierkegaardian "qualitative leap on to a different plane." Fielding returns to England—back to the "Mediterranean" norm with its decorum and harmonies. It appears that the novel might be finished at this point: "After such sundering, what reconciliation? After such disintegration what renewal?" But, no! We move on to a different plane and the Temple section presents new opportunities and fresh limitations. Many scenes and situations in "Mosque," "Caves," and "Temple" have a positive bearing on this essential link which is central to the religious significance of the novel. For example, the scene in which the personality of the dead Mrs. Moore is recreated by the imaginative and visionary Godbole. While he was engaged in the ecstatic dance on the carpet, Godbole "remembered an old woman he had met in Chandrapore days":

> Chance brought her into his mind while it was in this heated state, he did not select her, she happened to occur among the throng of soliciting images, a tiny splinter, and he impelled her by his spiritual force to that place where completeness can be found. Completeness, not reconstruction.

He loves the wasp, as Mrs. Moore does, but faced with the stone, a diminutive part of the hostile rocks which constitute the Marabar Caves, he withdraws from it and dances on the carpet. His dance and his trance symbolize his attempt, in the true spirit of Hinduism, at inclusion of the animate and the inanimate in his ideal cosmos. Whereas the Anglo-Indians and also one part of India represent the theme of exclusion, Professor Godbole as presented by Forster symbolizes man's attempt at inclusion and his innermost desire to become one with God.

Completeness is the key word for understanding the part Godbole plays in the temple ceremony. Yet the fact that the effect of the temple ceremony is transient makes it difficult for some to accept the view that Forster presents the solution of the problem in *A Passage to India* through the actions and ideas embodied in Godbole. While referring to the suggestive sign "God si love," Forster asks the central question: "Is this the final message of India?" Godbole's attempt at experiencing completeness and "the approaching triumph of India" symbolized by the Krishna festival are on the one hand an affirmation characteristic of the Hindu way of life and "a frustration of reason and form" on the other. In Forster's world it is believed that mystery and muddle are not far apart. Frederick C. Crews, Alan Wilde, and David Shusterman have expressed doubts whether Forster's solution to the philosophical issue presented in *A Passage to India* lies in any unqualified affirmation, though it seems clear that the essential vision as presented in the Temple section approximates it. I myself have taken the latter view, although this has been understood by some critics (notably by Benita Parry) to imply that I see the Temple section as the final solution to the problem presented while quietly claiming Forster for Brahman mysticism. This was not my intention. I was trying to reassess what I then believed to be a slightly unbalanced emphasis conveyed in Brower's essay. I am happy to note that none of the recent critics of Forster find any aesthetic or philosophical inadequacy in the Temple section.

This question of meaning contributes to the complexity of the novel. It is this complexity of vision in *A Passage to India* which seems so baffling to many critics. There are many moments of vision and anti-vision in it, the Krishna festival and the "boum" and "ou-boum" of the Caves, and neither the moments of despair and defeat nor the moments of hope and triumph lead to a distinct and clear understanding of a unified and lasting wholeness. Every attempt at synthesis is followed by (to borrow a term from Murray Krieger) a new anti-synthesis, for something is always left unaccounted for, the wasp by the missionaries and the stone by Godbole; the circle of completeness has to be indefinitely widened to accommodate new entrants. Thus are the apparently conflicting claims of Forster's own aesthetic, expansion and completion, to be reconciled. But, are they? This is the question that perplexes and nags the critics.

In Whitman's poem (from which the novel takes its title), the poet bids us

> Sail forth—steer for the deep waters only
> Reckless O soul, exploring, I with thee, and thou with me,
> For we are bound where mariner has not yet dared to go,
> And we will risk the ship, ourselves and all.

Forster's novel, too, bids us "steer for the deep waters only," to dare, to risk "the ship, ourselves and all," to experience the existential uncertainties without offering us the consolations of a certain victory or plunging us into the glooms of an equally predestined defeat. That is why the novel is one of the great classics of our time. It takes us so far into the extremities of experience where hope and despair alternate with such bewildering rapidity that we are never permitted to come to any facile conclusion. But here is no chaos either and even the twilight pessimism of the valedictory "No, not there" is subdued and redeemed by the hint of ultimate reconcilability implicit in the "No, not yet." Is it too generous to hope that a hundred voices will not prevail against the lone, dissenting voice of the sky?

V. A. Shahane

PMLA

PVBLICATIONS OF
THE·MODERN·LANGVAGE·ASSOCIATION·OF·AMERICA

Issued Five Times a Year

VOLUME LXVIII | SEPTEMBER 1953 | NUMBER 4, PART 1

A PASSAGE TO INDIA: ANALYSIS AND REVALUATION

By GERTRUDE M. WHITE

A PASSAGE TO INDIA, apparently the last, and certainly the best of E. M. Forster's novels, was published twenty-nine years ago, in, 1924. It was accorded instant recognition, as a fine novel and as a perceptive and sympathetic treatment of the problem of "Anglo-India." The years that followed saw the book established as a modern classic. It has reached a wide audience in the Everyman, Modern Library, and Penguin editions, and has challenged as well the attention of able critics. But, though the novel has received its just dues in many ways, there remains one aspect—and, I think, a fundamental one—still unexplored. It is acknowledged on all sides that thought is the most important element in Forster's novels;[1] yet the dialectical pattern of *A Passage to India* has never, to my knowledge, been fully and specifically recognized. This omission has resulted not only in a certain incompleteness in critical accounts of the book, but in not a little confusion and obscurity as well.

A score or more of penetrating studies have analyzed *A Passage* as a social document: "a book which no student of the Indian question can disregard."[2] Its plot, style, character-drawing, particular ideas and attitudes have likewise been exhaustively discussed, evaluated, and related to the body of Forster's work and to modern literature generally. Its author has been hailed as "the last survivor of a cultured liberal

[1] This point has been made by virtually every critic who has written on Forster. See specifically the following studies: E. K. Brown, "Revival of E. M. Forster," *Yale Review*, N.S. XXXIII (June 1944), 668–681; Virginia Woolf, "The Novels of E. M. Forster," *Atlantic Monthly*, CXL (Nov. 1927), 642–648; Lord David Cecil, "E. M. Forster," *Atlantic Monthly*, CLXXXIII (Jan. 1949), 60–65; Morton D. Zabel, "E. M. Forster," *The Nation*, CXLVII (22 Oct. 1938), 413–416; Rex Warner, *E. M. Forster* (London: Supplement to *British Book News*, 1950); et al.

[2] Peter Burra, "The Novels of E. M. Forster," *The Nineteenth Century and After*, CXVI (Nov. 1934), 583.

tradition" (Warner, p. 5) and "the only living novelist who can be read again and again."[3]

Even those who have written of him with most appreciation, however, have apparently failed to grasp fully the meaning and importance of the novel's theme, and thus have given only partial accounts of it. Penetrating and provocative as they are, such treatments as those of Burra,[4] Trilling, Brown,[5] Zabel, and Hoare[6]—to name a few of the best—still tend to be over-general, and to put a somewhat undue emphasis on the "mystery" of the novel. Burra seems to speak for all of them when he tells us that its "thought, like music's, cannot be fixed, nor its meaning defined" (pp. 586–587). Though this is, no doubt, true in a sense, I feel that the mistiness of the book has been exaggerated.

This same failure to apprehend clearly the framework of thought in the novel has led other critics into undue censure or misunderstanding. For example, we hear that, "He beats the bush with admirable dexterity, but nothing appears. No wonder his book leaves on our minds an impression of waste."[7] Or we are told, "In his comedy . . . he shows himself the born novelist; but he aims also at making a poetic communication about life, and here he is, by contrast, almost unbelievably crude and weak."[8] These are severe judgments indeed. And there are those

[3] Lionel Trilling, *E. M. Forster* (London, 1944), p. 9.

[4] Pp. 581–594. This article was later reprinted as the introduction to the Everyman edition of *A Passage to India* (London, 1942), pp. xi–xxvii. Forster himself has praised it very highly.

[5] E. K. Brown, "E. M. Forster and the Contemplative Novel," *Univ. of Toronto Quart.*, III (April 1934), 349–361.

[6] Dorothy M. Hoare, "E. M. Forster," *Some Studies in the Modern Novel* (London, 1938), pp. 68–97.

[7] Ranjee G. Shahani, "Some British I Admire," *Asiatic Rev.*, XLII (July 1946), 273.

[8] F. R. Leavis, "E. M. Forster," *Scrutiny*, VII (Sept. 1938), 185. This article offers a perfect illustration of the misunderstanding into which even a competent critic may be led by a neglect of the novel's pattern of thought. Mr. Leavis selects, for a criticism of Forster's style, the paragraph in Chapter XXVI which describes the reactions of Fielding and Hamidullah to the news of Mrs. Moore's death, directing particular attention to the "lapse in taste" responsible for the final phrase of the sentence: "How indeed is it possible for one human being to be sorry for all the sadness that meets him on the face of the earth, for the pain that is endured not only by men, but by animals and plants, and perhaps by the stones?" This is what he says: "Once one's critical notice has fastened on it . . . can one do anything but reflect how extraordinary it is that so fine a writer should be able, in such a place, to be so little certain just how serious he is? For surely that run-out of the sentence cannot be justified in terms of the dramatic mood Mr. Forster is offering to render?" (pp. 198–199). An understanding of the novel's thought and peculiar method makes it clear, on the contrary, that this phrase is one more echo in a book of echoes; as will be obvious to anyone who troubles to read carefully the account of Godbole's vision of Mrs. Moore, the wasp, and the stone in the final section of the novel. What Mr. Leavis describes as a fault in style is, in terms of thought, mood, and structure, a conscious, deliberate, and effective device.

who openly confess themselves at a loss: "One can re-read a dozen times and be no nearer a solution."[9]

Any attentive reader of *A Passage* has certainly realized that Forster indeed suggests more than can be explained; and to translate suggestive and poetic language into explicit statement is always to risk destroying one kind of reality without furnishing another. It is my belief, however, that there exists in *A Passage* a dialectical pattern, strong and subtle, by which the author attempts to bind social, psychological, and philosophical levels into a harmony and to relate the characters and events of the novel to each other and to the informing idea of the whole. Further, I believe that incompleteness and misunderstanding alike can best be avoided by a grasp of this design, and that a clear understanding of it will contribute materially to a revaluation of the novel. It is my purpose in this paper to analyze the basic thought of the book as closely as possible. But an acknowledgment and a warning is first of all in order.

"To summarize any good, developed idea is to betray it" (Trilling, p. 51). It cannot be too strongly emphasized that the *schema* of the novel that follows is not the novel itself, which, in richness and complexity, far transcends it. The importance of *A Passage* lies in the way Forster has given life and force to the philosophical pattern, and they are right who seek its chief meaning in character, idea, attitude, and atmosphere: in all the multitudinous richness of texture and substance which the book offers. My excuse must be, not that the theme is the *major* thing in the book, but that it is the *basic* thing; and that its neglect causes even the most gifted reader to fail, at least partially, in appreciation and understanding.

It is generally agreed that Forster is a writer of the "contemplative" novel; and further, that all his novels tend to be illustrations of a single idea. This single theme is, in the critics' various terms, "the chasm between the world of actions and the world of being" (Brown, *UTQ*, p. 352); "the search for the *wholeness* of truth," and the harmonizing of "the tragic antitheses of mankind" (Zabel, pp. 413, 416); the antithesis "between Real and not-Real, true and false, being and not-being."[10] Each book develops this single theme in somewhat different terms, and on many levels. The dominant idea of *A Passage* is best expressed by the Whitman poem from which the novel takes its title:

Passage to India!
Lo, soul, sees't thou not God's purpose from the first?
The earth to be spanned, connected by network,

[9] E. B. C. Jones, "E. M. Forster and Virginia Woolf," *The English Novelists*, ed. Derek Verschoyle (London, 1936), p. 262.

[10] Rose Macaulay, *The Writings of E. M. Forster* (New York, 1938), p. 10.

The races, neighbors, to marry and be given in marriage,
The oceans to be crossed, the distant brought near,
The lands to be welded together.

Then not your deeds only O voyagers, O scientists and inventors, shall be justified,
All these hearts as of fretted children shall be soothed,
All affection shall be fully responded to, the secret shall be told,
All these separations and gaps shall be taken up and hook'd and link'd together,
The whole earth, this cold, impassive, voiceless earth, shall be completely justified,

Nature and Man shall be disjoined and diffused no more,
The true son of God shall absolutely fuse them.

(O pensive soul of me—O thirst unsatisfied—waitest not there?
Waitest not haply for us somewhere there the Comrade perfect?)[11]

It is the theme of fission and fusion; of separateness and of desired union. The threefold division of the book, "Mosque," "Caves," and "Temple," which Forster himself tells us represent the divisions of the Indian year, the Cold Weather, the Hot Weather, and the Rains,[12] represent also a kind of Hegelian Thesis—Antithesis—Synthesis; or, more properly perhaps, the statement of the problem, and two opposite resolutions.

In Part I, "Mosque," the central problem, "all these separations and gaps," is set up and explored on many different levels. The most obvious gap, at first, is that between Indian and English. Chandrapore is two towns, the native section and the English civil station, from which the town "appears to be a totally different place."[13] The separation is complete: the civil station "shares nothing with the city except the overarching sky" (p. 8), the first hint of a division more fundamental than any human differences. The universe itself is to be a protagonist in the drama of the many and the one.

But these broad divisions are themselves divided. India is not one but a hundred, of which Moslem and Hindu are only the most noticeable. India is a muddle; nothing embraces the whole of it; no one race or creed or person can sum it up or know all of it; nor are differences clear cut: "Nothing in India is identifiable, the mere asking of a question causes it to disappear or to merge in something else" (p. 86). India, in fact, is

[11] *Leaves of Grass*, Incl. ed. (New York, 1924), pp. 343–351.

[12] "Author's Notes," *A Passage to India* (London: Everyman, 1942), p. xxxi.

[13] *A Passage to India* (New York: Modern Library, 1940), p. 8. All future page references to the novel are to this edition.

presented to us throughout as the very place of division; the unhappy continent where separations are felt more profoundly than in other places; and later we shall learn that Aziz's picnic fails "because he had challenged the spirit of the Indian earth, which tries to keep men in compartments" (p. 127).

If the continent and its conquered inhabitants are not united, neither are the conquerors. The English, in their club from which all Indians are excluded, are divided among themselves by the same barriers. Those who have been for some time in India are different in outlook from the newcomers, who have not yet retreated behind the defenses of tradition, race, caste, and position. Major official looks down upon minor official; wives of major officials look down upon their inferior sisters. The soldier's attitude differs from the civilian's. And though the Englishwoman does not live in purdah, as does the Indian lady, there is an antagonism between the sexes which raises a more subtle but as effective barrier between them: the women think their men "weak" in dealing with natives; the men believe, in their secret hearts, that it is their women who complicate matters.

The gaps and separations between human beings are not the only ones. Men themselves are separate from the rest of creation. Young Mr. Sorley, a missionary with advanced ideas, sees no reason why the mercy of God should not embrace all mammals; but he becomes uneasy if the conversation descends to wasps, and is totally unable to admit into the the Divine unity "oranges, cactuses, crystals, and mud" (p. 38). Yet men are only a small part of creation: "It matters so little to the majority of living beings what the minority, that calls itself human, desires or decides" (p. 114). And the universe itself, powerful, indifferent, is apart from or even hostile to the concerns of all sentient creatures.

If multiplicity is the fact, unity of some sort is the desire. Separated from each other by race, caste, religion, sex, age, occupation, and the hundred barriers of life, men still must strive to unite with each other and to achieve some harmonious resolution of their differences. And they desire as well, though some of them may not know it, to find that unity that shall embrace the whole scheme of things, from which nothing shall be excluded. "Mosque" is therefore not only a symphony of differences but of attempts at oneness. But this unity which is sought is of two different kinds, which must be carefully distinguished. One is the unity of negation, the other of affirmation; one of exclusion, the other of inclusion. The one emphasizes differences and separations; the other reconciles them in a larger synthesis. The one merely breeds misunderstanding, violence, and hatred; the other seeks peaceful resolution.

The first, of course, is the more easily come by. The Indians are united among themselves only by hatred and suspicion of the English, the one force strong enough to bind together the different races and creeds. Within separate groups, such as Moslem and Hindu, they are united by their traditions, their history, their religion, and their art. Aziz and his friends, quoting the poetry of Islam, feel that India is one and their own; Aziz, visiting his mosque, finds the home of his spirit in that faith. And these forces, which bind together members of the same group, by the same token set them apart from those of other groups. Aziz, embracing a Hindu friend, thinks, "I wish they did not remind me of cow-dung," at the same moment that his friend is thinking, "Some Moslems are very violent" (p. 267). The English, too, find the unity of exclusion, of suspicion, and of hatred. The anthem of the Army of Occupation reminds every member of the club that he is British and in exile, enabling them for the moment to sink their personal prejudices. Unity of this kind is achieved not *with* but *against;* it is essentially hostile and evil in nature, and the breeder of more hostility and more evil.

As the first kind of oneness affirms and ratifies the differences and separations natural to life, the second attempts to embrace and to reconcile them by good will, sympathy, kindness, and love. The effort may be on either a purely secular level, or on a religious basis. Fielding, the "holy man minus the holiness" (p. 121), believes that the world "is a globe of men who are trying to reach one another and can best do so by the help of good will plus culture and intelligence" (p. 62). Adela desires to "see the real India" (p. 24); to learn and to understand. But though she has true good-will, she is deficient in emotional response; in "the secret understanding of the heart" (p. 20). From this deficiency all her future troubles will stem. Mrs. Moore, on the other hand, a Christian mystic, is made up of intuitive understanding and sympathy, of an all-embracing charity. It is she who reminds her son Ronny of the necessity for love in all relationships, the political as well as the personal; that God is Love.

In this first section, every event, every character, every detail is a variation on the same theme. The gulf between English and Indians is shown from both points of view: at the dinner in Hamidullah's home, in the English club, at the farcical "Bridge Party." But what a different story when Aziz, the Indian, meets the newcomers, who wish to communicate, to bridge the gap, who offer genuine good-will, kindness, even love. Instantly he responds to Mrs. Moore's understanding on their meeting in the mosque; instantly he makes friends with Fielding; he accepts, though he does not really like, Adela; and generously and at infinite pains he makes plans for the visit of the ladies to the Marabar Caves.

At the end of the section, it seems that brotherhood is about to triumph. The omens are auspicious: East and West have met and embraced; friendship and love are in the ascendant. Islam, whose symbol the mosque gives the section its title, preaches the eternal oneness of God. Christianity, the religion of the English, teaches the oneness of all men in the Divine love. The season of the year is the Cold Weather, most suitable to human life and activity; the climate in which men can live and grow. But "April, herald of horrors" (p. 115) is at hand: the Hot Weather, dangerous and oppressive to all life. Professor Godbole, the Hindu, has sung his haunting song of invitation to Shri Krishna, Lord of the Universe: "Come, come, come, come, come, come" (p. 80). But the god refuses to come. And his refusal poses the problem for the next section.

If Part I has been Thesis, the problem of separation and attempts at bridging the gulfs, Part II is Antithesis; for in "Caves" we see the utter rout of the forces of reconciliation, the complete triumph of hostility, evil, and negation.

The central episode of this section, and of the entire novel, is the experience of the two Englishwomen, Adela Quested and Mrs. Moore, in the Marabar Caves. It is a shattering experience, calamitous to everyone: it destroys Mrs. Moore both spiritually and physically; it drives Adela to the brink of madness; it threatens ruin to Aziz, and actually alters his entire future; it imperils all relations between English and Indians; and it destroys all constructive relationships between individuals. Yet it is never satisfactorily explained by the author. The nature and meaning of Adela's and Mrs. Moore's experience is left in darkness, dealt with only in highly oblique and allusive language. What was the voice of the Marabar?

The Marabar Caves are the very voice of that union which is the opposite of divine; the voice of evil and negation; of that universe which is "older than all spirit" (p. 124). They are the voice of Chaos and Old Night, when "the earth was without form, and void, and darkness was upon the face of the deep"; long before the Spirit of God moved upon the waters and said, "Let there be Light." The answer they give to the problem of oneness is an answer of horror and despair, whether on the human or on the universal level.

To each lady, the voice of the Marabar speaks of a kind of oneness, but in different terms; terms appropriate to character, age, and situation. To the elder, the religious mystic who wishes to communicate with God, to become one with the universe, in the conviction that such union is beautiful and full of meaning, the echo speaks of a universe in which all differences have been annihilated, an infinity of Nothing. Good and evil are identical: "Everything exists, nothing has value" (p. 149). All has become one; but the one is Nothing. Here is unity with a vengeance! To the younger Adela, who has wished to understand but not to love India and the Indians, who has become engaged to a man she does not love, who is not convinced that love is necessary to a successful union, the meaning of the echo presents itself in different terms. To her, it speaks of the last horror of union by force and fear, without love. She believes that Aziz has attempted to assault her, goes nearly mad with horror, and sets in motion the machinery that shall prosecute and punish him. For the Marabar has revealed to her what such union is: Rape.

Upon Mrs. Moore, who had told her son that God is Love, the effect of the Marabar is immediate and profound despair. We have had hints of India's impact upon her previously. "God . . . had been constantly in her thoughts since she entered India, though oddly enough he satisfied her less. She must needs pronounce his name frequently, as the greatest she knew, yet she had never found it less efficacious. Outside the arch there seemed always an arch, beyond the remotest echo a silence" (p. 52). Since Professor Godbole had sung his queer song at Fielding's tea party, she had been apathetic. Already disillusionment is upon her, a sense of the futility of all attempts at union. "She felt increasingly (vision or nightmare?) that, though people are important, the relations between them are not, and that in particular too much fuss has been made over marriage; centuries of carnal embracement, yet man is no nearer to understanding man. And today she felt this with such force that it seemed itself a relationship, itself a person who was trying to take hold of her hand" (p. 135).

In this state of mind she enters the Marabar, and hears the echo of that oneness which is nothingness. "The mood of the last two months took definite form at last, and she realized that she didn't want to write to her children, didn't want to communicate with anyone, not even with God" (p. 150). From this moment, she takes no more interest in anything. She dismisses Adela's experience: "all this rubbish about love, love in a church, love in a cave, as if there is the least difference" (p. 202). Knowing Aziz to be innocent, she neither speaks nor stays to testify at his trial. She departs, in this season of the Hot Weather when travel is dangerous, and dies at sea. The echo has ended everything for her. To the Christian mystic the Marabar has said that the universe is muddle rather than mystery; the answer to its riddle is Nothingness.

To Adela the meaning of the echo has presented itself in terms very different, though nearly as disastrous. The keynote of her character, from the beginning, has been an honest but arid intellectualism. Unlike Mrs.

Moore, with her intuitive sympathies and responses, Adela approaches the problems of life by means of the rational intellect. Her good will, her kindness, come not from the heart but from the head. Fielding is to point out to her that she fails because she has no real affection for Aziz or for Indians generally; she herself confesses to him that her instincts never help her.

Adela's engagement to Ronny has taken place only because of the accident to the Nawab Bahadur's car. Previously, she has refused to marry him; but the accident has linked her to him in a spurious union. The same forces that unite the English against outsiders have united the young man and woman. She does not love him; but until the day of the expedition this question has not even occurred to her. But now, as she goes with Aziz alone to explore a cave, she thinks for the first time, "What about love?" (p. 152), a question in some way suggested to her by a pattern in the rock similar to that traced in the dust by the wheels of the Nawab Bahadur's car. For the first time, she realizes that she and Ronny do not love each other. "The discovery had come so suddenly that she felt like a mountaineer whose rope had broken. Not to love the man one's going to marry! Not to find it out till this moment! Not even to have asked oneself the question until now! . . . There was esteem and animal contact at dusk, but the emotion that links them was absent" (p. 152).

But Adela, being the person she was, "wasn't convinced that love is necessary to a successful union" (p. 152). Recovering herself, she drives Aziz from her side in embarrassment by her question, "Have you one wife or more than one?" and goes alone into the cave, there to undergo the ordeal, as she thinks, of his attempted rape.

The analogy here between the personal situation of Adela and Ronny, and the political situation between India and England is clear. It is almost as if she has felt about their personal relationship what Ronny feels about the union of India and England politically. He had told his mother that the English were not in India to be pleasant but "to hold this wretched country by force" (p. 50). Mrs. Moore had thought at that time that, "One touch of regret—not the canny substitute but the true regret from the heart—would have made him a different man, and the British Empire a different institution" (p. 51). The English are, for the most part, honest, sincere, incorruptible, earnestly attempting to do justice in administering India. But, as Mrs. Moore reminds her son. "Though I speak with the tongues of men and angels, and have not love . . . " (p. 52), it profits nothing. Aziz, in his illness, has told Fielding that what India needs is "Kindness, more kindness, and even after that more kindness. I assure you it is the only hope. . . . We can't build up

India except on what we feel" (p. 117). Instead, the English are holding India by fear and force, without kindness or love. "Mosque" has been full of this sort of union: hostile, evil, and negative. Now Adela, joined to Ronny without love, by the same forces which operate to link together the English in India against native and outsider, experiences symbolically the utmost degradation of such union.

The effect of their experience in the Marabar is to quench every little flame of kindness and good will in those around them. The bridges thrown across the gulfs crumble; the abysses widen and deepen. Evil and negative unity alone is left. The English draw together more firmly than ever against natives, in a union that annihilates all reason, all justice, and all mercy. Fear and hate unite the Indians in Aziz's defense. Fielding, throwing in his lot with them, realizes at that moment the profundity of the gulf that divides him from them. The evil spreads and propagates; the spirit of violence stalks abroad; the echo of the Marabar, spouting from its cave, has spread until it threatens to engulf the lives of everyone.

Adela, recovering from her ordeal, is troubled by the echo, which still sounds in her ears. She feels in some vague way, contrary to what her intellect tells her, that she has committed a crime, is leaving the world worse than she found it. Attempting to understand what has happened, she is puzzled by the difference between what she *feels* and what she *knows*, and says incoherently, "I shouldn't mind if it had happened anywhere else; at least I really don't know where it did happen" (p. 199). For it has not happened to her, in the Marabar; it has happened everywhere in India, it has happened in all places and at all times when men attempted union without love.

Mrs. Moore, engulfed in her own failure and her own despair, refuses help. Nevertheless, her mere presence helps Adela's echo, and suggests the possibility of a mistake. The machinery she has set in motion grinds on; and after Mrs. Moore's departure, though the question of an error still occurs to her intellect, it ceases to trouble her conscience. But at the trial, it is the name of Mrs. Moore, chanted like an incantation by Indians who do not know what the syllables mean, that shows Adela the truth, as in a vision: that nothing "in reality" had happened to her in the Marabar. The charge is withdrawn and Aziz saved. Adela's echo vanishes. Aziz, consulting Mrs. Moore's spirit, renounces the compensation that would have ruined his enemy. And Fielding and Adela, attempting to understand the whole muddle, have to give it up. "She was at the end of her spiritual tether, and so was he. . . . Perhaps life is a mystery, not a muddle; they could not tell. Perhaps the hundred Indias which fuss and squabble so tiresomely are one, and the universe they mirror is one. They had not the apparatus for judging" (p. 263).

Though the spirit of Mrs. Moore has averted the ultimate disaster, nothing good is left: the Marabar has brought nothing but evil. Political relationships have been imperiled; personal ones fare no better. Adela is rejected by the English community; Ronny breaks his engagement. Fielding, also cast out by his compatriots, is misunderstood by the Indians, his friendship with Aziz wrecked by the latter's suspicion of treachery. Kindness and good will have failed; of all the hopes and tentative gestures of union in Part I, nothing is left but hatred, force, and fear. The Marabar has triumphed.

"Mosque," symbol of Islam; of human desire for that unity which is the indubitable attribute of God; of the Cold Weather, favorable to human lives and hopes: the problem in its multifarious forms. "Caves" is one answer; the voice of chaos, of a universe of evil and annihilation, and of the Hot Weather, that climate in which men cannot live. But the caves are only one part of India. As Mrs. Moore's ship sails from Bombay, "thousands of coco-nut palms appeared all round the anchorage and climbed the hills to wave her farewell. 'So you thought an echo was India; you took the Marabar caves as final?' they laughed. 'What have we in common with them, or they with Asirgarh'?" (p. 210). It may be that the voice of the chaos older than all spirit is not the final one. "Temple," title of the third section of the novel, is the symbol of the Hindu religion; of a possible reconciliation of differences not in negation but in a larger synthesis; of a universe which is perhaps a mystery rather than a muddle, a riddle to which an answer exists; and of the Rains, token of renewed life, of regeneration, and of hope.

"Temple" opens with the enigmatic figure of the Hindu, Professor Godbole, who has appeared briefly in the first two sections. It is he who has invoked the god, at Fielding's tea party, in his song; he who has refused to answer Aziz's questions about the Marabar at that same time; and he with whom Fielding has had a curious and inconclusive conversation about good and evil at the time of the trial. Godbole, a Hindu mystic, is utterly immersed in the life of the spirit; so much so, indeed, as to be completely unfitted for practical action or decision. He dwells entirely in the world of being, and men of action, like the English generally and Fielding in particular after the Marabar expedition, find him maddening.

Godbole thus represents in his person the life of the spirit developed to its uttermost degree: he stands at the opposite pole from Ronny and the English in general, who excel at the practical life but are lost in the spiritual. Philosophically, he stands for that universality characteristic of Hinduism. Unlike Islam and Christianity, Hinduism makes no distinctions between humanity and the rest of the creation; its creed teaches that each particular part is a member of all other parts, and that all is one in the Divine. In his talk with Fielding, Godbole expresses the belief that nothing can be performed in isolation; that all perform a good action when one is performed, and when an evil action is performed, all perform it. Evil and good alike express the whole of the universe. Further, good and evil are both aspects of God. He is present in the one, absent in the other. "Yet absence implies presence, absence is not non-existence, and we are therefore entitled to repeat, 'Come, come, come, come' " (p. 178). Godbole, then, stands for the union in reality of all men, whether they will or no, and for a universe in which God exists, though he may at a particular time and place not be present; for a universe which may be a mystery but is not a muddle.

In the festival which opens the "Temple" section, the celebration of the birth of Shri Krishna, universality is the theme. At the birth of the god, "all sorrow was annihilated, not only for Indians, but for foreigners, birds, caves, railways, and the stars; all became joy, all laughter; there had never been disease nor doubt, misunderstanding, cruelty, fear" (pp. 287–288). The voice of the Marabar is drowned in this festival, in which "Infinite Love took upon itself the form of Shri Krishna, and saved the world" (p. 287). And Godbole, developing the life of his spirit, in a vision sees Mrs. Moore, united in his mind with a wasp seen he forgot where: an echo of an earlier discussion on the all-embracing mercy of God.

It is a prophetic vision, for what happens in "Temple" is reconciliation on the human level, the cancelling of the effects of the Marabar. Reconciliation, not real union; that is not possible on earth, whatever may be the truth about that universe of which earth is only an atom. The hundred voices of India say, "No, not yet," and the sky says, "No, not there" (p. 322). But the most painful human differences are soothed: Aziz and Fielding resume their friendship, though it can lead no further; Aziz finally makes his peace with Adela.

These things are brought about by Mrs. Moore, who returns to India in the guise of her children, Stella, whom Fielding has married, and Ralph, son of her flesh and still more of her spirit. It is the spirit of love, of intuitive understanding, which triumphs at last, in spite of her personal defeat. She had herself told Ronny, "I think everyone fails, but there are so many kinds of failure" (p. 52). Hers had been a failure of *understanding*, but not of *love*. Her memory, and the presence of her son, Ralph, completely change Aziz's attitude from hostility to homage: "He knew with his heart that this was Mrs. Moore's son, and indeed until his heart was involved he knew nothing" (p. 313). And at Mau, too, Fielding and Stella are brought closer together: "There seemed a link between them at last—that link outside either participant that is necessary to every relationship. In the language of theology, their union had been blessed" (p. 318). The Marabar has been wiped out.

"All invitations must proceed from heaven perhaps; perhaps it is futile for men to initiate their own unity, they do but widen the gulfs between them by the attempt" (p. 37). So Forster seems to be saying. *A Passage to India* is a novel of these gulfs, of the bridges thrown across them, of the tensions that hamper and threaten communication, of the failure and the horror of all efforts at union without love, and of whether Oneness when found is Something or Nothing. Since it is a great novel, it is, of course, far more than its dialectical pattern. But a grasp of that pattern in its full detail enables us to evaluate the novel more fully and fairly than has yet been done, and to arrive at an estimate of its author's achievement. We can now appraise Forster's apparently final effort to incarnate his difficult ideas; we can ask whether he has given them satisfactory aesthetic form, has successfully solved the problem which, as a novelist, he has set himself.

A Passage to India is not, as some critics have claimed, an expression of Forster's personal disillusion. Nor is it "almost unbelievably crude and weak" in its attempt at making a poetic communication about life. It is the last and best of Forster's attempts in that most difficult genre, the novel of ideas. It is an almost-successful attempt at an all-but-impossible task: an attempt to fuse the real world of social comedy and human conflict with the meaning and value of the universe which that world mirrors; to impose on experience the pattern of a moral vision; and out of these disparate elements to create a satisfying aesthetic whole. The wonder is not that it fails of complete success, but that it so nearly succeeds completely.

In *A Passage* appear the recurrent themes, the characteristic attitudes, and the peculiar gifts displayed by its author in his earlier fiction, integrated fully at last into the novel's structure and expressed in its characters, episodes, and atmosphere. Forster has found in it a thesis and a medium that enable him to use his full strength and to minimize or conceal his weaknesses. It is at once the finest and the most typical of his books, revealing most clearly his individual quality and distinction.

This is not to deny that, in some measure, the book is a failure. All good critics of Forster have remarked, in their different ways, upon the "double vision" apparent in his books: the contrast and often collision between the realistic and the symbolic, the two levels upon which characters and events exist and function. The most serious charge that has been laid at his door is that he is unable "to create realistic form, credible form, moving form" (Brown, *YR*, pp. 668–681); that his characters are inadequate to the ideas they incarnate; that his preoccupation with these ideas "leads him outside the limits of consciousness that his comedy would seem to involve" (Leavis, p. 185); that, in the words of Virginia Woolf, one of his most friendly critics, "his difficulty is to persuade his different gifts to combine into a single vision" (p. 643). He is both poet and satirist, both comedian and moralist, both preacher and artist. A mocking spirit of fantasy flouts his reality, poetry ruffles his prim surface, and his books, instead of being artistic wholes, are racked and rent by interior disharmony, the result of the tensions between his ill-assorted gifts and his contradictory aims.

From this charge, *A Passage* cannot wholly be absolved. Mr. Trilling, in his full-length study of Forster, has remarked upon the imbalance of its plot to its story. Its characters, he tells us, are right for the plot but not large enough for the story. By "story" Trilling seems to mean the thought I have just analyzed: the dialectical pattern of the book. The plot, as distinguished from this larger theme, is the story of Aziz; the tale of what goes on in his mind in the course of his tragically unsuccessful attempt to overcome the "separations and gaps" which divide him from Mrs. Moore and Adela. We see him progress from almost total ignorance to complete awareness of the unjust situation in which he is placed, and for which, as he comes to see, there is no remedy in human action. He retreats from Chandrapore to Mau, from the English and their Western science to a remote jungle where he can "let his instruments rust, [run] his little hospital at half steam, and [cause] no undue alarm" (p. 290). His failure and his disillusionment, humanly speaking, are the real center of interest in the novel.

Yet Aziz, however imaginatively realized as a man and an Indian, is, as Mr. Trilling observes, not large enough for the "story": for the cosmic stage on which his adventures are played. Though he comes to realize the uselessness of attempts at friendship and union, he never apprehends the real significance of his own ordeal nor relates it to the ordeal of India and of the whole world. Not for him, any more than for Ronny, Adela, or Fielding, is the world outside the arch, the silence beyond the echo. "It is useless discussing Hindus with me," he tells his friend during their last ride together. "Living with them teaches me no more" (p. 320).

On the other hand, the two "redemptive" characters large enough for the cosmic stage move among their human companions awkwardly, not wholly at ease with the world and the flesh. Mrs. Moore and Godbole are never really satisfactory as human beings, never vitally related to the people and events around them. Their human features are veiled by the larger-than-life masks they wear, like the actors in Greek tragedy playing at being gods. We perceive their effect without understanding or really accepting it; we take them at the valuation assigned by their author, but we do not put our own valuation upon them nor stamp them with the seal of our affirmation.

Thus, the gulf between symbol and reality, so often noticed in Forster's work, is again the chief feature, and in a sense, the chief failure of *A Passage to India*. The author tries hard to bridge it; but he does not quite succeed. Those who read the book as social comedy, or as an analysis of the Indian question, though they will find much to enjoy and admire, will be baffled and irritated again and again by the suggestion of a meaning far deeper than appears. To them, Godbole will be a nuisance, Mrs. Moore incomprehensible, Adela's adventure in the Marabar cave mere hysteria, and the Temple section irrelevant and incoherent. And those who perceive the larger "story," the immense and mysterious context into which the human adventures of Aziz and Adela are fitted, will also perceive more poignantly the crack between comic manner and cosmic meaning. "Between the conception / And the creation / Between the emotion / And the response / Falls the Shadow." The shadow of the double vision falls upon *A Passage*, as it does upon the earlier books: the real and the symbolic worlds co-exist independently instead of blending into one another and becoming a whole.

But only in this ultimate sense does the book fail. In all else it triumphs. Humor and poetry, those unlikely companions, walk arm in arm: tenderness and deep insight offer their balm to the sharp sting of satire. We have heard these themes—we have perceived these attitudes—we have met these people—we have watched these scenes—we have savored this delicate and lyric prose in Forster's earlier books. But we have never seen theme and character and attitude so clear, so free of ambiguity and doubt, we have never seen comedy so deft and light-handed, poetry so poignant. Not as a frieze but as a spirit, Anglo-India, India herself, pass before us. Their hundred voices sound in our ears, their pains and perplexities become our own and those of the whole world.

The value of personal relationships, the holiness of the heart's affections, always important in Forster's novels, is central to the theme, the characters, and the episodes of *A Passage*. Error and evil are the inevitable consequences of the failure of love between human beings: of the disastrous personal failure of Adela, and the no less disastrous social and political failure of the English officials and their wives. And whatever is saved from the wreck—Aziz's life, Adela's reason, Fielding's and Aziz's friendship—is saved by love alone: the love represented by Mrs. Moore's spirit. Whatever the level, human or divine, love is the only salvation.

"Kindness, more kindness, and even after that more kindness. I assure you it is the only hope." This theme is the dominant note of *A Passsage*, the keystone of its structural arch.

In the same way, in that "suspicion of action and of beliefs which sometimes seems to amount to passivity and defeatism"[14] which has been noted as characteristic of Forster, he is here leading from strength rather than weakness. For he here creates a world in which, whether it be on the social, the political, or the philosophical plane, sharply defined beliefs and active policies are productive of nothing but tension, hatred, strife, and disunion. Definite beliefs, Christian, Moslem, or Hindu, English or Indian, do but divide men more sharply from each other; and the world of action is the nightmare world of the English club, the Indian riot, the courtroom, the "world of telegrams and anger" shown at its most hostile and destructive. Neither beliefs nor action can save us, Forster says, and in *A Passage* compels us to believe, but only "the secret understanding of the heart," which may fail but can never be really defeated, and is our only answer to the voice of the Marabar.

So too Forster's dissatisfaction with civilization, with that humane and liberal culture which produced him and which he represents is, in *A Passage*, integrated into the plan of the book in a more vital sense than was true of the earlier novels. Did Margaret Schlegel really marry Henry Wilcox? We have never quite believed it. But we can believe in Fielding, in his effort and in his failure, for we see—how clearly!—what Fielding is up against, and we see too that his cultivated agnostic spirit is wholly unable to comprehend the awful mystery or muddle of the world beyond the arch. Fielding believes in good will plus culture and intelligence; but we see him baffled and wistful before the dim apprehension of something, he knows not what—something his wife knows and Mrs. Moore had known. *A Passage* shows, far more fully and satisfactorily than Forster's earlier books, the inadequacy, the collapse, of the liberal-bourgeois-agnostic mind face to face with the ultimate mystery at the heart of the universe. The hollowness of Margaret Schlegel's world stands for the first time fully revealed.

Even one of Forster's real weaknesses as a novelist, his "demurely bloodless gaiety,"[14] that embarrassment before the sexual relation which mars his other novels without exception, is a source almost of strength in *A Passage*. For his task here is not to portray a pair of lovers, and to fail at making them lovers, as was true, for example, of George and Lucy in *A Room With a View*. His intention is to show us a young man and

[14] "Morton D. Zabel, 'A Forster Revival' " (review of Trilling), *The Nation*, CLVII (7 Aug. 1943), 158–159.

woman who attempt to become lovers and who are temperamentally unequipped for their rôles. So, while it may be said that Ronny and Adela are one of the least attractive pairs in fiction, it may also be said that it is necessary to the purpose and effect of *A Passage* that this should be so. They are not there to show love and the life of the senses triumphant, as George and Lucy were—and to fail, as George and Lucy failed—but to show the horror and disaster of attempts at union *without* love.

The same thing is true of Forster's gifts of character-drawing, of social satire, and of that lyrical sensibility so oddly contrasted with it. A few deft strokes, and the English ladies—Mrs. Turton, Mrs. Callendar, Mrs. McBryde—are forever impaled in all their shallow and insular arrogance. Fielding, the holy man minus the holiness, is both more sympathetic and more vivid than his prototype, old Mr. Emerson. The portraits of the Indians, Hamidullah, the Nawab Bahadur, Mahmoud Ali, Mr. Das, form a varied gallery of individuals who never degenerate into types, and are crowned with that triumph of insight and imaginative sympathy, the figure of Aziz: most interesting, most human, most believable of all Forster's characters. Satirist of the collision between the English middle class and an alien culture, Forster creates in *A Passage* some unforgettable scenes: the discussions at the English club; the trial; the Indian riot; both comedy and satire given sharper edge and more pungent acidity by the deceptive lightness and grace of touch. And the poet who describes the Marabar caves, or the festival of Shri Krishna, evokes for us the very spirit of the Indian earth and conveys a sense of the ineluctable mystery of human existence.

It is true, as E. K. Brown has reminded us, that the end of fiction is the realistic representation of life, and that a novel is not saved by a great theme (*YR*, pp. 668–681). But a novel which displays such gifts of political penetration and social comedy, such beauty of language and depth of character-portrayal, is not rendered less great by a theme that is worthy of it, and which it manages so very nearly to subdue into a complete aesthetic pattern. In defiance of all modern canons of criticism, I believe it is sometimes preferable to fail of complete success in a great venture than to succeed wholly in a petty one; and by that token, I believe with Brown that *A Passage to India* is and will remain "the subtlest effort in our time to write the novel of ideas in English."

Detroit, Michigan

THE STRUCTURE OF *A PASSAGE TO INDIA*

HUGH MACLEAN

THE meaning of Forster's *A Passage to India* has been progressively illuminated by the chief critics of the novel. Rose Macaulay admired the book mainly for its "sheer beauty," but noticed also its merits as a psychological novel, though considering these "damaged by over-mystification and queerness." Lionel Trilling discovered that the book was not limited to India, but was "about all of human life." The late E. K. Brown demonstrated the presence of an intricate symbolic pattern which threads through the novel and gives it form. Any discussion of *A Passage to India* must depend heavily on Professor Brown's interpretation. The present article is no exception. But the methods of that study may be extended to throw further light on the novel. Specifically, it is suggested that *A Passage to India* reflects the approach and mood of Whitman's poem *Passage to India* more closely than has been indicated; that the claims of emotion, logic, and intuition to be central in man's search for the meaning of life are critically examined in successive divisions of the book; that the pattern of symbolism outlined by Professor Brown is capable of considerable elaboration; and that what happens to Mrs. Moore in the cave is not so much evil in itself as it is a necessary preparation for the consequent freeing of good influences to act in a way previously impossible.

Whitman's *Passage to India* begins by linking present with past, and by asserting the constancy of "God's purpose" through time. Praise of explorers and adventurers gradually gives way to an invitation to "the soul" to embark on parallel, but profounder, journeys. The poet suggests that only by plumbing the deepest mysteries of "primal thought," behind even the sacred books of ancient India, may the soul at last unite with divine all-embracing power, and so accomplish a "passage to more than India." The poem moves successively past action, emotion, and reason, to a satisfying intuition. The deeds of da Gama and his kind are praised, but

> not your deeds only O voyagers, O scientists and inventors, shall be justified,
> All these hearts as of fretted children shall be sooth'd,
> All affection shall be fully responded to . . .
> Nature and Man shall be disjoin'd and diffused no more. . . .

As an activeness which springs largely from emotional desire yields to a more scientific and thoughtful explorativeness, Whitman sings of

Vol. XXII, no. 2, Jan., 1953

> Doubts to be solv'd, the map incognita, blanks to be fill'd,
> The foot of man unstay'd, the hands never at rest . . .
> Something swelling in humanity now like the sap of the
> earth in spring. . . .

But the soul must go beyond this, seeking

> the voyage of the mind's return,
> To reason's early paradise,
> Back, back, to wisdom's birth, to innocent intuitions,
> Again with fair creation.

Not only the title of Forster's novel but its theme and even its structure are reflected in *Passage to India*. The second section sets out the three-part division adopted by Forster.

> O you temples fairer than lilies pour'd over by the rising sun!
> O you fables spurning the known, eluding the hold of the known,
> mounting to heaven!
> You lofty and dazzling towers, pinnacled, red as roses, burnished
> with gold!

This, in reverse, is Forster's approach to the various Indias: sensuous mosques, appealing to the emotional Aziz; fabled caves, "eluding the hold of the known," beyond Fielding's grasp; temples "fairer" to the soul than a beauty purely natural. The instruments of vision are parallel in Whitman and Forster. "Unloos'd dreams" prepare Aziz for his encounter with Mrs. Moore. She in turn finds completeness after death through the "far-darting beams of the spirit" emanating from Godbole. The novel's theme is stated in this same section of the poem.

> Lo, soul, seest thou not God's purpose from the first?
> The earth to be spann'd, connected by network,
> The races, neighbors, to marry and be given in marriage,
> The oceans to be cross'd, the distant brought near,
> The lands to be welded together.

Since Forster ironically compares Whitman's ideal with the meagre actuality of Anglo-India, this vision does not universally take place in the novel. The people in the first part are baffled and uneasy, as are Whitman's races of men:

> Wandering, yearning, curious, with restless explorations,
> With questionings, baffled, formless, feverish, with never-happy
> hearts,
> With that sad incessant refrain, *Wherefore unsatisfied soul?* and
> *Whither O mocking life?*

The first two parts of the novel are almost wholly negative and offer no path through the obstacles preventing mutual understanding. This is so because the central figures, each in his own way, attempt to force life within the limits of emotion or logic. Just so far as they relax this attempt do they achieve some measure of vision, though not necessarily beatitude, since the Westerners especially are extremely limited by personality. This is true obviously of the English of the Civil Station; less obviously but still powerfully of Adela and even Mrs. Moore. Mrs. Moore is a kind of sounding-board. By her reactions the reader may gauge the relative efficacy of viewpoints adopted by Aziz, Fielding, Godbole. In the first section, Mrs. Moore is passive, kindly, receptive, and a soothing influence, but she is bewildered by India and by the silence beyond the echo which she finds there. Later her soul grasps "reality," but is still shackled by physical personality, so that glancing insight alternates with exasperation and contempt. At last, through Godbole, her soul is "impelled" to completeness. Whitman's return, midway in his poem, to an age before the past, "to primal thought . . . To reason's early paradise, Back, back, to wisdom's birth, to innocent intuitions," is repeated in sombre tones by Forster's "Caves," which are timeless, and from which will come the vision which enlightens the soul of Mrs. Moore, and which indirectly will save Adela from herself. Aziz and Fielding are gripped throughout by their individual preconceptions and hereditary prejudices, which prevent them from assimilating more than "an occasional scrap of Godbole." Aziz longs for another time, the age of Babur; Fielding is at home only in another place, the Mediterranean, where resides "the spirit in a reasonable form." Neither can accept India, the muddle, where God "is, was not, is not, was." The Moslem is puzzled, though made to "glow," by Mrs. Moore; she eludes Fielding too. Only Godbole can encompass her soul.

Nevertheless, the implication of the book is, like that of the poem, optimistic of a resolution of the difficulties which in *A Passage to India* often seem hopelessly insoluble. Godbole's benediction is, after all, extended to Hindu, Moslem, and Christian alike. Forster's dimly seen time, "not yet . . . not there," to be brought about by "friendship . . . good will . . . kindness," Whitman has also imagined.

> Reckoning ahead O soul, when thou, the time achiev'd,
> The seas all cross'd, weather'd the capes, the voyage done,
> Surrounded, copest, frontest God, yieldest, the aim attain'd,
> As fill'd with friendship, love complete, the Elder Brother found,
> The Younger melts in fondness in his arms.

The soul of Mrs. Moore makes this journey and at last, through Godbole's mediation, finds completeness in the divine Elder Brother's arms. "Steer for the deep waters only": this too is Forster's appeal. The experience of Mrs. Moore must somehow be shared with all men. The faults and excesses of imperialism are easily ridiculed. More important is the land "where mariner has not yet dared to go," the brotherhood of an internationalism which must precede the soul's salvation. Godbole remarks of the one poem by Aziz which seems to suggest this, "Ah, that is bhakti; ah, my young friend, that is different and very good. Ah, India, who seems not to move, will go straight there while the other nations waste their time." The key to this ideal both Whitman and Forster suspect lies beneath and beyond India's past. Whitman cries, "Eclaircise the myths Asiatic, the primitive fables." Godbole's highest praise is that the poem by Aziz "might be rendered into Sanskrit almost." Future will link with past: "dreams of the ideal," a vision forgotten, will make new the lost "young maturity of brood and bloom" "below the Sanscrit and the Vedas." After "man's long probation," passively, intuitively will come into being the reconciliation of races which emotion and logic can only confirm in separation.

II

The opening section of the novel, "Mosque," appropriately deals with the Moslem Aziz. He is a creature of impulse, dashing everywhere, organizing parties and picnics, changing his mind continuously, loving passionately but as quickly despising the object of his love. His departure from Hamidullah's is as violent and impulsive as his arrival there. His first words to Mrs. Moore are a snarl; his parting, moments later, a happy acceptance of her as "an Oriental." His personality pervades the whole section. Since he is primarily an emotional person, the dominant tone of the section is one of emotion, impulse, even sentiment, based on the senses and on memory. Wandering in Hamidullah's garden, Aziz, deaf to politics, is conscious of the sweet-smelling trees, dreams of Persian poetry, and thinks increasingly of dinner. In the mosque, he recalls verses of a former Moslem age, and, carried away by the phrase "the secret understanding of the heart," he yields to tears, assigning to the mosque "meanings the builder had never intended." Appropriately, Aziz thinks in terms of black and white, good or bad. There is no middle ground of compromise. In the mosque, "the front—in full moonlight—had the appearance of marble, and the ninety-nine names of God on the frieze stood out black, as the frieze stood out white against the sky." This memory swims back to him at the close of the section, as he drops off to sleep in a haze of affection, sentiment, and emotion, all epitomized in his dream by "domes whereunder were inscribed, black against white, the ninety-nine attributes of God." This tendency to set up a rigid dualism, which pleases Aziz, is symptomatic. He is often mistaken. He fails to understand the English, even Mrs. Turton; with Fielding he has innumerable difficulties, psychological as well as linguistic, which lead him into blind alleys. "In every remark he found a meaning, but not always the true meaning, and his life though vivid was largely a dream." Further, his attitude to life is rickety and unstable. ". . . his belief in the life to come would pale to a hope, vanish, reappear, all in a single sentence or a dozen heart-beats, so that the corpuscles of his blood rather than he seemed to decide which opinion he should hold, and for how long. It was so with all his opinions. Nothing stayed, nothing passed that did not return. . . ."

Since Aziz is central at this stage, the note of black-and-white dualism accompanied by confused thought is evident throughout the section. After the Nawab's car bumps the ghost-hyena, "the torch created such high lights and black shadows that they could not interpret what it revealed. Moreover, Adela in her excitement knelt and swept her skirts about, until it was she if anyone who appeared to have attacked the car." The Bridge Party, a hopeless, because Western, attempt to find greys between black and white, breaks at once into the old division, whites on the verandah, Indians at the bottom of the garden. Mrs. Turton is contemptuous, Turton foolishly shrewd, Mrs. Moore baffled in her efforts to communicate with Indians. The latter seem willing to receive advances, but nothing comes of it: "a shapeless discussion occurred." Since this is the opening section of the book, such shapelessness remains.

The negative quality dominating this section is introduced and emphasized by the opening chapter.

> . . . the city of Chandrapore presents nothing extraordinary. . . . There are no bathing steps on the river front, as the Ganges happens not to be holy here; indeed there is no river front, and bazaars shut out the wide and shifting panorama of the stream. . . . There is no painting and scarcely any carving in the bazaars. . . . the civil station . . . charms not, neither does it repel. . . . It has nothing hideous in it . . . it shares nothing with the city except the overarching sky.

Everyone is baffled. The English are hopelessly at sea in India and with Indians, and content themselves with petty politics, amateur theatricals at the Club, and mean-spirited remarks on "natives." The Moslem community is equally mystified by the English, and hardly less uncharitable in its comments on the "whites." It is also bewildered by Hinduism: Aziz, trying to sound Godbole on the caves, is "defeated at every move by an opponent who would not even admit that a move had been made." The English Adela is unaware that "the comparatively simple mind of the Mohammedan was encountering Ancient Night." Nor is Godbole all-comprehending: "he had been silenced now; no doubt not willingly, he was concealing something." External nature itself is weak and baffled: even the Indian sun "failed to triumph . . . he was not the eternal promise . . . he was merely a creature, like the rest, and so debarred from glory." Restlessness clouds the section. Mrs. Moore's voice floats out "to swell the night's uneasiness." The night itself is "never tranquil." In this air Christianity is reduced to striking attitudes. The mercy of God may include monkeys, less probably wasps, hardly bacteria or mud. Only Godbole, who excludes nothing, will be able to encompass everything.

Harmony seems altogether absent. There are only false harmonies, or parodies of harmony. The Moslems, Hindus, and Christian, emerging from the house of Aziz, are drawn together only by fear of "the hot weather," and only momentarily. Adela and Ronny become engaged and believe themselves in love, but the typically cavalier announcement of this by Forster sufficiently instructs the reader. Aziz finds harmony only in dreams. The one harmonious character present is by Western standards peculiarly incongruous. Godbole "wore a turban that looked like pale purple macaroni, coat, waistcoat, dhoti, socks with clocks. The clocks matched the turban, and his whole appearance suggested harmony—as if he had reconciled the products of East and West, mental as well as physical, and could never be discomposed." He stands apart from the others, who willingly or not are continually isolated and thrown back upon the resources of self. There are certainly hints that this disunity need not be permanent. "Experience, not character, divided them," comments the author, noticing also "the little ineffectual unquenchable flames" of the Indians' separate efforts to understand one another. But the "kindness, more kindness, and even after that more kindness" which is for Aziz ideal, and which echoes Mrs. Moore's parallel appeal for "good will and more good will and more good will," is at this stage incapable of realization.

Forster prepares for later events by introducing a number of symbols, some of which will be associated with disharmony, separation, and evil, others with understanding, harmony, and peace. These are to be handholds on the difficult surface of the second section. The recurrence of certain symbols will guide the mind to Forster's meaning. The "hyena" bumped by the car, the tire-marks noticed by Adela after the accident, the snakes mentioned by Aziz in the mosque, the "hot weather" feared by most characters: each will in the second section announce or accompany a moment of disharmony or misunderstanding. Even in this section, events reflect the appearance of these symbols. The mention of snakes disturbs Mrs. Moore's equanimity; the "hyena" evokes "a loud cry of terror" from the Nawab Bahadur, and later a fearful shiver from Mrs. Moore; the "hot weather" continually oppresses, reminds of self, and dissipates efforts to establish harmony. One symbol is especially mysterious and withdrawn: the echo, discussed in detail by Professor Brown, is used at this stage to distinguish Mrs. Moore's insight from Ronny's obtuseness. Ronny, angry at a servant, makes a row; bustle and pandemonium result, but cease in time, since "the Englishman was appeased by their echoes." To Mrs. Moore, in contrast, India presents a mystery insoluble in terms of Christianity: "Outside the arch there seemed always an arch, beyond the remotest echo a silence." Finally there is a green bird, which counters by its appearance the forces of distrust and selfishness. Its appearance accompanies awakening mutual fondness in Ronny and Adela. Of course, Ronny is "no good at all at birds," and prefers the false birds of MacBryde's bird book, so that the liaison seems unlikely to prosper; yet the one true note of understanding seems to be due in a measure to the bird's presence. Godbole's song at tea-time, carrying a mysterious but certainly peaceful message, "was the song of an unknown bird." Adela's remark that she doesn't "know the animals any better than the birds here" may indicate her capacity for passive insight as well as hysteria, made fact in the following section.

The opening segment of the novel, in short, is primarily negative and unsatisfactory. It prepares for later events. The way of Aziz, of emotion, sentiment, memory, is weak, and even reinforces the influence of self-centredness in man and society. Godbole seems almost to be trying to tell the others this. In his song, the god "refuses to come," because the maiden's prayer is yearningly self-assertive in both its original and its revised form; the god will not come to her only, nor to her as an individual among others. The god in fact "neglects" to come. Such appeals arouse neither divine acquiescence nor divine rage, but indifference. India too, therefore, while under the spell of such influences, gets nowhere. "*In vain* did each item in it call out, 'Come, come.' "

III

Fielding is the spokesman of the second section. No individual, of course, can represent "Caves" as Aziz does "Mosque." Forster ironically selects a late-comer to India, one of the race least fitted to cope with the caves and their message. The opening chapter this time sounds the note of age. "The Ganges, though flowing from the foot of Vishnu and through Siva's hair, is not an ancient stream." A number of similarly suggestive phrases reinforce the atmosphere of unimaginable antiquity, and refer also to the mystery of these caves. "Nothing, nothing attaches to them. . . ." If their depths were finally plumbed, mankind would be wiser in no way. Fielding, though incapable of the finest insights, is remarkable among the English of the novel. He seems on first acquaintance to link East and West. The world he regards as "a globe of men who are trying to reach one another and can best do so by the help of good will plus culture and intelligence"; he likes to believe that "we exist . . . in terms of each other's minds." But he is no Godbole. His inclination to communicate with the older man after the trial is soon forgotten; the mention of Mrs. Moore's death which momentarily creates a bond between Fielding and Hamidullah has no lasting effect. "The soul is tired in a moment."

Being English, Fielding proceeds basically in terms of logic and intellect, and his thought gives the tone to this section, as the emotions of Aziz coloured the first. Fielding tends to be patronizingly amused at the emotional Aziz; and their conversations reveal his logical approach, largely responsible for misunderstandings. With Godbole, Fielding's logic is completely at a loss. Every attempt to get from Godbole some rational explanation of the cave-incident is thwarted, since he boggles at the echo and its significance, which "lay at the verge of Fielding's mind. He could never develop it." Though Fielding's quickness warns him of something "queer" at the picnic, and of the trial's result before other Englishmen grasp it, he cannot abandon his habitual manner of thought; lawyer-like, after the trial, he tries to solve the mystery by logical hypotheses, though Adela by then fully comprehends the futility of such methods. Fielding is to Aziz as spectator to actor. He is hardly more than a chorus, commenting on events the significance of which he cannot grasp. The vision of each man is incomplete; but the reader's expands in proportion as the shortcomings of Aziz and Fielding are revealed.

Neither Fielding nor Godbole is present during the central excursion to the caves. Partly for dramatic reasons, the participants hold the stage alone; harmonious influences are removed also, so that the three excursionists must depend utterly on their individual resources. The caves have nothing to say to Aziz, but a good deal to both women: what they say amounts to a riddle of negation for both, but the message seems different in each case because of the mental equipment and psychological condition of the two. Adela, well-meaning but comparatively shallow, has come to India to be married, and this is fairly continuously on her mind as she climbs with Aziz to the caves. His mind is on breakfast, hers on marriage—and love. She converses absently on these subjects with Aziz, and muses not very connectedly on his sensual appeal to women of his race. The notion of race differences leads her to ask a foolish question; he is insulted, sharply releases her hand, which he had been holding to help her ascend, and turns quickly into a cave, divided from her spiritually and physically. The ominous reappearance of the tire-marks made by the Nawab's car—as footholds in the rock climbed by Aziz and Adela—has warned of some threat. Now quite alone, Adela enters a cave and comes face to face with the age and mystery described earlier as incomprehensible even to Buddha, who "shunned" the caves with, it is implied, respect and awe. Adela succumbs at once to hysteria. Her mind is quite overcome by the impact of what amounts to a primordial image; the shock temporarily produces something like a mental black-out. Later, the three things in her mind when she entered the cave, love, marriage, and sensuality, suggest to her frantically groping senses and reason that an attack had been made on her in the cave. Aziz, the obvious culprit, is arrested, thus setting in motion the second part of this section.

Mrs. Moore is different from Adela. She holds views broadly Christian. She not only speaks of religion to Ronny (for whom "the conversation had become unreal as soon as Christianity entered it"), but wanders alone, actuated by a profound interest, into the mosque where she first encounters Aziz. She feels "kinship with the heavenly bodies." Accepted by Aziz as "an Oriental," she is potentially harmonious. But on the way to the caves, strange influences begin to work on her, partly because there is a difference between her nature and that of Adela. The latter had said, "I don't believe in the Hot Weather," to which Mrs. Moore had answered, "I believe in the Hot Weather, but never did I suppose it would bottle me up as it will," the unexpected phrase acting as a hint of what is to come. As Mrs. Moore nears the caves which are "older than anything in the world," she begins to doubt the power of love, or rather the forms which love takes in her civilization. "In particular," she feels, "too much fuss has been made over marriage." Jacques Maritain writes: ". . . of the two things which alone make life worth living, love is more valuable than intuition when it transforms us into something better than we are, but intuition is not liable to all kinds of illusion and moral defilement as love is: because intuition deals with knowledge . . . and, *qua* intuition, never misses the mark."[1] Mrs. Moore comes to realize

[1]J. Maritain, "Dante's Innocence and Luck," *Kenyon Review*, XIV, (1952), 305.

that even Christian love has not made her or those about her better; her intuition, seeking out true knowledge, is unsatisfied. She and her companions are steadily oppressed by feelings of inadequacy and disappointment; the expected glory of the sunrise results instead in dimness and "decayed" hues, a venomous black cobra rears up at the train (a tree-stump to Adela's glasses, it remains a snake for the natives and the reader); a "spiritual silence" closes down, and is not entirely pleasant. These signs lead up to Mrs. Moore's entry into the cave, immediately prefaced by her thought that the "Brahminy kite" flapping over the black entrance is a throw-back to a time "before birds."

Mrs. Moore's passivity and spiritual receptiveness are signs of her special insight, but the Christian form which her religion takes is unable to cope with the cave and its echo. Before the picnic, her gentle sympathy is ineffectual. Events take their course around and in spite of her. But after the cave, her knowledge first, and later her influence, actively move those about her. As a result of her encounter with "Boum," she undergoes an actual split of soul from body and from self. At first she feels merely physical revulsion, but soon the impact of the cave's echo begins to strike at all her previous beliefs, i.e., all the forms of her existence. The cave now seems to be "stuffed with a snake composed of small snakes." Despite a desperate effort to reassert her selfhood by clinging to physical sensation, she is forced to "surrender to the vision." Once having recognized and accepted the absolute which is "Boum," her soul is divorced, except for erratic and quixotic excursions into sense, from her body and from reason, sense, memory, feeling. Confronted with a new "Mrs. Moore," the others are taken aback. Ronny expects interest and finds irritability; Adela expects sympathy and finds apathy. But the soul of Mrs. Moore has passed beyond the need for forms and impatiently repels Adela's two efforts to reestablish understanding. Her soul is impatient to be loosed from the clinging and useless body.

"My body, my miserable body," she sighed. "Why isn't it strong? Oh, why can't I walk away and be gone? Why can't I finish my duties and be gone? Why do I get headaches and puff when I walk? And all the time this to do and that to do and this to do in your way and that to do in her way, and everything sympathy and confusion and bearing one another's burdens. Why can't this be done and that be done in my way and they be done and I at peace? Why has anything to be done, I cannot see. Why all this marriage, marriage? . . . The human race would have become a single person centuries ago if marriage was any use. And all this rubbish about love, love in a church, love in a cave, as if there is the least difference, and I held up from business over such trifles!"

Occasionally her insight glances through the shell. "Of course he is innocent," she replies to Ronny's inquiry about Aziz; but it is a matter of no moment to her. Like Godbole, "she really knew more than character but could not impart it"; unlike him, that part of her which is Christian, formal, and personalized, cannot be absorbed harmoniously into the soul's free vision. The earthly expression of her spirit is petulant and ill at ease. Content and form have in a flash been made aware of each other, and form is terrified and ashamed. Only death can free the soul; until then, "Mrs. Moore" cannot reassume the role of a peaceful and soothing influence. To observe what happens, it is necessary to return to Adela Quested.

Since the cave, Adela has been convinced that Aziz has made a physical attack on her. Shortly before the trial, birds make their final appearance, this time as harbingers of the outcome. As two sparrows fly about the room, Adela cries to Ronny that Aziz must be innocent. But the birds disappear, and insight abandons Adela until the trial. About the time Adela takes the stand, Mrs. Moore (the reader later learns) dies at sea; outside the court-room, the Indians break into their chant of "Esmiss Esmoor"; Adela acknowledges her release from the bondage of error by turning to her uncomprehending friends: "I shall be all right, and thank you all, thank you, thank you for your kindness." Buoyed by an insight granted by the soul of Mrs. Moore, she subsequently "withdraws" her accusation. Her nature is such that she cannot completely make over her attitude to life; forms, to Adela, are too strongly assertive; but she has gained something: "She was no longer examining life, but being examined by it; she had become a real person." No longer a virtual spectator, she has become an actor in life. It is precisely for this reason that Fielding, who remains spectator, cannot communicate meaningfully with Adela after the trial. Professor Brown has said that Fielding differs from Adela in that "he has, and she has not, some grasp of the nature of personal relationships."[2] This is true prior to the trial, but their positions are reversed afterward; she reaches a tentative hand to Fielding, but he withdraws. Yet it is right that Fielding should be the spokesman of this section, even though he is clearly at times an object of ridicule, for only Mrs. Moore and to a lesser extent Adela have participated in the cave's experience. The others are unenlightened, and Fielding, curious though bewildered, can best serve as the instrument through which the reader may try to assess what was in the cave. Forster invites us, if we can, to go on from the point Fielding reached and beyond which he could not proceed.

[2]E. K. Brown, *Rhythm in the Novel* (Toronto, 1950), 102.

But the last pages of "Caves" suggest the futility of this course. Fielding has listened to Godbole's wisdom glumly and without comprehension. Now he admits to himself, during the roof-top conversation with Aziz, that he has tried, in mind, "to kill Mrs. Moore"—an attempt which of course fails. "She still eluded him," just as the "thousands of stars" (with which Mrs. Moore has earlier been associated) silence Aziz when he attempts to communicate with her. And Fielding leaves India unsatisfied, relieved to move away from "muddle" and beyond Suez into the midst of formal beauty.

The second section is another blind alley on the road to discovery of the meaning of life. Aziz was unable to navigate "the deep water"; Fielding consciously recoils from it. But, as before, the answer waits for those who can accept it. "Truth is not truth in that exacting land unless there go with it kindness and more kindness and kindness again, unless the Word that was with God also is God." And there is a difference in Godbole's chant of "Come, come." At first, God came not; India called in vain. Now, India "calls 'Come' through her hundred mouths, through objects ridiculous and august. But come to what? She has never defined. She is not a promise, only an appeal." The tone has altered. Mystery remains; but refusal has become something in the nature of uncertainty as to what form the "coming" will assume and how it will be received. And, as Godbole says, "Absence implies presence, absence is not non-existence, and we are therefore entitled to repeat, 'Come, come, come, come.' " The two quotations presage the answer of the concluding section, in which Godbole, sitting among "objects ridiculous and august," imitates God.

IV

Forster begins this section ironically by emphasizing its changed place and time, passing at once to speak to the God who "is not born yet—that will occur at midnight—but He has also been born centuries ago, nor can He ever be born, because he is the Lord of the Universe, who transcends human processes." The conditions of which Aziz and Fielding are so conscious mean nothing to Godbole, who looks across a carpet at God. Emotion and logic are alike neglected; intuition has replaced them, and even that term is insufficiently descriptive of the mystical tone which pervades this section. Other things have changed too. The blasting heat of earlier sections has yielded, as in *The Waste Land*, to torrential rains which drench land, animals, and people. The black-and-white dualism of Aziz and the caves' complete colourlessness have been replaced by greys and greens. There is a grey lake near the Asirgarh railway station (Mrs. Moore's last sight of India), and the hills look "grey-green" and are "covered with temples." Greys and greens, suggesting a mysterious harmony of black and white, appear not only in the rain, but in a great number of "blurs." The Hindu crowd at the religious festival emanates music from so many sources "that the sum-total was untrammelled . . . melted into a single mass." These sounds later strike Aziz as "blurred." The town is "a blur of light." The whole occasion is "a great blur," of which "no man could say where was the emotional centre, any more than he could locate the heart of a cloud." These blurs suggest the new-found harmony which increasingly dominates people and events, but which is not explicable in Moslem or Western terms. God is of a piece with every person, action, and moment of the festival's apparent confusion, which reflects life. Singers chant, Indian bands play European melodies, Godbole clashes cymbals. At midnight, "Infinite Love took upon itself the form of Shri Krishna, and saved the world. All sorrow was annihilated, not only for Indians, but for foreigners, birds, caves, railways, and the stars; all became joy, all laughter; there had never been disease nor doubt, misunderstanding, cruelty, fear." The symbols of previous sections congregate and are unified in this gigantic free-for-all. "A cobra of papier-mâché now appeared on the carpet"; Mrs. Moore's wasp returns to Godbole's meditations; the flies earlier swept irritably aside by Aziz, "awoke and claimed their share of God's bounty." This religion does not balk at bees or bacteria but comprehends moods as well as beasts and men: the priests play games symbolic of God's sense of humour. The jar of rice-and-milk paste, broken over and into the howling throng, symbolizes the union of all things in this welter of commingled phenomena, and the blessing of that union by divine fiat. This "frustration of reason and form" is centred on yet another blur, the altar, "a jumble" of rose-leaves, bananas, plates, poems. On one is the legend "God si Love." In English to demonstrate God's universality, its error shows only that the desire serves for the deed, which, as most Westerners do not see, is of little account. Failure in this sense is and must be integral to life. And yet, as Mrs. Moore had observed, "I think everyone fails, but there are so many kinds of failure."

Aziz and Fielding seem momentarily to have been forgotten in the harmonious muddle. Aziz had never discovered the meaning of what he regards as "an annual antic." He seems to remain an outsider. ". . . he felt bored, slightly cynical, like his own dear Emperor Babur, who came down from the north and found in Hindustan no good fruit, no fresh water or witty conversation, not even a friend." Fielding too has been trying to reanimate his friendship with Aziz, but as usual by means of "irrefragable logic." He wants to "argue and reconstruct." But other influences have been at work. Godbole, imitating God, has recreated Mrs. Moore in his mind, and passively made her whole. "Completeness, not reconstruction," has absorbed her. The passive quality of Godbole's method is emphasized by his failure to impel in the same way other objects: "logic and conscious effort had seduced" him when he attempted too deliberately to impose his will. Mrs. Moore has also been recreated in a more tangible form. Her son Ralph, stung by bees, is soothed by Aziz, who involuntarily reacts to the hovering influence of "Mrs. Moore" by greeting Ralph in the same terms of comradeship employed years before in the mosque. Aziz is puzzled, but recognizes "the eternal goodness of Mrs. Moore," and his actions continue to be guided by her influence as he willingly guides the English out on the lake, unearthing the oars he had so maliciously hidden. On the far shore the ceremony approaches a climax, as the sacred symbols are given up to the beneficent water, swollen by the rains of "a magnificent monsoon," which will renew and save. Into the tray bearing the clay figures crashes the boat bearing Aziz, Fielding, and the young Moores. Comically but safely thrown into the water, they also become symbols of a promise of fulfilment for the hopes of men. All nature—artillery, drums, elephants, lightning—celebrates the miraculously renewed promise. Aziz and Fielding have thus at last been drawn, but not by any individual or personality, into the inclusive harmony, and are accepted in the union of Infinite Love. Echoes, hyena-ghosts, and hot weather disappear. To confirm the change, a cobra glides, but now peacefully, through a toy landscape, a "parklike scene," with "purple hills," "round white clouds," and "custard-apple trees." Riding together, Aziz and Fielding make way for the cobra in a friendly spirit. They too are "friends again," though as individuals they see only that "after the funny shipwreck there had been no more nonsense or bitterness, and they went back laughingly to their old relationship as if nothing had happened." Aziz "wants to do kind actions all round," beginning with a thank-you letter to Adela. Nature too breathes out love: "myriads of kisses around them as the earth drew the water in."

But Aziz and Fielding are too individual, too conscious of self, too perversely emotional or logical to forsake their course of life, nor would Godbole expect anything else. Fielding soon withdraws, remarking dully that "different people had different points of view." Aziz is as impatient of Hindus as ever: "Living with them teaches me no more." Both regard Godbole as an amusing grotesque.

"Does the old fellow still say, 'Come, come'?"
"Oh, presumably."

Even here Godbole moves them: Fielding wonders briefly about the attachment of Mrs. Moore's children to Hinduism, and Aziz is prompted to add a footnote to his letter to Adela, promising to remember her always in conjunction with Mrs. Moore. But neither pursues his train of thought; they turn together to more immediate problems, Aziz emotional, Fielding logical and matter-of-fact. Their friendship remains limited by their personalities. Nature rejects an extension of a relationship on these terms to wider spheres: buildings, dead and living beasts, the earth itself, "didn't want it, they said in their hundred voices, 'No, not yet,' and the sky said, 'No, not there.' " Forster might have added, "Not in that way," since the true friendship, kindness, and understanding of which Mrs. Moore had spoken is attainable only by abandoning the limitations inherent in the relationship between Aziz and Fielding.

Nevertheless, the ending of the novel, though phrased in negative terms, is a promise, not a denial, in the same way as Godbole's remark, "Absence implies presence." Like him, we are entitled "to repeat, 'Come, come, come, come.' " Professor Brown comments that in the novel the order of the universe "can be merely glimpsed, never seized for sure."[3] Aziz and Fielding indeed glimpse only when intuitive wisdom breaks through the customary veils of emotional and logical attitudes. But Godbole's mind certainly has seized this order, or he could not have impelled Mrs. Moore to completeness. Mrs. Moore eventually grasps its significance; that is why she acts as she does on her return from the caves. And the effect of the novel is to make us feel that the glimpses available to all may, though with difficulty, be converted to full and active vision. This may come about when men relax their efforts to impose form on life and allow life to take its own form, as Adela Quested was at least temporarily able to do. Only then will what is in the caves be seen not as evil but as merely a part of the order in the universe. Although the individual can to some extent determine the nature of things by his attitude toward them and toward himself, this is only a preliminary to absorption of the self within a transcendental frame of reference. In this sense, Forster's novel is "a passage to more than India."

[3]*Ibid.*, 114.

"A Passage to India": The Echoes in the Marabar Caves

KEITH HOLLINGSWORTH*

"*A Passage to India*": *The Echoes in the Marabar Caves*

Although the echoes in the Marabar caves have been commented on by nearly everyone who has written about Forster's *A Passage to India*, they continue to tantalize. They suggest strongly but are ringed with uncertainties; their power is felt but partly eludes explanation; and they seem to have more than one message, or at least to shift their import as they are met in different contexts. Since they are genuine symbols, every effort to explain them reduces and flattens them, and consequently seems less than the truth. The interpretation which follows cannot hope to be an exception. It is not presented, however, as being exclusive; it is rather to be taken along with other descriptions of the symbolic character of the echoes which are in harmony with the author's intention. Most of those in print deal scantily with the fascinating, sometimes puzzling texture of details. In the present exploration, what the echoes suggest on the open or upper level of the story will be noticed first; thereafter we descend, at certain points, to a subterranean level of allegory.

Forster's book, concerned with the relation of man to man and with the relation of man to something beyond himself, deals constantly with communication as the servant of relationship and love. The novel is filled with invitations and letters, with speech and reply; efforts at communication are always being made and are never wholly successful. Forster looks on with wistfulness and humor while people try to speak over all the barriers belonging to human life in a cosmos. How appropriate, then, is his choice of the echo, which is essentially a mockery of communication.[1] An echo is not a response from a listener; from wall or cliff the sounds are returned by a surface which cannot

* Keith Hollingsworth has degrees from William Penn College, the University of Chicago, and Columbia University, and is Associate Professor of English at Wayne State University. His book, *The Newgate Novel: Bulwer, Ainsworth, Dickens, and Thackeray* is soon to be published.

[1] Reuben Brower says, "Once the horrid tour has taken place, the Caves symbolize the failure of all communication . . ." (*The Fields of Light*, New York, 1951, p. 128). If, as seems possible, he means cave and echo together, his point is similar to mine; but I think it necessary to separate echo from cave.

receive them. The clearest of echoes consists merely of the original utterance, with no meaning added.

It is interesting to see, before going to the echoes of the caves, that the word " echo " occurs several times in the first section of the novel, " Mosque." At Mr. Turton's party, Adela, hoping to converse with the Indian ladies, " strove in vain against the echoing walls of their civility " (43).[2] The word comes a second time when Mrs. Moore, talking with her son, asserts that God is love and ends by quoting I Corinthians xiii. 1. (Incidentally, the verse describes the spirit which is necessary if human beings are really to speak to each other.) Only the first six words are printed: " Though I speak with the tongues. . . ." Ronny, turning his mind off, hardly hears the rest. His mother, who has thought constantly of God since she has been in India, is less than ever satisfied: " She must needs pronounce his name frequently, as the greatest she knew, yet she had never found it less efficacious. Outside the arch there seemed always an arch, beyond the remotest echo a silence " (52). Invocation of the Christian deity is thus followed by mention of an echo. Not quite at ease, Mrs. Moore wishes she had kept to the subject of marriage. Though much of the Mosque section is yet to come, this last paragraph of Chapter V anticipates the echoes of the caves.

On a third occasion, when Ronny Heaslop finds that a servant named Krishna has failed to come with files from his office, we have echoes in a context of humor. Heaslop repeatedly calls the man's name, with the noisy show of anger the servants expect. Then, " Krishna the earth, Krishna the stars replied, until the Englishman was appeased by their echoes, fined the absent peon eight annas, and sat down to his arrears in the next room " (97). There is a pleasant irony in the little episode when we recall Godbole's singing at Fielding's tea, some few hours earlier. The Hindu song, concerned not with office files but with spiritual solace, implored the divine Krishna, " Come, come, come, come, come, come " (80). In both instances, Krishna " neglects to come." Heaslop's shouts, unheard by his Krishna, create echoes. Godbole's song does not; if we cannot go so far as to say that it is heard, at least its appeal has meaning and importance. The word " echo " occurs nowhere in the third section of the novel, " Temple," where Godbole again sings and where the inclusive spirit of Hinduism issues a universal invitation.

[2] This and later numbers inserted in the text give page references to *A Passage to India* in the Modern Classics reprint of Harcourt, Brace and Co., New York.

The word occurs for the fourth and last time in "Mosque" when Aziz shows Fielding the picture of his dead wife, bringing her for the moment from behind the barrier of purdah: ". . . how bewildering she found it, the echoing contradictory world" (117). One recalls this phrase when reading later of Adela Quested and her echo; an emancipated English girl, she has entered the world which Aziz' wife only looks out upon, but for her too it is echoing, contradictory, and bewildering.

At the beginning of the second part of the novel comes a chapter-long description of the Marabar area, the ten hills, and the caves for which this section is named. Thereafter we follow Mrs. Moore, Adela, and Aziz on the famous picnic and through the distresses which come after it. The people continue to be realistic characters, utterly persuasive; and the echoes, when the women hear them, are real echoes attended, though in different ways, by loss of meaning and of the capacity to communicate or love. Mrs. Moore's response comes first. We have already seen her as weary on the train: while Adela chattered happily of plans for her wedding, Mrs. Moore entertained uncomfortable doubts of her accustomed values and reflected wearily on the futility of marriage (135). After she has been in a single cave, her low spirits are dramatically focused. In the dark and stifling place, she has been terrified by the echo, always "boum" or "ou-boum" no matter what the original sound, and she feels herself suddenly in a world without values. She sends the others on and sits down to write a letter: "Dear Stella, Dear Ralph" (149). Despair overwhelms her: with her life suddenly emptied of Christian belief, she cannot finish the letter to her children. She tries to think that she is only "an elderly woman who had got up too early in the morning and journeyed too far," but this does not help. Henceforth she is in a blank spiritual isolation. Both divine and human love have become meaningless. She who was generous becomes selfish; she who was sensitive almost ceases to notice others; she who benevolently undertook to preside over happy marriages becomes weary and cynical. During the remainder of her time in Chandrapore, everything about her is changed except her sibylline quality and her conviction that Aziz is innocent.

At her departure, the author asks, "What had spoken to her in that scoured-out cavity of the granite?" The answer he gives, cryptic and perhaps not intended to be complete, in part reiterates the change in her: "Something very old and very small. Before time, it was before space also. Something snub-nosed, incapable of generosity—

the undying worm itself. Since hearing its voice, she had not entertained one large thought . . ." (208). The curious echo has earlier been described with the metaphors of coiling worm, snake composed of small snakes, and serpent (147, 148, 150); here we have "undying worm," presumably unrelenting death.[3] Given this last of several warnings, we are not surprised when Mrs. Moore dies on the passage home. Before that happens, the "twilight of the double vision" is relieved by Mrs. Moore's double view of graceful Asirgarh as she goes on the train to Bombay; and coconut palms wave farewell to her as the ship leaves: "'So you thought an echo was India? you took the Marabar caves as final?' they laughed. 'What have we in common with them, or they with Asirgarh? Good-bye!'" (210) She does not know that her pronouncement, "God is love," drowned out by the echo, will be reasserted at Mau. Although some symbolism may be intended in this farewell chapter, Mrs. Moore first of all is an individual character–a woman who has felt the influence of Hindu India and who has heard a real echo in barren Indian caves.

Adela experiences cave and echo differently, but the echo again represents communication stopped and love denied. She explores caves with Aziz, but her thoughts are on marriage, on herself and Ronny; she is appalled to discover that she does not love him, but she has "her emotions well under control" (152). The exchange of question and answer between her and Aziz forms a classic of misapprehension; words have failed. She suffers the hallucination that Aziz has attempted to assault her in a cave. It is an irony both comic and pitiful: the young woman who cares for truth is thus caused to tell a falsehood; the person

[3] In the King James Bible, see Isaiah lxvi. 24 and Mark ix. 44, 46, 48. Glen O. Allen, in "Structure, Symbol, and Theme in E. M. Forster's *A Passage to India*," *PMLA*, LXX (1955), 944, connects the undying worm also with "Schopenhauer's blindly striving will." I do not feel sure that this makes a consistent interpretation of the passage, though Allen certainly shows that Schopenhauer is at hand elsewhere. If there is an underlying meaning in this chapter (XXIII) of the novel, probably it is that which Allen explains, though certain details are not dealt with. The serpent of eternity which may be made of maggots (208) seems to contrast with or parallel the snake composed of small snakes (148). Does "serpent of eternity" allude to the great serpent upon which Vishnu rests? At many points, Allen's interpretation and the one I offer are not incompatible; his information about Hinduism is helpful. He seems to me much more successful with Mrs. Moore than with Adela.

James McConkey follows Allen in certain important respects in *The Novels of E. M. Forster* (Ithaca, 1957), pp. 132-160. Gertrude M. White, in "*A Passage to India*: Analysis and Revaluation," *PMLA*, LXVIII (1953), 641-657, draws unnecessarily, I think, upon Hegel, but expresses insights of subtlety and value.

who most wanted to meet and know India becomes the agent of a greater division than any caused by Turtons and Burtons. Deeply affected by the shock of her experience, bruised, pierced by cactus needles, Adela remains with the McBrydes for some days, seeing few people and not much aware of the individuals about her. She goes over her memory of the dreadful incident again and again, trying to convince herself that her depression is without adequate cause. She breaks down, weeps, goes on, hears the echo, weeps again—and is disgusted with herself for weeping. At first we suppose that she simply hears the echo in memory; a little later, we become aware that a sound like the echo is constantly buzzing in her ears—a reality to her, though of course no one else can perceive it. Here, as elsewhere, the story has the quality of complete realism which Forster so easily commands. The echoing sound is a symptom of Adela's neurotic disturbance, to call her illness by no stronger name. (It resembles a type of auditory hallucination not uncommon in schizophrenia, in which disease, incidentally, the delusion of a sexual advance may be among those entertained.) She is not only cut off from the world—she is divided and out of communication with herself.[4]

Adela returns after a time to Ronny's bungalow and to Mrs. Moore; again in touch with the outside world, she still has the buzzing in her ears. She finds Mrs. Moore changed, but pays surprisingly little attention to the brusqueness with which she is received. Again the echo stops verbal communication: Adela begs to know the meaning of it—will Mrs. Moore say?

> "Say, say, say," said the old lady bitterly. "As if anything can be said! I have spent my life in saying or in listening to sayings; I have listened too much. It is time I was left in peace. Not to die," she added sourly. "No doubt you expect me to die, but when I have seen you and Ronny married, and seen the other two and whether they want to be married—I'll retire then into a cave of my own." She smiled, to bring down her remark into ordinary life and thus add to its bitterness. "Somewhere where no young people will come asking questions and expecting answers. Some shelf." (200)

---

[4] One finds Forster's usual modesty in his statement about how he acquainted himself with the new psychologies. In 1952 he said to two interviewers that he learned from Proust "ways of looking at character": "the modern subconscious way. He gave me as much of the modern way as I could take. I couldn't read Freud or Jung myself; it had to be filtered to me" (*Writers at Work*, ed. Malcolm Cowley, New York, 1958, p. 34).

Speech and marriage are two modes of entering into relationship, and Mrs. Moore, who has already felt doubts about the latter, henceforth despairs of both.

While Adela is with Mrs. Moore, she comes to think she has made a mistake, that Aziz is innocent; and the echo, she finds with delight, is better (202). But Ronny persuades her she is mistaken, and Mrs. Moore says ominously, " She has started the machinery; it will work to its end " (206). On the morning of the trial, the echo is worse; but she does, of course, recover her sanity. At the crucial moment, and after Mrs. Moore's name has been chanted, she communicates the fact that Aziz did not follow her into the cave. After the trial, she remarks that the echo is gone (239); it does not return. Indeed, this is the end of echoes in the book, except in Fielding's reflections, to be noticed a little later; she and Fielding do not further discuss the echo. With him she faces the explanation of what she has done: " You suggest that I had an hallucination there, the sort of thing–though in an awful form–that makes some women think they've had an offer of marriage when none was made " (240). Thus honesty and intelligence, for a time flouted, are not permanently displaced. As for love, though, Adela is further away from it than before, as we find in her last talk with Fielding. When he says, " I no longer want love," she replies: " No more do I. My experiences here have cured me. But I want others to want it " (263).

It is at the beginning of the second section, " Caves," and perhaps on a re-reading, that we begin to feel the presence of a lower level in the story, where counterparts of the real people move about as symbols or type figures and where the echoes have some additional meaning. (Remembering Forster's earlier fiction–*The Longest Journey*, for example, and the tales–we need not hesitate to look for allegory.) *A Passage to India* includes three groups of people; it has three sections, with the well-known titles. Mosque and temple, places of worship for Mohammedans and Hindus, are physical emblems of two religions and two cultures. Are we not to expect, then, that in some fashion the caves must be the place of worship of the English, the cultural focus of the west? [5] As we follow this lead, we find that the allegory under-

[5] I first made this formulation for my students some years ago, before the appearance of the article by Glen O. Allen already cited. He describes a " religion of caves " somewhat like mine (pp. 936-7); thereafter, his article proceeds in a different direction. One of the most interesting efforts to deal with these matters is that by George H. Thomson, " Thematic Symbol in *A Passage to*

girds a theme which is prominent in the open level of the story: the contrast between western order and Indian spirit.

How do the caves represent the west? No religious edifice—even if it could seem at one time cathedral, chapel, and meeting-house—would serve as the unique symbol of western culture. The characteristic cultural effort of Europe, from the Renaissance to the present, has been science; and the chief concern of science, at least until the twentieth century, has been the physical world. With no wish to discount the historical and present importance of religion in the west, we must recognize that the most lavish expenditure of intellectual energy has in modern times been scientific and technological, and that this effort, enormously successful, has given the culture of Europe and America the features which distinguish it most sharply from the cultures of other regions of the earth. There are, of course, people who have no direct involvement in science; there are large numbers of westerners who by our standards seem as innocent of scientific knowledge as any Indian chosen at random. But most of these have some contact with the technology; they live in the atmosphere of empiricism and rationalism which encouraged the development of science. All share, in varying degrees, the qualities of consciousness which permeate the culture. Nominally adhering to Christianity, the west adopted the religion of science. This is what we find, at the second level, in the Marabar hills and the caves.

This part of India, Forster says, has "been land since land began." The hills are primal matter, the stuff of the physical universe: "If flesh of the sun's flesh is to be touched anywhere, it is here, among the incredible antiquity of these hills" (123). The caves, "dark caves," are hollows in the center of rocks. These we must take to be the secrets of matter. The entrances to the caves are artificial:

> An entrance was necessary, so mankind made one. But elsewhere, deeper in the granite, are there certain chambers that have no entrances? Chambers never unsealed since the arrival of the gods. Local report declares that these exceed in number those that can be visited, as the dead exceed the living—four

India," *Twentieth Century Literature*, VII (1961), 51-63. Of the caves, he says (p. 53), "Just as the Marabar Hills signify the material universe void of life, so the Marabar Caves signify the universe of man void of spirit." Louise Dauner, in "What Happened in the Cave? Reflections on *A Passage to India*," *Modern Fiction Studies*, VII (1961), 258-270, works out an interpretation based on the premise that the caves are archetypal symbols. Thomson's and Miss Dauner's articles have appeared since my own essay was written.

> hundred of them, four thousand or million. Nothing is inside them, they were sealed up before the creation of pestilence or treasure; if mankind grew curious and excavated, nothing, nothing, would be added to the sum of good or evil. (125)

Human curiosity may cause more caves to be opened–scientific discoveries are yet to be made. The opening of them does not of itself add to good or evil, both of which are independent of science. These moral entities rest ultimately upon divine sanction or (for the non-believer) simply upon the unshakable conviction that human life is good and ought to be continued. The echo? It is the meaningless " answer " which necessarily is returned when people look to science for the meaning of life. Moral and ethical questions abound in science, but the foundation of morality lies outside it. Science has never pretended to explain the purpose of human existence. It excites us by its astonishing miracles; it helps us live–but cannot explain to us why we must.[6]

Mrs. Moore is the English, the western religious believer, in the midst of a rationalistic scientific culture, posing ultimate questions about values. To all of these, every Marabar cave returns the same meaningless echo:

> Coming at a moment when she chanced to be fatigued, it had managed to murmur, " Pathos, piety, courage–they exist, but are identical, and so is filth. Everything exists, nothing has value." If one had spoken vileness in that place, or quoted lofty poetry the comment would have been the same– " ou-boum." (149)

Mrs. Moore's distress represents what Forster sees as the defeat of Christian belief in the west, which is giving way before the appalling " ou-boum " which resounds when the culture devotes itself so exclusively to science. With meaning lost, so is the will to live: " the echo began in some indescribable way to undermine her hold on life." She tells herself that " the despair creeping over her [is] merely her despair, her personal weakness "–but at the moment we read this, we know that the despair is not merely hers. The great verbal expressions of Christianity lose their power:

---

[6] In another context, Forster writes in 1934 about G. Lowes Dickinson: " Science always attracted him, and he had, like many men of letters, hopes from it which are seldom cherished by scientists themselves " (*Goldsworthy Lowes Dickinson*, London, 1945, p. 58).

> But suddenly, at the edge of her mind, Religion appeared, poor little talkative Christianity, and she knew that all its divine words from "Let there be Light" to "It is finished" only amounted to "boum." Then she was terrified over an area larger than usual; the universe, never comprehensible to her intellect, offered no repose to her soul, the mood of the last two months took definite form at last, and she realized that she didn't want to write to her children, didn't want to communicate with anyone, not even with God. She sat motionless with horror. . . . (150)

At a later time, the burden which has fallen upon her is expressed by a method like that of some of Eliot's poems, such as "The Hollow Men," which have themes similar to Forster's. Mrs. Moore bursts out to Ronny and Adela, ". . . and Unto us a Son is born, unto us a Child is given . . . and am I good and is he bad and are we saved . . . and ending everything the echo" (205). In Mrs. Moore's last days in Chandrapore, she perhaps moves more than once from upper to lower level of the story, and back again, but in most of the "Caves" section she serves eloquently as both individual character and symbol.

Before we proceed in the allegory from Mrs. Moore to Adela, Godbole must be mentioned. In speaking of the caves to the English visitors, he does not mention the echo: "It never impressed him, perhaps."[7] But how could the real echo have failed to impress? The author's remark contributes, surely, to our interpretation. The value-destroying, hollow "ou-boum" of materialistic science, so alarming to the English Christian, is only what the westerners hear; it has no importance for Godbole. His philosophy, embracing matter, includes it with living things in a single continuum of existence. For him, an acceptable relationship with matter is achieved: he is frustrated but not discouraged when he attempts union with the stone (286). As one student of India wrote: "If Western scientists ever succeed in manufacturing life in a test tube—a feat which would probably have the most disastrous psychological repercussions at our present cultural level—the Hindu and Buddhist East will take the affair quite calmly."[8]

Just as Mrs. Moore is Christianity, Adela is English rationalism.[9] She

[7] Page 147. I cannot reconcile this remark by the author with Allen's suggestion (p. 942) that the echoing "ou-boum" is related to OM, the syllable upon which Hindu mystics meditate.

[8] Edmond Taylor, *Richer by Asia* (Boston, 1947), p. 263.

[9] Allen says, "The experience of the caves thrusts upon these western women the inadequacy of the Christian and the intellectual points of view" (946). Here

lives by intellect and common-sense inquiry, and represents them. Her great virtue is intellectual honesty, her defect the lack of warmth, sympathy, and responsive feeling. Hers is a type of character that may well be fostered in the country whose chief philosophical tradition stems from Locke. She is not religious; it is only in the period of her depression that, "after years of intellectualism," she "resumes her morning kneel to Christianity" (211). We do not, therefore, expect her to be affected as Mrs. Moore was. The echoing of materialistic nineteenth-century science might destroy the faith of Mrs. Moore's generation; but Adela, a young woman of the twentieth century, comes out of the first cave apparently unchanged.

But there are more caves—science has gone on. She tests the echo in others, and one of these proves to be her undoing. For Mrs. Moore, the higher criticism and Darwinian biology; for Adela's generation, new schools of psychology. Adela believes, quite as much as her elders, in the individual personality as an integer, whole; she believes in the availability of reason; she believes in the supremacy of the conscious mind and in the soundness of good intentions; she believes—or at least believes that she ought to believe—in the reality and nobility of human love. (Her personal misfortune—that she does not love Ronny—flashes upon her consciousness by means of a machine-age symbol: a series of notches in the rock which resemble the marks in the dust made by Miss Derek's tires.)

But if Christianity is a delusion, so is the self. Freudian psychology and its variants expose the divisions of the personality, one part of which is commonly at odds with another; they plumb a dark, unsuspected depth of irrational force, hidden from but influencing reason and conscious intention. They reduce (or as popularly understood they seem to reduce) love to a thin camouflage over ubiquitous sex, unromantic, undignified. This is the shocking echo, never heard by Mrs. Moore, which reverberates in Adela's cave and denies her cherished values. The scientific "ou-boum" goes on and on, the more caves one enters; the twentieth century has become no more comfortable for the trusting rationalist than was the nineteenth for the unsophisticated Christian.

The way to this interpretation is pointed by an incident which precedes the exploration of the caves. As the party approach the hills

we are quite in agreement. His explanation of Adela's defeat, however, is very different from the one offered here. As for one detail, sunstroke, that is Godbole's tactful suggestion—surely not Forster's.

on the elephant, everything seems "infected with illusion" (140). Villagers give contradictory answers about certain mounds: they are graves, they are "breasts of the goddess Parvati."[10] There is confusion about a snake, and it is important that the person concerned is not Mrs. Moore but Adela:

> Miss Quested saw a thin, dark object reared on end at the farther side of a water-course, and said, "A snake!" The villagers agreed, and Aziz explained: yes, a black cobra, very venomous, who had reared himself up to watch the passing of the elephant. But when she looked through Ronny's field-glasses, she found it wasn't a snake, but the withered and twisted stump of a toddy-palm. So she said, "It isn't a snake." (140-141)

The snake must be regarded as a phallic symbol; the little episode heralds the catastrophic delusion which will occur further on. Here, Adela's intelligence is still in control: her usual method of dealing with uncertainties is successful. They are in the open light, and her scrutiny with an instrument to aid the eye reveals the object for what it is.[11] In the cave, it is otherwise. She is alone and in the dark (alone with the Id, perhaps, Ego and Super-ego having been left at the entrance?). She scratches or strikes the wall, producing the echo; then come fear and delusion. The binoculars, symbol of the inquiring intelligence, are

[10] Parvati, "she of the mountains," is the consort of Siva and is the chief of Hindu female deities; worship of him, at the shrines containing the symbolic *linga*, is frequently extended to her. In this article, I try to read all the passages in the novel which disclose the allegory of the echo; I do not try to explain one or two which seem to me to involve some element of Hinduism. So far as I can discover, no such allusion contradicts the interpretation I give here; and sometimes, as in this sentence about Parvati, the allusion may be said to contribute to it.

[11] There is another cobra, a real one, at Mau; it has a connection with the illusory one but is outside the frame of the present allegory. Fielding and Aziz pause when they see it, and it goes harmlessly on its way (317). Just after this, Aziz produces the letter of reconciliation which he has prepared to send to Miss Quested; the delusions (first hers, then his) which began with a cobra are now wiped out. The cobra at Mau is noticed by Glen Pedersen in "Forster's Symbolic Form," *Kenyon Review*, XXI (1959), 231-249. One asks oneself, on examining these passages, whether the illusory cobra is to be connected with the snakes of the metaphors describing the echo. I think the answer is no. I cannot make a pattern of significance by forcing such a connection, and I do not believe the author intended it. Snakes are casually mentioned elsewhere in the book, and a viper is reported at Government College; I take this to be the natural result of there being many snakes in India.

torn from her, presumably by her own panicky efforts; she believes herself to have been pulled about by the strap, "and the climax was the falling of her field-glasses" (194).

Adela's mental illness, then, represents the disrupting intrusion of the new psychology, deeply felt during the early nineteen-twenties, when Forster was finishing the novel. The disturbance was widespread. Family relationships were reinterpreted and individual behavior analyzed. Freud was called upon to justify uninhibited sexual indulgence; affection between mothers and sons was suspected as a dangerous fixation; and friendships—no matter what their quality—between two men or two women were likely to be labeled homosexuality. The sub-surface psychology, along with the new anthropology, affected traditional explanations of historical events, political behavior, and social movements. Rationalization was detected running through the whole respectable history of philosophy. But what was happening to love seemed to many the most crippling injury, for human love, as literature said again and again from "Dover Beach" to *A Farewell to Arms*, remained the support for those who no longer found divine love present in the world. Among the intellectuals in the scientific culture, the dissolution of love proceeded furiously. Aldous Huxley is its best-known reporter. His lovers, "Quietly sweating, palm to palm," were in the volume, *Leda, and Other Poems*, of 1920; *Antic Hay* was published in 1923. The seriousness with which the destruction of love was regarded may be seen in Joseph Wood Krutch's *The Modern Temper*, published in 1928, four years after *A Passage to India*; one chapter is called, "Love: the Life and Death of a Value." (Another of Forster's themes appears in the chapter, "The Disillusion with the Laboratory.") Adela and her generation go on, of course, as they must, equipped with new self-knowledge but not better fitted for love. On the other hand, Forster, as we know, does not abandon it. In his novel, love persists, and reappears in the final section.

The echo belongs essentially to Mrs. Moore and to Adela; Aziz pays no attention to it, but it does occur twice in Fielding's thoughts. The first occasion is on the evening of the unhappy day of the picnic; he wonders about the echo which has disturbed Adela, and reflects briefly about his own life (191). The second occasion, and the last on which the echo is mentioned in the book, comes when Fielding has just revisited the club. New members are present, but the club remains the same:

> "It is no good," he thought, as he returned past the mosque,

> "We all build upon sand; and the more modern the country gets, the worse'll be the crash. In the old eighteenth century, when cruelty and injustice raged, an invisible power repaired their ravages. Everything echoes now; there's no stopping the echo. The original sound may be harmless, but the echo is always evil." This reflection about an echo lay at the verge of Fielding's mind. He could never develop it. It belonged to the universe he had missed or rejected. And the mosque missed it too. Like himself, those shallow arcades provided but a limited asylum. "There is no God but God" doesn't carry us far through the complexities of matter and spirit; it is only a game with words, really, a religious pun, not a religious truth.[12]

This passage, with Felding's remark about the eighteenth century, is a crucial test for any allegorical interpretation of the echoes. Why the emphasis upon "now" in contrast with the past? There seems but one answer. In the manner I have indicated, the echo is peculiarly modern. Fielding's "there's no stopping the echo" is the equivalent of Mrs. Moore's prediction that the machinery would work to its end; the technological society introduces a mechanization of human relations. So far as Indians adopt western modes of thought, they too may develop the factual, non-intuitive, emotionally insensitive qualities which modern science has bred in the English: "the more modern the country gets, the worse'll be the crash." [13]

[12] Page 276. Fielding's observation that in the past, relations between English and Indians were actually better has an interesting parallel in a comment by Sir Charles Brooke, second of the Brooke family to be rajah of Sarawak, in a pamphlet of 1907, *Queries, Past, Present and Future*: "All our possessions are too much Anglicised. Where good and friendly feeling—I might almost say love—existed in the early part of the last century, when black and white were combined in feeling, there has been a falling-off, a separation, in consequence of the English developing into higher civilisation—as it is termed—among themselves with wives and families and European luxuries, and so it has happened that though we govern, we only do so by power, and not by friendly intercourse of feeling" (quoted from Sir Steven Runciman, *The White Rajahs*, Cambridge, 1960, p. 227). Sir Charles predicted that Britain would lose India.

[13] Certain phrases in Adela's thoughts about the echo may now be recalled. The following may be only a quite realistic description of her disturbed state of mind while she is still at the McBrydes'; but the "evil" which she feels has brought may, allegorically, be the evils of the English intellectualism, the modernism, which Fielding deplores in the passage just quoted above: "The sound had spouted after her when she escaped, and was going on still like a river that gradually floods the plain. Only Mrs. Moore could drive it back to its source and

But Fielding's remarks are those of an observer. We must ask ourselves one more question about the allegory of the caves: Why is it that women—not men—suffer the destructive effects of the echo? The obvious answer lies in the chronology of women's general participation in the intellectual concerns of men. On other levels of interpretation, other answers might be given, other meanings suggested for the caves. Barren caves, barren wombs—of the old woman facing negation and of the young spinster who is unlikely to bear children? [14] Or wombs of Parvati? Possibly. It is appropriate enough that the reverberations which deny love should resound in cave-wombs which are and have always been empty; and that the scientific "boum" should be heard in a place where, though the Indian boulders may say, "I am alive," the English cannot think of themselves as children of earth. But in the pattern followed here we can say with more certainty that the presence of women in the allegory is peculiarly fitting for the twentieth century. Despite exceptions, the scientific reverberations came to women later than to men, and the full power of the echo was not known until the growing equality of women allowed it to be demonstrated. The men, generally, may be said to have hardened themselves and grown used to it; they will receive no aid from women, the life-bearers, if the culture produces only persons like Adela, who also succumb. But Mrs. Moore, though stricken, has transmitted her spirit through Stella and Ralph—marriage cannot be so hopeless as the weary mother had begun to think—and the Marabar caves are not to be taken as final.

For the book ends with the "Temple" section, not with echoes. The last sentences, it is true, record an aspiration denied, but we may if we like turn back to the words which precede the novel, its dedication: "To Syed Ross Masood, and to the seventeen years of our friendship." The cadences of regret on the last page do not destroy the resurgent hope which animates "Temple" nor the memory of the wall-motto, "God si love," in which the spirit triumphs over the letter.

We confront, finally, the question of how allegory, like this of the caves and echoes, comes about, especially since Forster, when asked whether he was aware of his technical capacities, replied: "People will not realize how little conscious one is of these things; how one

seal the broken reservoir. Evil was loose . . . she could even hear it entering the lives of others . . ." (194).

[14] Lionel Trilling suggests a womb symbolism for the caves, in *E. M. Forster* (Norfolk, Conn., 1943), p. 157.

flounders about. They want us to be so much better informed than we are. If critics could only have a course on writers' not thinking things out—a course of lectures. . . ."[15] Since Forster is always urbane, casual, deprecating, we may discount his statement a little; but we need not quite contradict him. He did not, we can agree, "think things out" in this sense: he did not plan an allegory and then allow the plan to tyrannize over the complexities of creation. Interviewers report him as saying, "I knew that something important happened in the Malabar [*sic*] caves, and that it would have a central place in the novel—but I didn't know what it would be."[16] He is a writer of genius, with a rich mind and a sensitive awareness of life; such a writer finds incidents developing themselves, draws them out, chooses some which are emotionally and intellectually magnetic, and arranges them—in a way that seems afterward unexplainable and miraculous—so that they form patterns of several kinds, not solely in one plane. At moments, the process may be quite consciously directed; at other times, the several layers, the many strands of significance produce themselves from such a mind, and the writer seems merely to discover them as they come. *A Passage to India*, with all its complexities, does not smell of the lamp. There is no need to claim perfection for it, but it is one of the greatest of novels, by an author who, finding himself unable to take passage beyond it, has published none after it.

[15] *Writers at Work*, p. 34.
[16] *Writers at Work*, p. 27.

WHAT HAPPENED IN THE CAVE? REFLECTIONS ON *A PASSAGE TO INDIA*

WHAT HAPPENED IN THE CAVE? REFLECTIONS ON *A PASSAGE TO INDIA*

Louise Dauner

A PASSAGE TO INDIA is E. M. Forster's best known and most popular novel; yet it remains a work which, more than forty years after publication, still leaves us with a vague sense of frustration. Forster *is* elusive, sometimes through subtlety, occasionally through infirm control of structure, and, notably, as in *A Passage to India,* through ability to seize upon and fully realize the potentials of an archetypal symbol—here, the Marabar Caves. Thus, though critics agree that the caves are the central symbol of the novel, interpretations of their meaning are widely diverse. Furthermore, we are still, literally and metaphorically, in the dark as to what really happened to Adela Quested in the cave; and yet this episode is the structural core of the novel.

Perhaps we may arrive at some illumination in these matters if we explore what the caves themselves imply. I wish therefore to examine the caves viewed as natural phenomena or nature symbols, and as archetypes or psychological symbols. Then we may attempt an interpretation of Adela's experience in the cave, the synaptic point for plot and story.

The differentiation between plot and story is, of course, Forster's. In a Forster work the story, which may be thought of as lying beneath and extending beyond the consummation of the plot, is the "real thing." In the story, which is an insight or a "perception," lie symbolic representations of experience upon which Forster has a firm intuitive grasp, no matter how loose at times may be his control of plot. To use the word *intuitive,* however, is to touch the heart of the difficulty; for Forster belongs to that small group of writers—one thinks within the last century of Melville, Hawthorne, D. H. Lawrence, and Dostoevsky—whose deepest wisdoms transcend temporal and racial boundaries because their insights derive not so much from the conscious mind as from what Jung calls the Collective Unconscious, that source for creativity which gives rise to a vision of genuine primordial experience common to humanity. Rex Warner, in his *E. M. Forster* (1950), locates the sources of Forster's power in "a combination of vision and nightmare," as particularly apparent in *A Passage to India*. Thus an exegesis of a Forster work which focuses only upon the patterns structured by the conscious mind, the plot, and which relies only upon the techniques and terms of conventional literary analysis must leave undefined perhaps the deepest significances, which reside in the story, and which may be carried by symbolic elements such as the caves. Concepts and insights which derive from non-literary but pertinent systems of knowledge such as archeology and Jung's analytical psychology should provide appropriate means for an exploration of the story. Before such an attempt is made, however, it is well to note briefly representative interpretations of the meanings of the caves.

Lionel Trilling, basing his interpretation upon the psychic and emotional changes wrought by the caves upon Adela and Mrs. Moore, calls them "wombs." Gertrude White calls them "the voice of evil and negation . . . of Chaos and Old Night. . . . The answer that they give to the problem of oneness is an answer of horror and despair, whether on the human or the universal level." William York Tindall sees them as including "the primitive, the unconscious, and the sexual." To Austin Warren they suggest "eternity, infinity, the Absolute." Glen O. Allen considers them 1) as representing a kind of religion, "a devotion to reason, form, and the sense of purpose as the *sine qua non* of right behavior and attitude"; 2) as equating to "the ultimate identity of Brahma and Atman"; and 3) as representing, in Mrs. Moore's and Adela's experiences of them "the inadequacy of the Christian and the intellectual points of view." And James McConkey suggests that the symbol of the caves, though still a mystery, may be read on one level as representing, in their emptiness, "the absolute Brahman" in Hindu philosophy. Taken literally, their effect upon Mrs. Moore, Adela, and Fielding is, of course, completely negative. "Yet, the caves suggest, too, that a reality exists beyond time and space to which man's consciousness cannot fully reach."[1]

Now certainly these readings contribute much to the potentiality of meaning, but they are not entirely satisfactory because they approach the caves as rational elements. Actually, the caves are not only the setting for *irrational* experience, but they are themselves archetypal. We mean by this first that the caves function in a situa-

---

[1] Sources cited in this paragraph are as follows: White, "*A Passage to India:* Analysis and Reevaluation," *PMLA*, LXVIII (Sept., 1953), 647; Tindall, *The Literary Symbol* (New York: Columbia University Press, 1955), p. 144; Warren, *Rage for Order* (Chicago: University of Chicago Press, 1948), p. 136; Allen, "Structure, Symbol, and Theme in E. M. Forster's *A Passage to India,*" *PMLA*, LXX (Dec., 1955), 934-954; and McConkey, *The Novels of E. M. Forster* (Ithaca, New York: Cornell University Press, 1957), p. 140.

tion involving elements which derive, not from Forster's rational or conscious mind, or even from Adela's conscious mind, but from the dark ambiguous soil of the unconscious, which disguises its meanings in symbols, as in myths, fantasies, fairy tales; and second, that the cave, *as cave,* is itself a primordial image in mythology and psychology, hence as an archetype it is a constituent of the collective unconscious and not of the purely personal and conscious psyche.

Thus, it need not surprise us that, within the novel, we find no rational answer to Adela's question to Godbole and Dr. Aziz, "What are these caves?" Aziz frankly does not know; and Godbole the Brahmin replies only in enigmatic negatives which deny to the caves anything remarkable at all: they possess neither sculpture, holiness, nor ornamentation—not even stalactites. There is only "an entrance in the rock . . . and through the entrance is the cave."[2] Yet they also figure as "extraordinary" in both the opening sentence of the novel and the opening chapter of Part II, "Caves." And early in this section Forster does tell us that the Marabar Hills, in which are the caves, "are older than anything in the world" (p. 123). Thus they are primordial. What does this mean?

Recent archeological discoveries, as noted by G. R. Levy in *The Gate of Horn* (1948), suggest "the profound significance of the cave in the race-memory and traditions of more advanced peoples." The cave, it now appears, functioned in the most critical events in the life of early man—as far back, indeed, as Mousterian and Crô-magnon man. Bodies of Mousterian men were buried in trenches in the floors of their caves, with implements and offerings which, Miss Levy concludes, "indicates the existence, if not of the family, at least of the group or clan, whose uniting bonds were felt to extend through time . . . and suggest continuous relationship. . . . This is the earliest indication in Europe of belief in a non-physical existence."[3] Thus, at the beginning, we see the cave identified with the concepts of unity and of a belief in an aspect of the spiritual. These suggestions are pertinent to *A Passage to India.*

A Passage to India presents, on the surface, a theme the opposite of unity and relationship. It is a novel of barriers—between matter and essence, between races, castes, religions, and sexes; and though some of the tensions are somewhat relieved in the resolution, we are left with a re-assertion of the barriers: "Why can't we be friends

[2] E. M. Forster, *A Passage to India* (New York: Harcourt, Brace and Company, 1924), p. 123. All references in the text are to this Harbrace Modern Classics edition.

[3] G. R. Levy, *The Gate of Horn* (London: Faber and Faber, 1948), pp. 3-6.

now?" Fielding asks Aziz, during what both know to be their last meeting. "It's what I want. It's what you want."

> But the horses didn't want it—they swerved apart; the earth didn't want it, sending up rocks through which riders must pass single file; the temples, the tank, the jail, the palace, the birds, the carrion, the Guest House . . . they didn't want it, they said in their hundred voices, "No, not yet," and the sky said, "No, not there." (p. 322)

Yet the underlying theme of *A Passage to India* is that which characterizes and charges all of Forster's novels: the implication of unity, togetherness, "connection." So in *Howards End* Margaret Schlegel muses, "Only connect! . . . Only connect the prose and the passion, and both will be exalted, and human love will be seen at its height. Live in fragments no longer. Only connect, and the beast and the monk, robbed of the isolation that is life to either, will die."[4]

The cave, then, ambivalent in its combination of primal functions, both shelter and tomb, testifies to man's early sense of unity, both material and spiritual, and symbolizes here that unity of individuals, races, spirits which, Forster implies, is the only real solution to the problems, not only of an England and an India, but of all men. But as the place of burial the cave also means death or separation. Unity and separation, as basic aspects of the human experience, are also basic themes of *A Passage to India*.

The separation or death-aspect is translated in the novel into Mrs. Moore's experience in the small black hole. Already in a strange depression when she enters the cave, she faces the darkness, is caught up in a momentary panic caused by the dark, the smell, and the strange pressures, she hits her head "and for an instant she went mad, hitting and gasping like a fanatic." There is also an echo, a sound which reduces everything to indistinction and futility: "Whatever is said, the same monotonous noise replies . . . 'Boum' is the sound . . . utterly dull. Hope, politeness, the blowing of a nose, the squeak of a boot, all produce 'boum' " (p. 147). The echo undermines Mrs. Moore's life; for, coming at a moment of fatigue, it murmurs to her, "Pathos, piety, courage—they exist, but are identical, and so is filth. Everything exists, nothing has value" (p. 149).

From this "double vision" Mrs. Moore never recovers her sense of the positive. As a Westerner, whose rational heritage discriminates between polarities, she is lost in a concept which sees good and evil, not as irreconcilable opposites, but as hyphenated; as essential, though

---

[4] E. M. Forster, *Howards End* (New York: Vintage Books, 1954), p. 187.

contrasting, aspects of the same all-pervasive divinity. She could then have made no sense of Godbole's "explanation" to Fielding of Adela's experience in the cave: "Good and evil are different, as their names imply. But, in my own humble opinion, they are both of them aspects of my Lord. He is present in the one, absent in the other, and the difference between presence and absence is great. . . . Yet absence implies presence, absence is not non-existence, and we are therefore entitled to repeat, 'Come, come, come, come!' " (p. 178). As Mrs. Moore experiences it, however, this basic paradox can only paralyze her spirit, a blend of Western rationality and oriental intuition; for the intuitive part of her nature, though real, is not sufficiently developed to sustain and protect her. The moments in the cave simply reduce her to ill temper, cynicism, and an apprehension of spiritual decay and death which, only a little later, is paralleled by her physical death on the sea. Yet even this death is paradoxical; for even as her body is committed to the Indian Ocean, her spirit manifests itself to Adela during her testimony at the trial of Aziz; she is transmuted by the crowd in the street into an Indian goddess, Esmiss Esmoor; and still later she assumes identity as a cosmic aspect in the memory of Godbole.

The cave, then, is thematic in its implication of good-and-evil. But because this theme is so highly complex, it can be explored and dramatized only through a series of "variations." These variations, both negative and positive, are reflected in both Adela's experience in the cave and in its own implicit qualities.

Taken literally, Adela's experience adds up to hallucination, hysteria, and physical and psychic illness—to negation and evil; but this experience, though highly distressing to Adela and others, does not change the positive implications of the cave as symbol. Perhaps just here is an instance of the difference between plot and story in a Forster work. For we must differentiate between what Adela *thinks* happens—an attempt by Aziz to assault her—between, then, the *facts* of the *plot,* and the underlying truth, the *story,* which is carried by the cave-symbol. It is the old difference again (not confined to a Forster novel) between objective reality and a subjective interpretation of that reality. Here an ancient parable may help us.

Another cave has left its mark upon our imaginations, Plato's cave, in the seventh book of *The Republic.* This is the cave of Illusion, where "reality" is merely the shadow of a shadow, for the objects that cast the shadows are themselves artificial. And this cave too, like Forster's cave, has an echo. Because of Forster's long devotion to Greek thought and attitudes, we may logically assume that Plato's cave of Illusion underlies other symbolic implications of Forster's cave.

Yet *A Passage to India* is rooted in Forster's intimate knowledge of India, which he first visited in 1912-1913, and to which he returned in 1921, serving for nearly nine months as secretary of the Maharajah of Dewas State Senior, Sir Tukoji Rao III. *A Passage to India* was begun before the 1921 visit and completed after Forster's return to England. The story is given in detail in *The Hill of Devi* (1953). Here we need note only that Forster's immersion into Indian life—his contacts with the Maharajah, with the Maratha nobles and their women, even his dressing as a Hindu and participating in the eight-days' feast in honor of Krishna, the Gokul-Ashtami—all of this contributes significantly in theme, characters, events, and attitudes to the "rightness" of the novel. But even more important, this record of the Indian months suggests that the conceptual texture of *A Passage to India* is inevitably a blend: it is a combination of concepts both Greek and Indian. To the Platonic cave, with its concepts of earthly life as illusion and as the betrayal of the senses, we must now add a corresponding Indian concept—Māyā.

In *Philosophies of India* (1956) Heinrich Zimmer defines Māyā as "the illusion superimposed upon reality as an effect of ignorance." Māyā is the net of sense entanglement. In the Vedantic philosophy, to understand its secret, to know how it works, to transcend its cosmic spell, "breaking outward through the layers of tangible and visible appearance, and simultaneously inward through all the intellectual and emotional stratifications of the psyche"—this is conceived to be the primary human task. For this task the intellect alone is insufficient, for it sees life and experience as a dualism. But "it is a sign of non-knowing to suppose that because the dualistic argument is logical and accords with the facts of life, it is therefore consonant with the final truth. Dualism belongs to the sphere of manifestation, the sphere of bewildering differentiation through the interaction of the gunas, and is but a part of the great cosmic play of Māyā."[5]

Adela's experience in the cave of Illusion is an instance of Māyā. This state is corrected during the tense moments of the trial in her clear if temporary recognition that, whatever happened in the cave, it was not any act of Aziz, though it may well have been something entirely real, if entirely inward. Thus the critical question of what did happen in the cave includes both Adela's illusion, her misconception of the truth, and the reality; and obviously the reality includes

[5] H. Zimmer, *Philosophies of India,* ed. Joseph Campbell (New York: Meridian Books, 1956), pp. 27, 394.

all the value-implications which the cave symbolically carries. Adela's hysterical flight from the cave is a rejection of these values. But since this rejection grows inevitably out of her total personality, we are also involved with the problem of what totality of psychic elements, what kind of personality, can apprehend truth or reality.

Adela is one of those persons to whom life must "explain" itself rationally. She wants to "know" India, to harmonize all of its paradoxical voices into one clear harmonious chord of being. Yet, unlike Mrs. Moore, Adela lacks the intuitive capacity which alone can grasp the disparaties and resolve them into an image of cosmic wholeness. Only love, through intuition, Forster suggests, can do this; and with all the good will in the world, it is Adela's incapacity to love, her emotional and intuitive deficiency, which is her essential limitation.

When she enters the cave, Adela has just realized that she does not love Ronny, her fiancé. Her decision to marry him has never been based on strong physical or emotional need; it has been a restrained, rational decision, an on-again-off-again mattter, revived, for instance, by an automobile accident which momentarily threw them into close contact. Preoccupied during these days with the question of love and marriage, she is also psychically involved (though on a below-rational level) with the physical contact implied. Her essentially virginal nature is obscurely troubled by this implication; yet she is also fundamentally honest, and now she sharply sees the incongruity: "Not to love the man one's going to marry! Not to find it out till this moment! Not even to have asked oneself the question until now! Something else to think out. . . " (p. 152).

In the first moments of this shocking recognition, she puts a blunt question to Aziz, which so embarrasses him that he darts into a cave to recover his poise. She enters still another cave. The emotional context of the moment is thus confused and negative. From her cave Adela emerges in deep psychic and emotional distress, half-falling down the hillside into cactus plants, hundreds of needles of which penetrate her body. This too is meaningful: it is as though nature itself enacts a violent impingement upon this woman who "hitherto had not much minded whether she was touched or not: her senses were abnormally inert and the only contact she anticipated was that of mind" (p. 193). It is not exaggerated perhaps to see some phallic symbolism in the penetration of the cactus-needles, a delicate irony. And it is significant that Adela's movement down the granite hillside is a wild descent, the physical plane correlating at the moment with the psychic plane.

Now from what "reality" has Adela fled? Her panic must have

arisen out of what she felt to be a peril—primarily, the danger of contact or union. This brings us back to the cave in its implications of union with either the human or the divine.

The ancient cave consists of a shallow grotto which leads to a deeper recess. The Marabar Caves have a similar form: "A tunnel eight feet long, five feet high, three feet wide, leads to a circular chamber about twenty feet in diameter" (p. 124). Crô-magnon man used his grottoes, which were open to the daylight, as shelters and workshops. These represent the mundane activities of the group. But in the deeper recesses behind the entrance were enacted the essential ceremonies, what we may call the psychic life, of early man. Miss Levy tells us that these ceremonies were of a religious nature, "as yet inseparable from art, magic, and social and economic experiment," and that here "the signs of daily activities . . . are strikingly absent." This, then, is the place where early man enacted the rituals which celebrated critical moments in his life, moments during which he intuitively felt some aspects of cosmic truth. The cave was considered "the repository of mystic influence," in that both animal souls and divinity were felt to exist here. This aspect of the cave, as the site of divine power, underlies the other positive aspects. But these other aspects have each their special property and significance.

As the site of divine power, the cave is also the site of the masked religious or ceremonial dances, a deliberate means of approach to the animal nature and therefore to the divine nature. Again, it was a common belief that the primal emergence of the mythic ancestors was from caverns in or under the earth. To the cave the novice magicians repaired for their sleep of death and rebirth. The cave was the site of the sanctuary where were kept the churingas, the incised or painted objects of wood or stone which were believed to hold in union both animal and human divinity, and which were shown to every initiate at the moment of his passage from boyhood to clan membership. Since amulets and engraved blocks bearing female symbols have been found lying face down in contact with the earth, the cave is associated with female potency. "The cave was already a Mother." Both primitive and later civilized races, performing their ceremonies in caves or crypts, considered the cave the mother from whom they were born again. Such rites aimed at renewal through union with divinity, and were among the major ceremonies in the "rites of passage," celebrating the individual's birth, initiation, death, and rebirth. The initiation rites linked the religious and social aspects of group solidarity, and signified the spiritual rebirth of the individual (sometimes known as the moment when he "received his soul"). "The primary group-relationship known to us was not that of blood, but of a willed participation in a life both physical and non-physical, which stretched through time to include the dead and the unborn."[6]

Thus as a nature-symbol the cave is polyvalent: it appears as the site of the divine power; as the Mother, or female potency; as the link to mythic ancestors, thus to the past; as the place of initiation into adult and group privilege and responsibility, hence as a symbol of maturity and of the future, of rebirth and resurrection. Cumulatively, the cave appears as the site of the Divine Mystery, the creative life-force. Thus it implies the continuity between the past and the future.

Many of the archeological implications of the cave are supported by modern psychology, which sees the cave as an archetype, a psychic image of an inherited, unconscious tendency. Freud sees any object which has the property of enclosing a space or acting as a receptacle as a female symbol. Such objects as pits, hollows, caves, boxes, chests, and ships are, furthermore, "constant" symbols, occurring in dreams, mythology, folk-lore, religion, and art. And such activities as dancing, riding, climbing, being rhythmical in nature, may symbolically represent the sexual act. From this standpoint, it is pertinent to note that the physical aspects of Adela's experience—the climb up the hill (which would be seen as a male symbol), the violence in the cave (somehow the strap of her field-glasses is broken, a significant detail suggesting her loss of "sight"), and her frenzied descent down the hill—all constitute a kind of parody on the sex-act, really a symbolic rejection of it. This equates with Adela's rejection of the implication of union, which again is thematic.

According to Jung, the cave is an archetype for the Great Mother. "Phylogenetically as well as ontogenetically we have grown up out of the dark confines of the earth. . . . The protecting mother is . . . associated with the . . . protecting cave. The symbol of the mother refers to a place of origin such as nature, to that which passively creates, to matter, to the unconscious, natural and instinctive life."[7]

Neumann also conceives of the cave as a Great Mother symbol, linking it, through its "elementary containing character" with the womb. "The vessel lies at the core of the elementary character of the feminine. At all stages of the primordial mysteries, it is the central symbol of their realization. In the mysteries of preservation, this sym-

---

[6] Levy, pp. 8-35 and *passim*. E. O. James (*Myth and Ritual in the Ancient Near East* [New York: Frederick A. Praeger, 1958], p. 22ff) would agree with Miss Levy on the general significance of the cave, seeing it as a tribal sanctuary in which magico-religious fertility and hunting rites were performed, as well as rituals intended to "establish a beneficial relationship with the supernatural source of the food supply."

[7] Quoted in Patrick Mullahy, *Oedipus: Myth and Complex* (New York: Grove Press, 1955), pp. 149-150.

bol is projected upon the cave as sacral precinct and temple."[8] But the cave is also a tomb, the "container" that "holds fast and takes back." So the elementary character of the Archetypal Feminine is also terrible. And the Terrible Female is one symbol for the unconscious. "The womb of the earth becomes the deadly devouring maw of the underworld, and beside the fecundated womb and the protecting cave of earth . . . gapes the abyss of Hell, the dark hole of the depths, the devouring womb of the grave and of death, of Darkness without light, of nothingness."[9] Forster notes of the caves, "Nothing, nothing attaches to them."

Finally, Neumann sees the cave as an archetype for the Way. "In a ritual still largely unconscious, the Way led prehistoric man into mountain caves, in whose recesses they established 'temples'. . . . The 'hard and dangerous way' by which these caves could be reached formed a part of the ritual reality." Later, this archetype of the Way became a conscious ritual, until in Calvary, "the way of destiny becomes the way of redemption."[10]

Thus, as a psychological archetype, the cave is, again, the site of divinity; a symbol of the Good Mother; an aspect of the Terrible Mother, hence a symbol of the unconscious; and a symbol of the Way of spiritual rebirth. But because here it is also the cave of Illusion or Māyā, to Adela's vision these positive implications are distorted and obscured. Nonetheless, it is from these mythic potentials that she flees. Details of plot and character support this interpretation.

Neither very mature emotionally nor very profound, Adela's contemplations about love and marriage have occurred only at the top of her mind: in terms of herself as an Anglo-Indian, of the place where she and Ronny will live, of the kind of social and domestic life they will have. As she tells Fielding later, "I was bringing to Ronny nothing that ought to be brought. . . . I entered that cave thinking: 'Am I fond of him?' . . . Tenderness, respect . . ." (p. 263). These she has tried to make take the place of love. The cave forces violently upon her an experience involving her emotions, her unconscious psyche, her sense of herself as a woman. This, her undeveloped feminine psyche, is her basic limitation. Her disturbance in the cave is thus fundamental, for all of the cave's feminine implications—

[8] Erich Neumann, *The Great Mother* (New York: Pantheon Books, 1955), p. 282.

[9] Neumann, p. 149. It is further interesting to note that the experience of the Terrible Mother finds its most grandiose form as Kali. "In the very earliest Indian culture, . . . in the temple sites of the Zhob River Valley, of northern Baluchistan, we find figures of the Terrible Mother" (Neumann, p. 150).

[10] Neumann, pp. 8, 9, 177. Adela's approach to the caves is, of course, on foot; her descent, in its irrational violence takes on something of the exaggerated movement often characteristic of the primitive dance.

union, initiation, potency—are experienced as an attempt at rape, an ironic perversion.

Thus Adela must reject the cave as the spot of the mystic initiation, achieved through the individual's "willed participation" in some significant ritual. The cave *is* evil for her simply because in her flight she rejects all of its positive potentialities.

But Adela has other limitations. Frankly she admits to Fielding her lack of religious faith. Both, they confess to each other, are atheists; yet both sense a basic lack. "Were there worlds beyond which they could never touch, or did all that is possible enter their consciousness? They could not tell" (p. 263). Communicating at last on a rational level, they feel their friendliness is yet that of "dwarfs shaking hands," and they sense a wistfulness that marks the absence of something significant though indefinable.

So Adela can only fail to realize the religious implications of the cave. *The Secret of the Golden Flower,* speaks of *"the cave of power,* where all that is miraculous returns to its roots."[11] But Adela must reject the cave of power, the finitely unknowable, for she is never able to define rationally what did happen to her there.

She does, however, confront something there. Since it is not rationally definable, let us call it the unconscious. Jung's system postulates for the woman, as for the man, a balancing element in the psyche. In the woman the masculine side is personified by the Animus, which thus represents the opposite of the dominant attitude in female consciousness. According to Jung's "function compass," Adela's dominant function is Thinking; thus her compensatory unconscious function is Feeling. Now, says Neumann, "the spiritual aspect of the unconscious confronts woman as an invisible stimulating, fructifying, and inspiring male spirit, whether it appears as totem or demon, ancestral spirit or god. In the woman, every psychic situation that leads to an animation of the unconscious . . . sets in motion the unconscious patriarchal structures of the animus."[12] I suggest that what Adela really encounters in the cave, what is symbolized there so violently that her unconscious (Feeling) function is activated, is the Animus, the male principle. Recognized and integrated into her consciousness, this principle would have initiated for her a greater psychic completeness, productive eventually of a real Self.

The Truth, then, was implicit in the situation; but only the Fact was experienced. Possibly evoked by her half-conscious ruminations as

[11] *The Secret of the Golden Flower,* trans. Richard Wilhelm, trans. into English by Cary F. Baynes (New York: Harcourt, Brace and Co., 1932), p. 62.

[12] Neumann, p. 294.

she entered the cave, some force which her intellect could make nothing of, spirit or flesh, denied god or demon, was objectified to her. But because she had never been really aware of her Feeling-self, she could only view this manifestation as evil, and reject it in panic and flight. In addition to the mythic implications of the cave itself, Adela has, then, also rejected the beginning of a meaningful Self-hood, or, in Jung's term, of the process of individuation.

Thus again we return to the cave as the place of Illusion, Māyā, of the false testimony of the senses. *What happened in the cave is a dramatization of the dualism in which cosmic truth states itself when seen only through the half-vision of the intellect alone.* The reality behind the illusion, the integration of the paradoxes, could appear only when not merely the intellect, the conscious psyche, is invoked, but also the intuitive powers of the unconscious.

Part of the significance of Adela's experience in the cave is that its implications transcend the limitations of an individual and/or fictional character. In her partial vision, Adela represents perhaps the major neurosis of modern man, the "split" between the conscious and the unconscious psyches. She cannot "connect," either within herself, or without.

In his psychological commentary on *The Secret of the Golden Flower,* Jung interprets this sort of experience, suggesting that such separation of consciousness from "the laws of life represented in the unconscious" is peculiarly characteristic of the Western Christian, and especially the Protestant "cult of consciousness." The more the intellect is developed, the greater is the gap between consciousness and the unconscious. Furthermore, "danger arises whenever the narrowly delimited, but intensely clear, individual consciousness meets the inner expansion of the collective unconscious, because the latter has a definitely disintegrating effect on consciousness." Although this danger may manifest itself as a "complex"—an autonomic psychic content—it may also appear as "more complex emotional states which cannot be described as pure and simple affects but are complicated partial-systems which have . . . the character of persons. . . . As we know, activated unconscious contents always appear first as projections upon the outside world." If, however, one denies the existence of the partial-systems, "they then become an inexplicable factor of disturbance which one assumes to exist somewhere or other outside. . . . *The disturbing effects are now attributed to a bad will outside ourselves.*"[13]

[13] C. G. Jung, "Commentary" to *The Secret of the Golden Flower,* pp. 96-111. (Italics mine.)

So far as one may attribute psychological reality to a fictional character, the above comments seem remarkably pertinent to Adela's experience in the cave. Confronted in her low-toned state by the inexplicable "collectivity" of the cave, she can "know" her activated unconscious only as a projection upon the outside world—as, literally, an evil will directed against her, Dr. Aziz. Actually what she experiences suggests itself as a manifestation of her own state of psychic disunity.

What, then, did happen in the cave? Nothing. And everything. For negation and disunity are real too. Confronted by a deep and unprecedented experience of her unconscious, Adela is frightened, and rejects. Her engagement to Ronny is broken, and she can only return to England and to her orderly rational life there. True, she does develop under her ordeal. Fielding sees that she is no longer examining life but being examined by it, and that in this degree she has become a "real person." But India, the land of the intuitive and the mystical, can remain for her only an enigma, though not a Mystery.

Thus we may see Adela's experience in the cave as ambivalent: having both subjective and objective meanings. Subjectively, it reveals to her the painful knowledge of her own limitations. Objectively, it poses Western rationality against Eastern mysticism; time against eternity; the conscious against the unconscious. But for modern man, or at least for Western man, no integration of these polarities seems yet possible. Perhaps this is why, in the last lines of *A Passage to India,* Forster leaves us without any neat comforting resolutions of the basic tensions, knowing that, until our disparate psychic selves find some real integration, the voice of the cave, the mysterious echo, speaks still its "No, not yet."

Yet here, in the Cave, in the silence of the OM, the Mystery, is the site of the "transformation" that may produce the Self. For the cave is the Mother and the Tomb, the beginning and the end.

THE WITHERED PRIESTESS
MRS. MOORE'S INCOMPLETE PASSAGE TO INDIA

By EDWIN NIERENBERG

THE WITHERED PRIESTESS
MRS. MOORE'S INCOMPLETE PASSAGE TO INDIA

By Edwin Nierenberg

Mrs. Moore, in E. M. Forster's *A Passage to India,* is, if not a failure, certainly not a heroine. And yet much of the criticism of this novel stresses this lady's benevolent and even superhuman qualities. J. K. Johnstone, for example, recognizes Mrs. Moore's great, universally significant, intuitive powers and maintains that the evil echo of the caves is overcome by her influence because she accepts and understands it, and because she herself is truly religious and good. E. K. Brown, Walter Allen, and Gertrude M. White have also praised this Magna Mater figure, and James McConkey writes of her detachment and resignation, her great and encompassing love. Others, Lionel Trilling and Austin Warren among them, have suggested that the spirit of Mrs. Moore survives in her good will.[1]

My own view is that Mrs. Moore, a principal figure in a novel that celebrates the necessity of facing up to the complexity of life, is neither a saint nor a devil, neither an altogether redemptive nor yet a fallen character, but a figure with concurrent attributes of sincerity and self-deception, of true and false virtue. She often displays a potential for tolerance and wisdom, and certainly she wishes to do good deeds, to create good will, and to establish a bridge between Indians and Englishmen. Yet her considerable failure to help others and herself toward

[1] J. K. Johnstone, *The Bloomsbury Group* (London, 1954); E. K. Brown, "The Revival of E. M. Forster," *Forms of Modern Fiction,* ed. William Van O'Connor (Minneapolis, 1948); Walter Allen, *The English Novel* (Baltimore, 1958); Gertrude M. White, "*A Passage to India:* Analysis and Revaluation," *PMLA,* LXVIII (1953); James McConkey, *The Novels of E. M. Forster* (Ithaca, 1957); Lionel Trilling, *E. M. Forster* (London, 1944); Austin Warren, *Rage for Order* (Ann Arbor, 1948).

an understanding of love, on an individual let alone an international basis, recalls Samuel Johnson's charge against the uninformed heart: "He that voluntarily continues ignorance, is guilty of all the crimes which ignorance produces."

Mrs. Moore graciously attempts to be tolerant and understanding on her visit to India, but she fails because she is not wise enough in her good will to accept muddle or mystery in a friend, a God, or India. " 'I like mysteries but I rather dislike muddles,' " she says (p. 69),[2] to which Fielding replies that a mystery is a muddle. This truth Mrs. Moore must discover for herself within the Marabar caves—to her utter despair. Earlier, in Chapter 2, she meets Aziz at a mosque. To a complicated, if muddled, Aziz, the mosque is attractive for its "contention of shadows," its hint of religious subtleties. On the other hand, Mrs. Moore's summary expression, "God is here," is, as she shall also discover in the caves, a terrible oversimplification of the universal mystery of good and evil. Later the climactic Mau religious festival will celebrate, crudely but freely, "God si love"—a not at all mistaken spelling or crudeness in not trying to pin down God, which is precisely Mrs. Moore's error. She cannot accept what Forster himself appreciates in the ancient Greeks or in a Renaissance Sir Thomas Browne or in some modernly muddled Hindus of India—namely, the ability to live in the blurred worlds of fact and value, of reason and imagination, the ability to envision a God who comes and yet does not come, a God of mystery that is a muddle.

At the same time, Mrs. Moore is self-deluding in her naïve piety, in her oversimplified conclusion that "God had put us on the earth in order to be pleasant to each other" (p. 51). Her religiosity is incomplete because, as Graham Greene would appreciate she has an innocent conception of evil, and because her piety is unfulfilled by *acts* of love. She is not wise or intuitive enough to help her son, Ronny, who has come to look upon life and love in the narrow terms of British officialdom. And despite her apparent awareness of a lack of true love between Adela and Ronny, Mrs. Moore continues to act the dutiful matchmaker, until, in the caves, Adela herself breaks down because she senses that her match with Ronny will not be a marriage, but merely another official arrangement. From behind her own shield of duty, Mrs. Moore fails to perceive the duty-free demands of love.

Few will deny the abstract nobility of Mrs. Moore's belief that God

[2] *A Passage to India* (New York, 1924). All page references are to this edition.

is love. But when and where does Mrs. Moore, even within the limitations of an elderly lady on foreign soil, show love in action? She is *annoyed* by the spat between Adela and Ronny in Chapter 8, yet she offers them no guidance toward a truer understanding of each other. After the couple renew their engagement, Mrs. Moore tells herself: " 'My duties are evidently finished, I don't want to see India now; now for my passage back' " (p. 95). In terms of true love, Mrs. Moore is even more a failure than is Adela; instead of love, Mrs. Moore has a sense of duty in a universe of obligation and due reward. After all, she muses, Adela came from good, conventional, English stock, and "On and on! the number of such unions would certainly increase as education spread and ideals grew loftier, and characters firmer" (p. 95). Mrs. Moore suffers from an incomplete, blind faith in progress and duty, a mechanical certainty of upward and onward; not until she enters the caves, does she begin to sense that the truth about the advance of civilization may be closer to creeping and crawling than to forward march.

Once Ronny has been "suited" to Adela, however, Mrs. Moore must go home to help others dutifully: "She was past marrying herself, even unhappily" (p. 95). Even unhappily! Forster could not be more specific about Mrs. Moore's incomplete (and even un-Christian) awareness of love. She replaces it with a belief that her function is "to help others, her reward to be informed that she was sympathetic. Elderly ladies must not expect more than this" (p. 95)—unless, of course, they expect and demand more of life and personal relationships, like Adela or an equally elderly Miss Raby in Forster's story, "The Eternal Moment." But between the poles of function and reward, Mrs. Moore finds little if any attraction to the pursuit of self-insights upon which true personal relationships may be established. And when a troubled Adela seeks guidance about her coming marriage to Ronny, Mrs. Moore continues her game of patience and dutifully advises Adela not to worry (pp. 98-100).

Mrs. Moore attends to the letter rather than to the spirit of her Bible. Before she enters the caves, she directs her actions by the belief that she will earn a duty-rewarded niche in Heaven; after visiting the caves, she abjures all duty as well as action because she has lost her belief—not in love, but in rewards. Earlier she had been troubled by Professor Godbole's belief that one must ever sing "Come" to a never-coming God (p. 80). After her experience in the caves, her disillusion over God's never-coming and never-rewarding reality is too pitiable for Forster or any reader to condemn. This old lady, who has in her fashion attempted good will, has lost the only thing left for her this side of the grave: her sure expectation of reward on the other side. She is pitiable, but she is not heroic or great.

Although we may flinch at Mrs. Moore's apathy and cynicism, her "just irritation against the human race," we sympathize with her bankrupt soul, shriveled by "the cynicism of a withered priestess" (p. 208). Forster makes it very clear, however, that Mrs. Moore had accepted much false spiritual coin before entering the caves, for she "had always inclined to resignation," while at the same time trying "to be one with the universe! So dignified and simple. But there was always some little duty to be performed first, some new card to be turned up from the diminishing pack and placed, and while she was pottering about, the Marabar struck its gong" (p. 208). Mrs. Moore's reward for her uninformed good will is to be remembered after her death by Godbole, Aziz, and Mr. Forster.[3] It is an unexpected reward, perhaps given her for at last coming upon the excruciating awareness of the wasp-like nature of the universe, the truly choppy tides of the sea. But it is not a heroine's due reward for inspirational greatness.

The deficient, unfulfilled nature of Mrs. Moore is further signified by her relationship to the novel's motifs of tributary waters, the rivers and streams and water-tanks of India with their offer of ablution through self-immersion in the mysterious sea of life. In Chapter 3 Mrs. Moore, accompanied by Adela and Ronny, views the moonlit Ganges: "Below them a radiance had suddenly appeared. It belonged neither to water nor moonlight, but stood like a luminous sheaf upon the field of darkness" (p. 32). But Mrs. Moore's perception of radiance is blurred when she learns from Ronny that the river's banks are impermanent and that Indian bodies float down the river—if they get past the crocodiles.

Here the Ganges becomes an emblem not only of India but of the universe: a mixture of beauty and horror, good and evil, death and crocodiles and radiance. " 'What a terrible river! what a wonderful river!' " Mrs. Moore cries, but she cannot now or later reconcile her opposing views, the opposition of destiny and desire. "The radiance," Forster narrates, "was already altering, whether through shifting of the

[3] For a full discussion of how it remains not for Mrs. Moore herself but for Professor Godbole, another most incomplete person, to fulfill her spirit, see David Shusterman. "The Curious Case of Professor Godbole," *PMLA,* LXXVI (1961), 426-35.

moon or of the sand; soon the bright sheaf would be gone, and a circlet, itself to alter, be burnished upon the streaming void" (p. 32). Just as in the scene in *The Longest Journey,* when Rickie and Ansell discussed squares within circles within squares, Forster is here suggesting the enigmatic, changing nature of reality. The scene also prefigures the alteration in Mrs. Moore when the crocodiles become the eternal echoing serpent of the caves and she, buried at sea, "a circlet . . . burnished upon the streaming void."

In Chapter 2 the mosque in which Mrs. Moore first meets Aziz contains "an ablution tank of fresh clear water, which was always in motion, being indeed part of a conduit that supplied the city" (p. 18). The waters here and yet to flow are by no means still waters; nor is the mosque—or India—a place of repose. Coursing through the novel and emptying into the Mau tank, a motif of water-tanks suggests various degrees of incomplete ablution, of unfulfilled immersion into a life stream of muddle and mystery, out of which the characters of the novel may revive some dark but precious truth about love and life and the universe.

The water-tank motif reappears in Chapter 7, as Mrs. Moore and Adela, and later Godbole, join Aziz and Fielding for an attempted "bridge party" between East and West. Aziz, to impress the Englishwomen, tells a lie about the water-tank in Fielding's garden: " 'You remember the water by our mosque? It comes down and fills this tank —a skillful arrangement of the Emperors' " (p. 71). The truth or falsity of Aziz's defensive statement is not the point, which is that, in bridge parties anywhere in life, a complicated man like Aziz must be understood as an individual, and in terms of the human heart. But Adela in her ignorance "regarded him as 'India,' and never surmised that his outlook was limited, and that no one is India" (p. 72). Like Mrs. Moore, Adela seeks the false ablution of clear, simple answers about India and the muddle of life. For both women their journey is toward the ablution of truth, or as much of reality as they can stand.

The water-tank motif recurs in the account of the expedition to the Marabar caves. Aziz and the Englishwomen ride on elephants toward the hills, and then, "Here, more or less, was their goal. A ruined tank held a little water which would do for the animals, and close above the mud was punched a black hole—the first of the caves" (pp. 141-42). Later, Professor Godbole tells Fielding the legend of this Tank of the Dagger. It is the story of a Rajah who killed his nephew, but could not let the dagger fall from his hand; years later the Rajah came to the Marabar hills, where, despite his own great thirst, he allowed a cow to drink first, whereupon " 'dagger fell from his hand, and to commemorate miracle he built Tank' " (p. 179).

The meanings of this legend may be ambiguous and therefore to Forster's purpose; but at least one important significance of the legend concerns a moral complexity in which evil and good are mysteriously mixed, in life generally and in individuals, so that moral ablution cannot be a simple matter of ritual, but must proceed from human kindness without expectation of reward. At the caves both Adela and Mrs. Moore suffer from having sought a false, rewarding ablution: Adela in the name of a reasonable marriage, let alone a reasonable universe, and Mrs. Moore in terms of a tangibly just God who exhibits His earth as continual proof and clear promise of His simple goodness. Both women seek the ablution of happiness without first facing up to their crimes—Adela and her truth-thwarting reason, Mrs. Moore and her love-killing and pitiably incomplete reliance upon a dutiful universe of function and reward. Each of them has failed to comprehend the water-tank's truth, a mystery and a truth as elusive as India itself. Then each one enters the punched hole of her cave, where at last the daggers of naïveté fall from them, and they are left defenseless against the disorder of an unreasonable universe.

Of the two women, Adela remains in India and suffers a breakdown through which she comes to realize, as did Philip Herriton at the end of *Where Angels Fear to Tread,* that life was greater than she had supposed, yet it was even less complete. Mrs. Moore, to whom the Marabar had boummed its message of "Everything exists, nothing has value" (p. 149), chooses to flee from India, from the mysterious sea of life. Up in the Marabars, "A gully, or rather a crease, showed among the rocks. . . . The crease continued as a nullah across the plain, the water draining off this way towards the Ganges" (p. 159).

The message of the cave-connected river, a message of truth through and beyond disillusion, is lost upon a despairing Mrs. Moore as she takes her passage from India. Aboard the train, "As she left Chandrapore the moon, full again, shone over the Ganges and touched the shrinking channels into threads of silver, then veered and looked into her window" (p. 209). The moonlighted river is as radiant as it had been upon Mrs. Moore's first view of it, but now the river and life are not wonderful, they are terrifying. She has succumbed to one-sided despair. All the next day, across the baked and bleached landscape of India, she watches "the indestructible life of man and his changing faces, and the houses he has built for himself and God, and they appeared to her not in terms of her own trouble but as things to see" (p. 209). She cannot perceive that, through despair like her own, man struggles to achieve meaning and value upon the earth, and that the struggle is worthy of man. " 'I have not seen the right places,' " she deludes herself, for she has seen them, but she is unable to connect despair with hope. She cannot see how this land and this sun, this sea and this universe—this India—fail simply to vanish, nor why, when she sails from India, the trees and hills "wave her farewell," but scornfully laugh: " 'So you thought an echo was India; you took the Marabar caves as final?' " (p. 210). The helpless Mrs. Moore, secure only in her despair, sails into the hazy tropic sea, where she is to die and be buried.

And yet the dead Mrs. Moore will have a life of sorts in the memories of those like Adela and Godbole who, out of whatever false or incomplete knowledge about their friend, think of her as they attempt to exercise love, to complete their natures through remembrance of Mrs. Moore. If this can be called Forster's mysticism, it is rooted not so much in Christianity as in an ethical humanism; it remains for the living to complete themselves, and as much of mortal life as is possible, by their memory-in-life of dead and worthy friends. Forster himself has "evoked" the qualities of some of his dead friends, in his books on Marianne Thornton, Goldsworthy Lowes Dickinson, and the Maharajah of Dewas (in *The Hill of Devi*). The waters of such love and friendship flow deep, cutting across national boundaries, offering the ablution of hope at least to the living.

At the end of *Passage,* the joyous and muddled Mau rituals suggest a peace and a love that pass understanding, as well as a separation between men and between nations. In the Mau water-tank, in the Grand Collision between East and West, pure connection is unattainable; yet Love, the Beloved Republic, remains Forster's hope, whereby man may act and create, be a friend to himself and to others and thus to the universe. India, the universe of sun and cave, of desert and sea, of an appeal rather than a promise, offers passage to all: "a passage not easy, not now, not here, not to be apprehended except when it is unattainable" (pp. 314-15). Mrs. Moore's failure to achieve such a passage for and by herself affords hope and impetus to others.

San Francisco State College

//

ADELA QUESTED'S DELUSION:

THE FAILURE OF RATIONALISM IN *A PASSAGE TO INDIA*

TED E. BOYLE

THOUGH MANY of the enigmatic problems of Forster's most important novel dictate somewhat complicated solutions, one of the most frequently discussed of these problems —the significance of Adela Quested's experience in the Marabar Caves—seems one of the most readily soluble. To assess correctly Adela's Marabar experience, thus capturing the full force of Forster's indictment of rationalism, we need only note Forster's description of Adela's obviously sexual frustrations prior to the visit to the caves and his subtle employment of an unobtrusive symbol—the fieldglasses which Adela has borrowed from Ronnie.

Adela Quested, of course, comes to India to see her fiancé, Ronnie Heaslop, at his work. She is to decide whether she should indeed marry Ronnie, and all concerned, especially Adela herself, assume the trip is a mere formality. After several days in India, however, Adela is disappointed by her almost excruciating boredom: "She was particularly vexed now because she was both in India and engaged to be married, which double event should have made every instant sublime" (133).[1] In an attempt to alleviate her boredom by knowing "the *real* India" (24), Adela mingles freely with the Indian guests at Major Turton's "Bridge Party," yet she still feels vaguely dissatisfied about her Indian experiences. Thus, her acceptance, with Mrs. Moore, of Aziz's invitation to visit the Marabar Caves is not only a manifestation of her naive desire to know "the *real* India," it is a subconscious recognition of her unsatisfactory relationship with Ronnie. Adela has expected mystery and excitement from her engagement. She has experienced only boredom, and though she fails to come to terms with her boredom rationally, she goes to the caves in a subconscious search for the adventure which she senses she has missed.

The sensational result of the Marabar expedition is, of course, Adela's accusing Aziz of attempted rape. Adela later withdraws her charge, but the reader who is in doubt as to its falsity may misinterpret Forster's message concerning the failure of untempered rationality to solve basic human problems. That the charge is false can clearly be seen when one understands the symbolic implications of the field glasses which Ronnie lends to Adela. On the tedious train journey to the caves, Adela notices a strange object out of harmony with the undulations of the parched hills: "Miss Quested saw a thin dark object reared on end at the farther side of a watercourse, and said, 'A snake!' . . . But when she looked through Ronnie's fieldglasses, she found it wasn't a snake, but the withered and twisted stump of a toddy palm. So she said, 'It isn't a snake'" (141). In this landscape where "everything seemed cut off at its root, and therefore infected with illusion" (140), Adela's first cognition of the "thin dark object reared on end" clearly represents the working of her subconscious, her irrational mind. This young woman who has approached marriage as though it were essentially a rational business transaction has been overwhelmed for a moment by her emotions, by her very real desire to experience the purely physical facet of marriage which her rational code will not allow her to recognize. The irra-

[1] Numbers in parentheses refer to page numbers in the Harbrace Modern Classics edition of *A Passage to India* (New York, 1924).

Mr. Boyle is professor of English at Southern Illinois University and the author of Symbol and Meaning in the Fiction of Joseph Conrad.

tional and the emotional will not be denied, however; thus Adela's readiness to see the "thin dark object reared on end" as a snake with all its symbolic implications of sexuality. The fieldglasses function here as a symbol of Adela's shallow rationalism. When she views the "thin dark object" through the glasses, she perceives the "withered and twisted stump of a toddy palm." Her British middle-class training has triumphed through contact with the mechanical things of Western civilization.

Later, only moments before she enters one of the Marabar Caves, Adela realizes she does not love Ronnie. Her rational mind again triumphs: "Ought she to break the engagement off? She was inclined to think not—it would cause so much trouble to others; besides she wasn't convinced that love was necessary to a successful union" (152). She is, however, curious about that which she has decided is impractical and unnecessary. With a mixture of rudeness and fascination she questions Aziz closely about his marriage, and as she enters the cave she is "thinking with half her mind 'sight-seeing bores me,' and wondering with the other half about marriage" (153).

In the caves, the subconscious, the irrational, the emotional, the very soul of India wins out over the conscious, the rational, the intellectual—all that Adela has been taught by Western society. The "real India" which Adela sought to know has reversed the situation completely, has, in fact, "known" her. She runs in panic from the caves, leaving behind Ronnie's fieldglasses, the symbol of shallow rationality. Again, however, the victory of Adela's subconscious, that deeper soul which she will not acknowledge, has been only temporary. She accuses Aziz, and her accusation is symptomatic of her refusal to admit that a marriage is not a rational business contract, that love is necessary. The British police, in their haste to confirm the validity of their rational approach to things Indian, interpret the fact that the eye-piece of Adela's fieldglasses is jammed and the strap newly broken as incontrovertible evidence of Aziz's guilt. They arrest Aziz and it seems certain that the gods of the conscious life and the intellect shall be served.

When Mrs. Moore, who has also had her experience in the caves, who has learned of the flabbiness of traditional Christianity, is questioned by Adela as to the significance of the frightening echo of the caves, she replies: "Don't you know? . . . If you don't know, you don't know; I can't tell you" (200). Mrs. Moore cannot explain because she realizes that the message of the caves has meaning only in terms of the individual experience. The echo of the caves pierces the unplumbed depths of each individual and there uncovers his most deeply felt doubts and needs. Mrs. Moore has had her belief in shallow Victorian Christianity—in the God that saves the King. This faith has been destroyed and the echo of the caves has substituted a larger, though less activist and optimistic, faith. Adela has had her faith in the rational and intellectual way. Counter to this faith, the caves have asserted that the emotions, the flesh, must not be denied.

Fight against her emotions Adela must, else she would be untrue to her training. Yet, during the trial she admits, quite emotionally, quite irrationally, that she has falsely accused Aziz. This is not to say that Adela has integrated the experience of the caves into her view of the world, but she is, in fact, a more complete person now than she was before her Marabar experience. She is now capable of insights not dependent upon the intellect. After the abortive trial, Fielding, whose acuity in character analysis is limited to the characters of others, asserts, "I believe that you yourself broke the strap of the fieldglasses; you were alone in that cave the whole time" (239). Of course, Fielding's remarks are in keeping with his notion that the world is a logical place where effect can be explained by readily discernible cause. Fielding believes that "a mystery is only a high-sounding name for a muddle" (69). Yet, his judgment is more relevant to Miss Quested's case than he suspects. It was she, in fact, who broke the strap of the fieldglasses, who was forced by the welling up of her emotions to admit her physical desire. As Adela tells Fielding: "I had an hallucination there, the sort of thing—though in an awful form—that makes some women think they've had an offer of marriage when none was made" (240).

Thus, through his artful description of Adela's partial realization that the emotions cannot be denied, Forster offers an insight into the larger theme of the novel—the failure of untempered rationalism to destroy the barriers which isolate man from his fellow. As Adela, to fulfill herself, must strike a balance between the intellect and the emotions, so man, be he English or Indian, Moslem or Hindu, must approach the realm of human relationships with a proper balance of head and heart.

The Prophetic Novel: A Passage to India

James McConkey

The last novel is his great novel, the one that most fully realizes its potentialities, and it does so partly at least because in it Forster is most keenly aware that the division does exist, that what he attempted without full success in *Howards End* is totally impossible now. Fielding has supplanted Margaret Schlegel as the protagonist who is concerned with the problem of human relationships; but earth no longer supplies a link between man and the transcendent unity. The voice remains, it can still remind of that unity, but without the aid of earth it cannot give to Fielding a sense of his own connection with it.

For the separation of man from earth and hence from ultimate reality which threatened in 1910 has become accomplished by 1924, a disaster which has had, for Forster as novelist, at least one brighter feature: it has meant that the two commitments which he could never quite reconcile have been divorced fully by forces not his own and that what has been perhaps his individual psychological inability has become the fault of an age; it has meant that Forster's own detachment from human reality has become the only means of sensing, however partially, the divine order. Fielding's achievements in the realm of personal relationships, inconclusive as those achievements finally become, are possible because he, as opposed to Margaret Schlegel, can "travel light"; he has no roots in society nor place and he desires none; he is associated with no sense of tradition.

Not that all the characters in the novel are completely without root. Aziz, we are told, "was rooted in society and Islam. He belonged to a tradition which bound him, and he had brought children into the world, the society of the future. Though he lived so vaguely in this flimsy bungalow, nevertheless he was placed, placed"; and it is because he is so placed, because he is aware of such a tradition, that, in spite of the brevity of his acquaintance with Mrs. Moore, the two make immediate and lasting connection. For she also is placed: she, like Aziz, has two sons and a daughter, and to her, "it is the children who are the first consideration"; too, she is equally rooted by tradition—in her case, that of western Christianity.

But Aziz, though placed, "was without natural affection for the land of his birth" and must make a conscious, willful attempt to love it; and Mrs. Moore is in a countryside which is alien, even hostile, to her spirit. That is the difference that the years between *Howards End* and *A Passage to India* finally have forced upon Forster. India is more than a foreign land which the English may leave at their wish: it is the contemporary condition, the separation between all mankind and all earth. In her awareness of continuity and tradition, in her capacity for detachment and resignation, in the greatness of her encompassing love, Mrs. Moore is, indeed, Ruth Wilcox once more; but she is a Ruth Wilcox whose intuitive love remains after the major contributing factor to that love—a harmony between her spirit and the earth—has ceased to exist. Although she is fated to failure, we believe in her as we never believed, despite all of Forster's efforts, in Ruth Wilcox.

There is a paragraph in *Howards End* which stands as a foreshadowing of *A Passage to India* and will even do as a partial statement of the latter novel's intent. Marriage, we are told, "had not saved" Margaret

> from the sense of flux. London was but a foretaste of this nomadic civilization which is altering human nature so profoundly, and throws upon personal relations a stress greater than they have ever borne before. Under cosmo-

politanism, if it comes, we shall receive no help from the earth. Trees and meadows and mountains will only be a spectacle, and the binding force that they once exercised on character must be entrusted to Love alone. May Love be equal to the task!

In *A Passage to India*, no longer does man receive "help from the earth"; quite the opposite is true, for the earth even seems to increase the friction between men: "It was as if irritation exuded from the very soil. Could one have been so petty on a Scotch moor or an Italian alp? . . . . There seemed no reserve of tranquillity to draw upon in India. Either none, or else tranquillity swallowed up everything, as it appeared to do for Professor Godbole." The English Lake Country is referred to at various times in the novel, and it stands, in its contrast to the land around Chandrapore, as a symbol of the harmony that once existed between man and his surroundings; Wordsworth is in the background, Forster has acknowledged,[3] in the reference to Grasmere, whose "little lakes and mountains were beloved by them all. Romantic yet manageable, it sprang from a kindlier planet." But in India, beauty is lacking; Fielding "had forgotten the beauty of form among idol temples and lumpy hills; indeed, without form, how can there be beauty?" With the approach of the hot season, the sun returns "to his kingdom with power but without beauty—that was the sinister feature. If only there had been beauty! His cruelty would have been tolerable then."

[3] In a letter to the author of this study.

"*May Love be equal to the task!*" For Mrs. Moore, as we have seen, it is not: "God . . . is . . . love," He "has put us on earth to love our neighbours and to show it, and He is omnipresent, even in India, to see how we are succeeding," she tells Ronnie Heaslop. Yet God has not proved to be the satisfaction to her He was before her arrival in India: "She must needs pronounce his name frequently, as the greatest she knew, yet she had never found it less efficacious. Outside the arch there seemed always an arch, beyond the remotest echo a silence." And in the cave, in the unattractive, shapeless hills, she undergoes a psychic experience in which she loses totally the sense of values that her mystical divination of unity, related to the Christian tradition, has afforded her; she loses interest in Aziz, in her own children, in God. Yet Mrs. Moore has made a lasting effect, and she acts—*after* her negating vision, after her death—as an influence even more pervasive than that of Ruth Wilcox in *Howards End*. The Hindus at the trial of Aziz invoke her name in an echoing chant, for she has seemed like a goddess to them; she influences Adela toward realization that her accusation of Aziz has been false; her presence is felt throughout the final section of the novel and helps weave the achieved unity—transitory though it may be—that we find there.

In the important essay, "Art for Art's Sake," Forster, after commenting on the apparent impossibility of man's achievement of harmony "with his surroundings when he is constantly altering them," finds:

> The future of our race is, in this direction, more unpleasant than we care to admit, and it has sometimes seemed to me that its best chance lies through apathy, uninventiveness, and inertia. . . . Universal exhaustion would certainly be a new experience. The human race has never undergone it, and is still too perky to admit that it may be coming and might result in a sprouting of new growth through the decay.

One sees in the depiction of Mrs. Moore a concept similar to this. She, who has always inclined toward resignation, must die through spiritual exhaustion—and this is achieved in the cave and not in her actual death on the sea—in order that a new birth, a new growth, may be achieved: the birth and growth which are portrayed for us in the final section of the novel. *Must* die—for the earth has become alien to man; the God, the order, the unity, which had been perceived through that earth must perforce be discovered again.

It is hence as a rebirth after exhaustion that we need to read the final section of *A Passage to India.* The novel's three sections represent, Forster tells us in his notes to the *Everyman* edition, the "three seasons of the Cold Weather, the Hot Weather, and the Rains, which divide the Indian year"; it is the recurring cycle of birth through death, commencing, in this novel, with the culmination of the period of fullest realization and maturity, proceeding thence through death to rebirth. The symbolic rites connected with the birth of Krishna, which relate to the Christmas observance in Christian tradition, even if they are primitive, even if they are muddled (perhaps partly *because* they are muddled), reach out in an attempt to encompass everything, to encompass the order which lies beyond chaos; and, because the ceremony is so all-inclusive, it prohibits anyone's discovery of "the emotional centre of it, any more than he could locate the heart of a cloud."

Obviously such a rebirth as this last section represents is one to be achieved neither through Christianity nor through the earth-relationship. Though one should not read the novel as a statement that Hinduism as such will solve the Indian dilemma, much less the dilemma of the world, Hindu metaphysics bears a number of definite relationships to the stabilized Forsterian philosophical position, a position which does not require place worship and which has always been hostile to organized Christianity. Certainly the redemptive power that Mrs. Moore possesses after death signifies chiefly in regard neither to place nor to her Christian religion; she becomes such a power, indeed, primarily only to the extent that she is merged with the small and elderly Hindu professor, Godbole.

Godbole, the central figure in the last section of the novel and the one most responsible for whatever sense of hope is granted there, is the only truly prophetic *character* in all the novels; for he is the only one who ever becomes the human counterpart of the Forsterian voice. To no locality on earth is Godbole indebted: he "always did possess the knack of slipping off," and he would be, one assumes, no less tranquil in London or even Chicago than he is in Chandrapore or Mau. For, like the voice, he is detached, though never to the extent of the full mystic. He remains, in his contact with human and transcendent realities, at precisely the midpoint of voice, and his is the same imperfect intuition: he is capable of comprehending the transcendent unity, but not completely. Thus, during the Krishna rites at Mau, he can love a wasp equally with a human figure recollected from his Chandrapore days—it happens to be that of Mrs. Moore—but he cannot equally love the stone on which the wasp rests: "no, he could not, he had been wrong to attempt the stone, logic and conscious effort had seduced, he came back to the strip of red carpet and discovered that he was dancing upon it."

Basic to the Mau ceremonies and to Godbole's desire "to attempt the stone" are the dual realities of Hindu metaphysics. Brahman is the unseen metaphysical absolute; the triad of Vishnu, Siva, and Brahma is the manifestation of Brahman. The metaphysical absolute is to be approached through the triad, but since Brahman is devoid of attributes, such an approach is, from the standpoint of logic, impossible. The triad, indeed, as is true of the phenomenal universe itself, offers a reality which is but illusory; hence identification with the absolute comes only with the extinction of individual consciousness, with the final and total separation of soul from the physical realm. One may love other existence within that realm in proportion to the extent of his own remove from the phenomenal universe; thus the detachment and self-abnegation of Godbole are qualities which impart to him his extensive, though necessarily incomplete, sense of love and unity—even as they have always been the qualities of the Forsterian voice, imparting much the same incomplete vision.

And so the rebirth suggested in the final pages of the novel is one to be brought about by a love which, in turn, can be obtained only through as great a denial of self and the physical world as it is possible for mankind to make. Is such a price too dear? Does the cost of the love make that love prohibitive? A recent critic of *A Passage to India*, Glen O. Allen, says that to Forster the Hindu Way of Love is a "good," although "not in its extreme nor to the exclusion of all other goods." The renunciation and loss of individuality which the Hindu must achieve in order to gain unity is, Allen believes, the "repugnant extreme"; and he feels that Forster in *A Passage to India* is asserting, as he did in *Howards End*, the need for proportion: love is but one of the "ingredients of the good life."

But such a proportion as Margaret Schlegel seeks between seen and unseen worlds in *Howards End* simply isn't a factor in this novel, for the seen world has become meaningless through man's own perversity and decay. The cost of love, to put it simply, has already been paid; man has already become the alien wanderer on earth's surface. Fielding and Godbole those entirely different men, represent the division that exists between seen and unseen worlds; and they represent as well the disparity to be found between Forster's commitment to human relations and his commitment to the insight and love gained through a remove from those relations. No hope for a spiritual rebirth, for a new awareness of unity, can come from an emphasis upon the values of the human world; for, without the agency of earth, no valid sense of connection among men can be obtained. Fielding, despite his efforts in behalf of Aziz, still is denied brotherhood with him; thus those efforts, admirable though they may be, can produce no lessening of the spiritual sterility.

Harmony between man and nature may be gained at some time in the future, and perhaps once more there will be a reconciliation of seen and unseen worlds—we are given some slight indication of this by the landscape at Mau, which, while queer, is less alien than the rest of India; and we are granted some hope—it is, however, never stressed—in the as yet unborn child of Stella and Fielding. Stella, the daughter of Mrs. Moore, is her heir, so far as the possession of intuitive love is concerned; and hence Stella is also of spiritual kin to Godbole. Through the child of Stella and Fielding, mankind may once again achieve proportion and a balance between realms of reality. But, if so, the initiating power *must* come from a love which draws no sustenance either from nature or from human relations. Godbole and the Hindu Way of Love, absurd though they may seem to the western rationalist, can provide that power.

As is apparent by now, the major mythological referent of *A Passage to India* is that of Hinduism. Since the method whereby this referent is presented to us is primarily that of recurrent symbolism, the intricacies of the subject are best left to the following chapter on "Rhythm"; here what primarily needs to be noted is that such a referent has given Forster a framework totally in keeping with the implications of his voice and that the prophecy of the novel results from such a relationship.

A word of caution, however, is perhaps necessary. One can easily overemphasize the importance of Hinduism in *A Passage to India:* what we need to recognize, I think, is not that Forster accepts Hinduism, but rather that he selects from its metaphysics and attitudes those things which always have been most congenial to him. Reason, while important to Forster, has always been relegated by him to a position beneath that of love; and man's relationship to the physical world in *A Passage to India* is such that reason no longer can operate in conjunction with a spiritual insight. Other attitudes of Forster's which give him an affinity with Godbole have already been suggested. And clearly the Hindu division of realities—a division which, while affirming the existence of an absolute, makes its approach impossible to conscious man—offers a parallel to Forster's own philosophical view.

Toward the ceremonies of Hinduism, on the other hand, he shows little attraction. One assumes that Forster, with Stella and her brother, likes Hinduism while taking "no interest in its forms." Such an assumption is documented by *The Hill of Devi* (1953), an account of Forster's experiences in India in 1921 while he was serving as a personal secretary to the Maharajah of Dewas Senior. The description in *The Hill of Devi* of a Gokul Ashtami festival which he attended, and which provided him with the description of the Mau rites in *A Passage to India*, certainly indicates that the festival itself made no profound religious impression upon him. "There is no dignity, no taste, no form, and though I am dressed as a Hindu I shall never become one," he writes concerning his participation in the festival. What he chiefly responded to during the festival was the fact that it "touches something very deep in their hearts." [4]

Once we have discovered Forster's attitudes in *A Passage to India*, we can perceive the thematic progres-

[4] *The Hill of Devi* presents many of Forster's experiences which later were to be incorporated into *A Passage to India:* there is an account of an automobile accident which becomes the accident involving the Nawab Bahadur in the novel; there is a description of Mau (the Gokul Ashtami rites witnessed by Forster actually did not occur there); and there is always the sense of strangeness and lack of form in India. But *The Hill of Devi*, despite its wealth of background material, offers little new insight into the richness and depth of *A Passage to India:* for it is what Forster's creative faculty has done to the material which chiefly matters. In this respect, it is interesting to note in *The Hill of Devi* a comment on *A Passage to India:*

"I began this novel before my 1921 visit, and took out the opening chapters with me, with the intention of continuing them. But as soon as they were confronted with the country they purported to describe, they seemed to wilt and go dead and I could do nothing with them. I used to look at them of an evening in my room at Dewas, and felt only distaste and despair. The gap between India remembered and India experienced was too wide. When I got back to England the gap narrowed, and I was able to resume."

sion to be found in his novels, for it is a progression from a complete trust in physical reality to the denial of it in a Marabar cave, that cave, in its lack of attributes, representing the "nothingness" of the metaphysical absolute itself. It is a progression marked by Forster's choice of redemptive characters, from the elder Emerson to Gino, Wonham, Ruth Wilcox, and finally Godbole; and the disparity that separates the first from the last is, largely, the philosophical distance which Forster has covered within the relatively brief course of five novels.

Yet even the Forster who finds a parallel of his values in a Godbole and in Hindu metaphysics is not a writer who represents what we normally would consider the mystic state of being; he is, rather, a writer most keenly aware of discord and lack of harmony in his world who nevertheless senses, however obscurely, a harmony beyond and strives for identification with it. He never (or rarely) succeeds; it is difficult to determine whether or not Forster has ever attained the mystic vision, and Forster himself could never accurately tell us, as his account of the moment of birth during the Mau ceremonies indicates:

> But the human spirit had tried by a desperate contortion to ravish the unknown, flinging down science and history in the struggle, yes, beauty herself. Did it succeed? Books written afterwards say "Yes." But how, if there is such an event, can it be remembered afterwards? How can it be expressed in anything but itself? Not only from the unbeliever are mysteries hid, but the adept himself cannot retain them. He

> may think, if he chooses, that he has been with God, but as soon as he thinks it, it becomes history, and falls under the rules of time.

And, in Forster's belief, if we lose a sense of unity with the earth, if we lose a sense of a divine plan in the stars, the loss, though profound, is ours only; it constitutes no denial of that ultimate order. For Forster's is a Shelleyian view, with the important exception that the veil cannot be fully penetrated to the absolute forms. All that Forster can do is suggest the presence of a transcendent verity. To do more is to absolutize what man cannot decipher; any absolute would be of man, not of the divine. Such a dissociation between man and ultimate truth is a basic distinction between Forster and the English Romantics and one reason that Forster's romanticism, idealism, can exist into the twentieth century while theirs cannot.

THE CURIOUS CASE OF PROFESSOR GODBOLE: *A PASSAGE TO INDIA* RE-EXAMINED

BY DAVID SHUSTERMAN

ALTHOUGH many critics of E. M. Forster's *A Passage to India* have mentioned that Professor Godbole, the Hindu educator, behaves somewhat queerly during the course of the novel, no one, so far as I can discover, since the book's publication in 1924 has seemed to have any serious doubt that Godbole is a man of genuine goodwill or that he is the source of much that is good. This conventional attitude has been expanded upon within recent years by several critics who have put Godbole forward as Forster's primary spokesman for cosmic and divine truth. Forster's point, they claim, is that Hinduism is closer to this truth than any other religion; the author is using Godbole to make this revelation known. To James McConkey, one of the proponents of the Godbolean viewpoint, "the full measure of the success" of Forster's Indian novel "suggests that Forster has finally come to terms with himself and his universe." These terms are imparted through Godbole "the only person in all the novels who becomes the character-equivalent of the Forsterian voice." Godbole's position is "one of detachment from human reality and from the physical world, a detachment obtained by as complete a denial of individual consciousness as is possible, that denial and remove bringing with them a sense of love and an awareness of unity." Hindu metaphysics "bears a number of definite relationships to the stabilized Forsterian philosophical position." It is Godbole who is "the one most responsible for whatever sense of hope is granted" in the last section of the novel. The "way of Godbole is the only possible way: love, even though to exist it must maintain a detachment from the physical world and human relationships, offers the single upward path from the land of sterility and echoing evil."[1] To Hugh Maclean, another Godbolean adherent, Mrs. Moore, the elderly Englishwoman, finds completeness only after death through the intercession of Godbole; the latter "excludes nothing" from his spiritual life, and because of this he "will be able [ultimately] to encompass everything." It is only Godbole whose mind has seized on the order of the universe. Forster is advocating above everything else that people should become like Godbole, one who is able to accomplish the "absorption of the self within a transcendental frame of reference."[2]

It is my opinion that this attempt to turn Forster into a transplanted Hindu and his novel into little more than a tract for the glorification of Hinduism and Godbole represents a grave misreading of the novel and of Forster's writing in general. First of all, it becomes necessary to stress one fact: if anything can be said of Forster it is that nowhere explicitly or by implication does he advocate complete detachment from human reality and from the physical world. It is true that, in recent years, Forster has asserted the overwhelming importance to man of the aesthetic element; and he has insisted, particularly in war time, that the ivory tower is not to be looked upon with scorn but with great respect. This attitude may be considered by some as a form of limited detachment. In his "Art for Art's Sake" address in 1949 he admits the possibility of a "mystic harmony, which *according to all religions is available for those who can contemplate it*" (italics mine). The existence of this divine order "though it cannot be tested, has never been disproved." There is one other possibility of order, however, and this is the one Forster is primarily interested in: "the order which an artist can create in his own work." The work of art is unique "because it is the only material object in the universe which may possess internal harmony." The artist who pursues his art as he should, for its own sake, Forster admits, "will tend to be an outsider in the society to which he has been born."[3] Believing so fervently in the importance of art, Forster elsewhere asserts that it is good for the artist to withdraw occasionally into an ivory tower where he can labor undisturbed in fashioning his work of art. Many writers achieved their greatest creative efforts in strict solitude.[4]

This is the limit of Forster's advocacy of withdrawal: it is a specialized type of behavior, good only for the artist at certain periods in his career. And Forster is not advocating a mystical renunciation of self as a necessity for new spiritual growth, as has been claimed, when he says in the "Art for Art's Sake" address that the best chance for the future of the race "lies through apathy, uninventiveness, and inertia. Universal exhaustion might

[1] James McConkey, *The Novels of E. M. Forster* (Ithaca, 1957), pp. 11–12, 86, 159–160.

[2] "The Structure of *A Passage to India*," *Univ. of Toronto Quarterly*, XXII (January 1953), 157–171.

[3] *Two Cheers for Democracy* (New York, 1951), pp. 88–95.

[4] "The Ivory Tower," *Atlantic Monthly*, CLXIII (January 1939), 51–58.

promote that Change of Heart which is at present so briskly recommended from a thousand pulpits." This statement has been cited as proof of the advocacy of Godbole's love, "the only kind of love which can survive in the world that Forster depicts."[5] In this context Forster was speaking of the impossibility of any real harmony within man's social structure because of the "implacable offensive of Science," which is constantly bringing into being new inventions. "How can man get into harmony with his surroundings when he is constantly altering them?" Forster asks. It is true that the change of heart must come from within, but in this connection Forster was definitely thinking of man as a social being. To jump from this completely social statement to the advocacy of renunciation of the individual self as a prerequisite for union with godhead is to misunderstand Forster's whole point.

We must clarify our thinking about Forster's attitude towards love. To him it is almost a regenerative force in modern life, but it is not at all a love detached from the physical world or from human relationships, not at all a love separable from the individual self. Forster believes solidly in the mental and physical development of the individual. That his leading characters do not always exemplify this all-around individual development is another matter; their failure cannot be equated with the beliefs of their creator. To do so would be to commit the biographical fallacy. Under this type of reasoning Forster becomes an Indian mystic like Godbole. But just because Godbole's love is detached from the self and seeks union with the nonhuman Divine element, there is no reason for believing that Forster advocates it. In "What I Believe," written in 1939, he starts his series of affirmations with the maintenance of his belief in the importance of personal relationships: "Here is something comparatively solid in a world full of violence and cruelty." In theory we cannot put our trust in personal relationships in such a world, but "in practice we can and do. . . . For the purpose of living one has to assume that the personality is solid, and the 'self' is an entity, and to ignore all contrary evidence." One must, he insists, be fond of people and trust them if one is not to make a mess of life. Forster is most fond of people who belong to "an aristocracy of the sensitive, the considerate and the plucky." Members of this select group "are to be found in all nations and classes, and all through the ages. . . . They represent the true human tradition, *the one permanent victory of our queer race over cruelty and chaos*" (italics mine). Forster would prefer that this aristocracy not be ascetic: "I am against asceticism myself. I am with the old Scotsman who wanted less chastity and more delicacy. I do not feel that my aristocrats are a real aristocracy if they thwart their bodies, since bodies are the instruments through which we register and enjoy the world."[6] One could go through Forster's writings, fiction and nonfiction, and cite a considerable number of similar affirmations of the importance of the individual and development of his whole nature—mind and body. The love that these developed individuals engender will be the means of regeneration for the tired human race, if regeneration ever comes; these individuals, Forster has written eloquently, are the lighthouses that reach across the barriers of race and nationality to keep alive the best in human history. This individual "seems to me a divine achievement and I mistrust any view which belittles him."[7]

This type of love is not the kind that Professor Godbole indulges in or aspires to. Godbole's love does not even begin to approach the conditions which Forster has laid down for his aristocracy. Nor can one believe for a moment that Forster thinks that Godbole's is the only kind that can survive in the world he describes. Though more despairing, the world of his last novel is essentially the same one that he has written about in his earlier novels; at the center always stands the sensitive, considerate, plucky aristocrat (such as Fielding in *A Passage to India*) who aspires to complete individual development and to a love with such another one as himself, though he seldom, if ever, attains his aspiration. There is no equivalence between his love and Godbole's.

Forster's general philosophical position perhaps does bear some resemblance to Hindu metaphysics, but it has resemblances also to many other metaphysical positions, since Forster has absorbed eclectically through his reading and contemplation a variety of approaches to man's problems. I am unable to understand how anyone can speak of Forster's having a "stabilized philosophical position." The adjective is a complete misnomer, for stabilized is exactly what Forster's philosophy is not, as anyone who takes the trouble to read all of Forster's writings carefully and with an open mind will ascertain. But whether stabilized or not, Forster's position has little resemblance to that of Godbole. There is very little in "What I Believe," Forster's most extensive statement of his beliefs,

[5] McConkey, pp. 140–144.
[6] *Two Cheers for Democracy*, pp. 67–76.
[7] "The Challenge of Our Time," ibid., p. 57.

which Godbole could or would accept. Could, for example, a fervent Hindu, like Godbole, have anything in common with the man who said that his lawgivers are Erasmus and Montaigne and that his motto is "Lord, I disbelieve—help thou my unbelief"? Is there anything much in common between Godbole and the man who wrote: "One must be fond of people and trust them if one is not to make a mess of life, and it is therefore essential that they should not let one down"? My paper will show that Godbole is the very type of person Forster is condemning in this statement, for Godbole shows very little fondness or trust in people and is almost always letting them down.

If it is true—and I think it is—that Forster does have an interest in mysticism, and in this respect has a resemblance to Godbole, the evidence of his writings indicates that his interest has been somewhat vague, not very intense. The important point, however, is that he could just as easily have been stimulated in this direction by the Neo-Platonists, on whom he has written, by the English Christian mystics, whom he has read, by the experiences of his friends G. Lowes Dickinson and Frank Vicary,[8] by Madame Blavatsky, under whose influence it has been claimed he once came,[9] or, perhaps, by the Moslem poet Mohammed Iqbal, on whom he has written an appreciative essay.[10] I stress Forster's eclecticism for I think it is relevant; if one reads Forster closely, it will become evident that his is a mind that has absorbed many intellectual strands. On the question of metaphysical doctrines, he has shown, as in almost everything else, an ever-inquiring, ever-searching mind, not content to remain fixed in any one position. One cannot deny the possible influence of Hinduism, which may have colored to some extent the pattern of his great Indian novel. It is my belief, however, that Hinduism has really much less importance in the novel than has hitherto been believed. A close consideration of the novel will also show that the role of Professor Godbole, though important, is important in a manner different from that which has ever been claimed: far from being an influence for good, his is an influence which is non-beneficial and, if not primarily and consciously evil, is at least in the direction of evil.

There are valuable bits of evidence of Forster's shifting viewpoint in the years preceding *A Passage to India;* they indicate clearly that Hinduism was possibly less important to him at the time than was Mohammedanism. In a letter of 26 September 1921, Forster wrote of how impressed he was by his second visit to the Taj: "I do like Islam, though I have had to come through Hinduism to discover it. After all the mess and profusion and confusion of Gokul Ashtami, where nothing ever stopped or need ever have begun, it was like standing on a mountain."[11] On 12 November 1921, he wrote: "I have passed abruptly from Hinduism to Islam and the change is a relief. I have come too into a world [Hyderabad] whose troubles and problems are intelligible to me: Dewas made much ado about nothing and no ado where a little would have been seemly."[12] There are other statements in *The Hill of Devi* denigrating Hinduism, especially with reference to Gokul Ashtami, but these will be brought out later in my discussion.

In assaying the role of Professor Godbole in *A Passage to India,*[13] it is most important to notice that the author a number of times states that no one is India. It is obvious that Forster is using the word India on at least two levels of thought: the literal earthly reality and the transcendental reality. In no other book has his double-visioned interest in these two divided and distinguished worlds been more paramount, as G. Lowes Dickinson pointed out. There is the literal India, the earthly Asiatic nation with its millions of people striving towards national independence and self-government; and there is the figurative India, the transcendental cosmic clarity towards which all humanity is striving. Forster sometimes uses India in one sense, sometimes in the other, and sometimes in both senses simultaneously. By the end of the book

[8] Dickinson's great interest in mystic experience and in psychical research is shown in a number of places in Forster's biography, *Goldsworthy Lowes Dickinson* (London, 1934); Forster also occasionally mentions his own much more tepid interest. As to Vicary, see p. 216 of this biography.

[9] Paul Fussell, Jr., "E. M. Forster's Mrs. Moore: Some Suggestions," *PQ*, XXXII (October 1953), 388–395. If Forster did come under the influence of Mme. Blavatsky (which, in my opinion, is highly doubtful), he would also have learned much about Hinduism, for her Theosophy embodied the doctrines of Ramakrishna and Vivekanda, two Hindu leaders of the 19th century. See in this connection Frederic Spiegelberg, *Living Religions of the World* (Englewood Cliffs, N. J., 1956), pp. 204–205.

[10] "Mohammed Iqbal," *Two Cheers for Democracy,* pp. 288–291. In this essay Forster discusses Iqbal's brand of mysticism, which he doesn't like, but nevertheless he finds Iqbal's writings enjoyable and more congenial than any other Indian's. The article was written in 1946 on his hearing of the poet's death, but Forster says that he met Iqbal thirty years before and had read his works in translation.

[11] *The Hill of Devi* (New York, 1953), p. 193.

[12] Ibid., p. 235.

[13] E. M. Forster, *A Passage to India* (New York, 1924). All references to this novel will be from this edition and will be cited in my text.

the two Indias become intertwined so that the concluding words apply to both. Just before Godbole is shown for the first time, we are told that Adela Quested, in her ignorance, never surmised that Dr. Aziz had a limited outlook "and that no one is India" (p. 72). What is this but a warning by the authorial voice against falling into the belief that any one character in the novel or any one creed can stand for, or can ultimately be taken as an accurate guide for, anything so complex, so multiform as India? Godbole is then described as wearing a turban "that looked like pale purple macaroni" and socks with clocks. "The clocks matched the turban, and his whole appearance suggested harmony—as if he had reconciled the products of East and West, mental as well as physical, and could never be discomposed" (pp. 72–73). His appearance "suggested" harmony: the author does not say that he was in reality harmonious. As a matter of fact, Godbole, in this scene and throughout the novel, by his whole attitude and behavior makes for disharmony; he becomes in reality a disruptive force. When Adela and Mrs. Moore insist on knowing what the Marabar Caves are like, Godbole starts to describe them. But Aziz, who knows almost nothing about the caves himself, realizes that Godbole is keeping something back: "no doubt not willingly, he was concealing something." And Adela has no conception of the underdrift of the conversation. "She did not know that the comparatively simple mind of the Mohammedan was encountering Ancient Night." Aziz, we are furthermore told, was "defeated at every move by an opponent *who would not even admit that a move had been made,* and further than ever from discovering what, if anything, was extraordinary about the Marabar Caves" (p. 76; italics mine).

Harmony? One who had reconciled East and West? Perhaps Forster, in his quiet ironical way, has been throwing out hints about Godbole at the very outset. A combination of socks with clocks matching a turban that looks like pale purple macaroni, even if, perhaps (a long perhaps), moderately harmonious, seems hardly stimulating to people with aesthetic sense. And certainly this combination can never be a vehicle that will harmonize East and West, can never be in a state that will successfully resist discomposition. Even if one's aesthetic sense is not offended by Godbole's appearance, is there anything remotely near being Western in Godbole's behavior in the entire novel? As I shall show, his behavior is entirely inexplicable to Westerners, as well as to some Orientals, from his first appearance to his last. Can it be that Forster has been having great fun with his readers and that all these years we haven't been able to see Godbole for what he is? No one is India, not even Professor Godbole.

It is truly Ancient Night, as the author says, that Aziz and the Western people are encountering in Godbole: not light but darkness, not clarity but impenetrable confusion. Had Godbole told the others what they would find at Marabar, had he been at all truthful with them, they would have been saved all the grief, all the turmoil and further confusion that ensued: Aziz would not have been falsely accused of rape and would not have known the subsequent loss of his medical position at Chandrapore; Adela would not have suffered so horribly and have found that her marriage to Ronny was impossible; Mrs. Moore would not have come face to face with the truth about herself and her relationship to the cosmos—she would not have been disillusioned—and probably she would not have gone to her death at sea; Fielding would not have been forced to take the stand which ultimately drove him out of India and disrupted his whole program of Indian education. There would have been, in short, no novel, which, of course, would have been a pity; but aside from that, it is important to realize that the groundwork for almost all the evil that is established in the novel is laid by Godbole's reluctance, whether deliberate or not, to say anything that matters about Marabar. It is possible that he doesn't know anything about Marabar; but we are distinctly given the impression that he knows a great deal, and at least one of the party assembled that day, Aziz, senses that the Professor is withholding valuable information. Nevertheless, despite his uneasiness, Aziz extends his invitation to take them all to Marabar. Everyone, except Godbole, leaves the party feeling cross or wretched: "It was as if irritation exuded from the very soil. Could one have been so petty on a Scotch moor or an Italian alp? Fielding wondered afterwards. There seemed no reserve of tranquillity to draw upon in India. Either none, or else tranquillity swallowed up everything, as it appeared to do for Professor Godbole" (p. 78). The instigator of the wrongs and of the confusion that result from the misunderstandings about the true nature of Marabar "appeared" to exude tranquillity as he leaves the gathering that day.

It is then, when leavetakings are already made, that Godbole decides to sing. It is a religious song which baffles the Western ear repeatedly. Godbole explains that in the song he implores Shri Krishna to come to him only. The god refuses to come, and so, growing humble, he begs the god to multiply himself into a hundred Krishnas and "let one go to each of my hundred companions" but at least come to him also. But Krishna refuses to come at all. And when Mrs. Moore suggests that perhaps he will come in another song, Godbole states bluntly that he refuses to come. We are told by the author that "perhaps" he did not understand her question. But Forster does not say that he really did not understand; "perhaps" he did understand. In any case, Godbole declares: "I say to Him, Come, come, come, come, come, come. He neglects to come" (p. 80). The salient aspect of Godbole's song is that Krishna, the god whom Godbole worships, does not come to him at all, and the Professor for some reason is underlining that fact. He, too, like the others in *A Passage to India,* is in a condition of bafflement because his implorings for the clarity of religious and cosmic knowledge have been met with silence by his god. Perhaps, the confusion that Godbole engenders arises not from any deliberate intentions on his part; it may only be caused by the confusion that is an integral part of his nature. Perhaps, also, the tranquillity which he alone appears to exude on this occasion is only an appearance and not an inward element of his being. Of such a chain of "perhapses," of ambiguities, is this whole scene composed.[14] Looking back, then, to the beginning of the scene, we can echo the author in saying that no one is India, neither Aziz nor Godbole nor anyone else; the India that is sought here, the cosmic clarity that will bring light to human minds, is not to be found by Godbole, who is himself lost in the confusion of the Ancient Night of which he is a part. The whole chapter is an intricate and harmonious design expressive of Forster's point: that neither Godbole nor anyone else can speak for something that is too complex for easy analysis. The chapter which follows, dealing with the ride of Adela and Ronny along the Marabar road, helps also to reinforce this theme: the whole scene "suggested that the countryside was too vast to admit of excellence," for "In vain did each item in it call out, 'Come, come' " (p. 87).

On the day of the expedition to Marabar, Fielding and Godbole miss the train by a moment. As the train pulls away from the station, Aziz, as if sensing the disaster that will come to him, calls out, "Bad, bad, you have destroyed me." And Fielding calls out to him, "Godbole's pujah did it." But the "Brahman lowered his eyes, ashamed of religion. For it was so: he had miscalculated the length of a prayer" (p. 131). Later, when Mrs. Moore has her terrifying experience within a cave, the author says: "Professor Godbole had never mentioned an echo; it never impressed him, perhaps" (p. 147). The position of the "perhaps" at the end of the sentence, the place of greatest emphasis, makes one wonder whether it had impressed him and whether he had deliberately kept back mention of the echo. This may have been what Aziz sensed the Professor was holding back. One begins to wonder, therefore, whether Godbole had really miscalculated the length of the prayer: "perhaps" he knew what would happen at Marabar and wanted to dissociate himself from the experience.

Again there are sentences which contain ambiguities. Take the authorial comment that Godbole "lowered his eyes, ashamed of religion." This comes immediately before the statement that he had "miscalculated the length of a prayer." It is unthinkable that Godbole is ever ashamed of his religion; it is not in keeping with anything else about Godbole that we learn throughout the novel that he would feel ashamed of his religious beliefs—unless we are to assume that on religious matters he is a hypocrite. And this assumption, no one, including myself, is prepared to make. No, he is a devout Brahman, and as such he could never be ashamed of his religion. The author is again deliberately casting dust into our eyes, but leading us through devious paths to the sentence which follows; this sentence I prefer to read as a piece of Forsterian hocus-pocus and as really saying that Godbole had not miscalculated the length of the prayer.

It is perhaps significant also that when Fielding later that day goes to Marabar with Miss Derek, Godbole stays behind. We are never told why he does not go after all, but his absence further stimulates wonder. Could it be that the Professor didn't really want to go to Marabar? And the talk that Fielding has with Godbole near the end of the hectic day is very peculiar also; not only does Forster say that the day concluded "in a queer vague talk with Professor Godbole," but Fielding's manner indicates that he too thinks that Godbole is behaving in a very queer way, queerer than usual. After all, we know that Fielding has been associated with Godbole for a long time and therefore is

[14] More than one critic has pointed out that one of Forster's most obvious characteristics, shown throughout his whole literary career, is his ambiguous approach to much of his material; some critics have attributed it to his liberalism. I would agree with Arnold Kettle, in *An Introduction to the English Novel* (New York, 1953), II, 163: "The 'perhapses' that lie at the core of his novels, constantly pricking the facile generalization, hinting at the unpredictable element in the most fully analysed relationship, cannot be brushed aside as mere liberal pusillanimity." This characteristic, says Kettle, is an indication of Forster's "scrupulous intelligence," his toughness. I would add also that it is an indication of Forster's fundamental scepticism, which cannot see any solution in human affairs as easy.

presumed to be well acquainted with the Professor's idiosyncrasies; if Fielding thinks that he is acting more than a little odd, then the reader should take careful notice of what occurs. Godbole says to Fielding: "I must tell you how glad I am to hear that after all you succeeded in reaching the Marabar. I feared my unpunctuality had prevented you, but you went (a far pleasanter method) in Miss Derek's car. I hope the expedition was a successful one." And the scene continues:

"The news has not reached you yet, I can see."
"Oh yes."
"No; there has been a terrible catastrophe about Aziz."
"Oh yes. That is all round the College."
"Well, the expedition where that occurs can scarcely be called a successful one," said Fielding, *with an amazed stare.*
"I cannot say. I was not present."
He stared again—a most useless operation, for no eye could see what lay at the bottom of the Brahman's mind, and yet he had a mind and a heart too, and all his friends trusted him, without knowing why. "I am most frightfully cut up," he said.
"So I saw at once on entering your office. I must not detain you, but I have a small private difficulty on which I want your help; I am leaving your service shortly, as you know." (pp. 175–176; italics mine)

Forster's statement about trust comes at the precise moment when Fielding is certainly beginning to wonder at Godbole's extraordinary behavior; it serves surely to cast doubt upon the Professor's honesty, upon his trustworthiness. Furthermore, if Godbole says that he had perceived on entering the office that Fielding was "most frightfully cut up" about what happened at Marabar, then why did he say that he hoped the expedition was successful, especially since he knew what had happened that day? The remark about Godbole's friends trusting him without knowing why cannot have been stated by the author or thought by Fielding (whichever it is—authorial comment or Fielding's thought—is not clear) as just a random statement or thought without any implications. The implications are certainly intended. These are reinforced by Godbole's subsequent remarks to Fielding which indicate that Aziz' plight and that of the others do not seem to concern him in the slightest. We are reminded of the comment that he had a heart too. The inescapable truth is forced onto one who reads this passage carefully that Godbole is not trustworthy; he has deliberately contrived the events of the day, insofar as it is possible for one man to contrive them, and now, after all the awful things have been done, wants to dismiss the whole matter coldly, with as few words as possible. No wonder that Fielding stares at him amazedly.

Another interesting example of Forster's great ability to throw the reader off the scent is the chapter which follows (xx). The charge is made by Major Callendar at the English Club that Aziz, through Mohammed Latif, has bribed Godbole to make Fielding late by prolonging his prayers. One can, of course, deny the accusation. There is much guile in Godbole's behavior, as I am trying to show; but one cannot believe that he would allow himself to be bribed by Aziz for evil or for any kind of motive. We must reject this implication just as we must reject any thought that he was ashamed of his religion. And no one can believe for a moment that Aziz would instigate such a course. This chapter shows the extreme lengths to which the prejudice of the Anglo-Indian officials would go; probably that is its main purpose in the development of the plot. But there may be a secondary purpose: since the sympathetic reader at this point would indignantly reject any suggestion that Godbole, as well as Aziz, would be guilty of accepting a bribe, his rejection would have the effect of helping him forget the real defects in Godbole's character. Yet because the English official, even though prejudiced, has openly projected the belief that Godbole consciously prolonged his prayers, the reader would be led to wonder again if there was any guile on Godbole's part in that connection—not, I repeat, because of bribery, but because of some other motive personal and inexplicable. Forster's skill in confusing the reader was never better; this is part of the game which he has admitted he enjoys.[15]

Regardless of Godbole's possible treachery, it seems to me that one of Forster's main intentions is to show that Godbole, like the other principal characters, is one of the baffled, unsatisfied children of the earth, attempting to penetrate into the mysteries of existence, but never quite finding the true path to the ultimate knowledge, never really reaching the passage to India. The first view we

[15] When recent interviewers, in *Writers at Work: The Paris Review Interviews,* ed. Malcolm Cowley (New York, 1958), p. 33, asked Forster if he likes having secrets from his readers, they remarked that he appeared to brighten at the suggestion. Forster has admitted elsewhere that his is the type of mind which likes to be taken unawares: "The frontal full-dress presentation of an opinion often repels me, but if it be insidiously slipped in sidewise I may receive it." This is a technique which he enjoyed in Samuel Butler's *Erewhon* and which he has often tried to copy: "I like that idea . . . of muddling up the actual and the impossible until the reader isn't sure which is which, and I have sometimes tried to do it when writing myself." *Two Cheers for Democracy,* p. 222.

get of Godbole at Mau in the last section of the novel shows him as one who is standing in the presence of God. "He and Professor Godbole stood at opposite ends of the same strip of carpet." Literally, the Professor, who is now Minister of Education at Mau, stands on a red carpet as he goes through his religious ceremony. At the opposite end, "indistinguishable in the jumble of His own altar," is a silver representation, the size of a teaspoon, of the God to be born in the ceremony. As a hymn is sung, Godbole thinks of Mrs. Moore, and he impels her image in the direction of the God, "where completeness can be found." And in this mystical, or semi-mystical, state he also remembers a wasp which he had once seen on a stone. Trying to imitate God, who encompasses all in His completeness, he also impels the mental image of the wasp. Then he attempts to do the same with the stone; but "no, he could not, he had been wrong to attempt the stone, logic and conscious effort had seduced, he came back to the strip of red carpet and discovered that he was dancing upon it" (pp. 283–286).

If the carpet is symbolic of the entire universe, of God's completeness, as it clearly seems to be, then truly Godbole and God stand at opposite ends. For in God's completeness He is capable of encompassing the stone, just as He can encompass Mrs. Moore and the wasp. But Godbole, despite his attempts to imitate God, is unable to do so completely; his human mind, because of its limitations, is left merely with the physical body which is dancing on the end of the carpet. Godbole is truly, as his name implies (Greek, bōlōs, lump of earth), a lump of God's universe like all the others, and is only capable of occupying a minute portion of it. This carpet image, hitherto little noticed by Forster's critics, is the key to the meaning of the last section of the novel; it comes at the very beginning of the section and, if read rightly, reinforces the ending of the book where Fielding and Aziz are shown faced with many of the elements of the man-made and the natural universe which are instrumental in dividing them and their descendants. The "Temple," symbolic of the Hindu way of belief, is thus far from being a means of reconciliation or a means of synthesis, as some have believed. The temple, like the mosque and the Christian church, is to be taken as offering a possible passage to the primal knowledge which all men seek; but it is not *the* passage, the sole way to God. It is merely one among many passages which, since they are human passages, bound down by human conditions, are ultimately fated to end in dilemma and confusion.

According to this reading of the "Temple" section of the novel, Godbole is revealed as inadequate to carry the burden of reconciliation and of synthesis. As if to emphasize Godbole's failure, and the failure of all humans, immediately after Godbole is shown dancing on the edge of the carpet after failing to impel the stone, the author describes the ceremony enacting the birth of Shri Krishna:

> Infinite Love took upon itself the form of SHRI KRISHNA, and saved the world. All sorrow was annihilated, not only for Indians, but for foreigners, birds, caves, railways, and the stars; all became joy, all laughter; there had never been disease nor doubt, misunderstanding, cruelty, fear. Some jumped in the air, others flung themselves prone and embraced the bare feet of the universal lover; the women behind the purdah slapped and shrieked; the little girl slipped out and danced by herself, her black pigtails flying. Not an orgy of the body; the tradition of that shrine forbade it. But the human spirit had tried by a desperate contortion to ravish the unknown, flinging down science and history in the struggle, yes, beauty herself. Did it succeed? Books written afterwards say "Yes." But how, if there is such an event, can it be remembered afterwards? How can it be expressed in anything but itself? Not only from the unbeliever are mysteries hid, but the adept himself cannot retain them. He may think, if he chooses, that he has been with God, but as soon as he thinks it, it becomes history, and falls under the rules of time. (pp. 287–288)

Could Forster be more explicit? This is surely the voice of the sceptical Westerner, and in it there is little or no *rapprochement* with the attitude, words, and the behavior of Godbole. Notice, also, the subtle jibe at the Hindu mind which would forget, under the throes of religious ecstasy, the realities in this world of sorrow, disease, doubt, misunderstanding, cruelty, and fear. One can now more readily understand what Forster meant in *The Hill of Devi* when he said that, while attending a Gokul Ashtami festival (feast in honor of Krishna, who was born at Gokul), "though I am dressed as a Hindu I shall never become one." And though his response to the festival was mildly emotional because he saw that it "touches something very deep in their [the Hindus'] hearts," he knew that it was not for him. The tenor of the whole description of the festival is highly critical, and again reveals Forster as the sceptical Westerner and the sensitive, aesthetic man who could not bring himself to respond wholeheartedly because he found "no dignity, no taste, no form" in the ceremony. Almost every detail of the eight-day feast he found distasteful: "What troubles me is that every detail, almost without exception, is fatuous and in bad taste." It is revealing that he uses the word "fatuous" over and over again in his description. Finally, near the end of his account, he writes: "But by now you will have heard enough of religion of sorts. I have, and am ashamed that the good people here should have felt I was so sympathetic. The mere fact that I did not hold aloof seemed enough—they did not the least mind my saying that it all meant nothing to me."[16] *The Hill of Devi,* a rich sourcebook for background material to his Indian novel, indicates clearly that he found Hinduism at most only mildly interesting. Though he responded to it lukewarmly for a time when in Dewas, his interest had turned to Moslemism by the time he left India in 1921. This perhaps partly explains why he dedicated the novel originally to his great friend Syed Ross Masood, the Moslem educator, of whom he has said that without Masood's aid he could never have written his novel.[17] If Forster had meant to exalt the role of Hinduism, he would hardly have dedicated the novel to a Moslem. These facts must be stressed in light of the knowledge that there are some who would depreciate *The Hill of Devi* as an index to Forster's mind in the years preceding *A Passage to India* in order, possibly, to maintain their somewhat untenable positions.[18]

At the end of the first chapter of the "Temple" section, Forster brings our attention again to Godbole, who, covered with grease and dust, had once more tried to develop the life of the spirit:

He had, with increasing vividness, again seen Mrs. Moore, and round her faintly clinging forms of trouble. He was a Brahman, she Christian, but it made no difference, *it made no difference whether she was a trick of his memory or a telepathic appeal.* It was his duty, as it was his desire, to place himself in the position of the God and to love her, and to place himself in her position and to say to the God, "Come, come, come, come." *This was all he could do. How inadequate! But each according to his own capacities, and he knew that his own were small.* "One old Englishwoman and one little, little wasp," he thought, as he stepped out of the temple into the grey of a pouring wet morning. *"It does not seem much, still it is more than I am myself."* (pp. 290–291; italics mine)

Godbole feels that it is his duty to pretend that he is like God, and he has the desire to become one with God. But again we see him in his failure. It is clear that he recognizes vividly his own inadequacies. Moreover, it is hinted that Mrs. Moore's image may very well be a trick of Godbole's memory. He has been able to project in his mind an "old Englishwoman and one little, little wasp" in the direction of the God; but that is all. One must remember, while reading this passage, that shortly before he had been unable to project the stone. And now he recognizes that what he believes he had been able to accomplish was something greater than himself; he had been able to get away from the restricting bonds of his own ego and to come into contact with the essence of the divine nature for a brief moment. But he could not go the whole distance across the red carpet of the universe and merge completely, as he desired, into the nature of God. His mystical experience, he knows, is only partially a success. Of him it may be said in Forster's own words only a few pages before: "He may think, if he chooses, that he has been with God, but as soon as he thinks it, it becomes history, and falls under the rules of time." The words apply to Godbole so well that Forster must surely have had him in mind when he wrote them.

It is in this troubled frame of mind, as he is leaving the temple, that Godbole meets Aziz, and he tells the Moslem physician that Fielding had arrived at Mau. It is revealed now that Godbole had extended a helping hand to Aziz in the latter's predicament after the trial; Godbole had aided Aziz in obtaining his post as court physician. Aziz now considers him a dear friend: "he was well assured that Godbole was a dear old man" (p. 292). Though Aziz was as unable to understand Hinduism at Mau as he was before, and though there could really be no real religious meeting ground between the two Indians, yet the relationship between them seemed to have become harmonious. The reader's probable feeling at this juncture of the novel is that Godbole has an element of greatness in him, however undefinable, and is definitely a man of good will; without talking about it, he had silently done something tangible in improving the lot of a man who needed help, a man at that who was of a different faith. For a brief moment we are given a glimpse into a way of harmony between human beings that is so seldom seen, and we feel momentarily gladdened at the sight.

But then immediately the author snatches this harmonious outlook away and, instead, disillusions us. We see that Aziz is not very contented at all. At Mau, however much he may pretend, he does not altogether fit into the strange and alien

[16] *The Hill of Devi,* pp. 159–171.

[17] *Two Cheers for Democracy,* p. 292.

[18] Thus McConkey writes, p. 91 of *The Novels of E. M. Forster:* "But *The Hill of Devi,* despite its wealth of background material, offers little new insight into the richness and depth of *A Passage to India:* for it is what Forster's creative faculty has done to the material which chiefly matters."

Hindu society; and we soon see that even his relationship with Godbole is not as amicable as it could be. As the festival continues, there is a vivid little scene in which Aziz is shown colliding with Godbole as the former averts his eyes at the Hindu procession, "for he never knew how much he was supposed to see." It is then that Godbole informs Aziz that he had known for a year that Fielding had not married Adela Quested, as Aziz had believed, but rather Mrs. Moore's daughter. Aziz, in consternation, asks: "Why did you not tell me? Your silence plunged me into a pretty pickle." We are then told: "Godbole, *who had never been known to tell anyone anything,* smiled again, and said in deprecating tones: 'Never be angry with me. I am, *as far as my limitations permit,* your true friend; besides, it is my holy festival.' Aziz always felt like a baby in that strange presence, a baby who unexpectedly receives a toy" (pp. 304–305; italics mine).

This last conversation between Godbole and Aziz in the novel indicates that the ways of Godbole are beyond the comprehension of Aziz or of any person who acts and thinks in a reasonable manner. Perhaps the main thesis upon which the novel rests is that human beings can never fully understand one another; for it is in the nature of the human to be ultimately mysterious, arising from mystery and going down to the grave in the same aura of the unknown and incomprehensible. But aside from that general theme, it is also clear that Godbole, although he may extend the helping hand to Aziz at times, is, for some unfathomable reason, not completely Aziz' friend. He is, as he admits, his true friend only so far as his limitations permit. Translated into blunter terms, this means that he will let Aziz down whenever it serves his own peculiar purposes; in the final analysis this means he is really no friend to Aziz at all. For this type of friendship is very far from the friendship enunciated by Forster: "One must be fond of people and trust them if one is not to make a mess of life, and it is therefore essential that they should not let one down. They often do. The moral of which is that I must, myself, be as reliable as possible, and this I try to be. . . . It is a matter for the heart, which signs no documents. In other words, reliability is impossible unless there is a natural warmth."[19] There is no reliability in Professor Godbole anywhere in the novel; and as for natural warmth, he seems to lack even an iota of it.

In considering the problem of Godbole and the evil he engenders, one must recall that it was Godbole who told Fielding that evil is as much a part of God as good, that good and evil are almost inextricable parts of His nature. The main point of the Marabar Cave episode, as I see it, is the expression of the same almost inextricable mixture of the very nature of God's universe. The essence of Godbole, like the cave a lump of God's universe (remember his name), comes almost ultimately to "Ou-Boum," the hollow, dull echo which makes everything appear to be identical, entirely devoid of distinction. "Almost," I say in all these sentences, but not entirely; for as Godbole says, though good and evil are "both of them aspects of my Lord," He "is present in the one, absent in the other, and the difference between presence and absence is great, as great as my feeble mind can grasp" (p. 178). The distinction is too much for Fielding's mind to grasp also. But the distinction, though extremely subtle, is there nevertheless. We mortals can never believe that good and evil are inextricably joined forever in the nature of God; ultimately, beyond the ken of the human and the terrestrial, in the transcendental realm, we can suppose that the mixture of good and evil can be altogether separated—but it would take God himself to do it! In the realm of the human, the mixture is there, is at times tangible, and becomes merged, often indefinite and devoid of distinction. It is, though Godbole does not say this, only in their reverberations—only in their effects on the lives of others—that we humans can distinguish, if we try hard enough, between good and evil. Godbole, for example, has good in him, no doubt, and much of this good is conscious; but he also has evil, whether conscious or not, and in its reverberations this evil far outweighs the good. He is the human exemplar, more than anyone else in the novel (they are all exemplars, but it is a question of degree), of the principle of good merging into evil, even though the converse may also be true in a lesser amount. Godbole is, in short, a very complex character in Forster's most complex novel; he is probably the one who best illustrates the author's belief that human beings are creatures of mixed motives, thoughts, and actions. As such, Forster has presented him with the objectivity and with the deliberate care of the fully mature artist in absolute control of his materials.

In stressing Godbole's complexity, we must be careful not to assert that in the over-all dimensions of the novel he is more important than Aziz or Fielding or Mrs. Moore; he is certainly not developed on as large a scale as the first two, what-

[19] *Two Cheers for Democracy,* p. 68.

ever else we may say about him. But for intricacy of development within a limited scale and for expanding reverberations within his created limits —that is, the implications of his total character not only grow far beyond the time and space given him by the author but also have an immense effect on the other characters—Godbole may well be Forster's best creation. He is a real triumph of Forster's artistry; he has been introduced, sustained, involved in the lives of the other characters, and finally allowed to disappear without ever being overdrawn or mishandled at any place in the novel. Forster handles him with just the right amount of irony, humor, and deft sleight-of-hand maneuvers so as to intrigue the curiosity of the serious reader. Forster demands alert, objective readers; the unwary and the casual will be hopelessly entrapped and confused by his treatment of Godbole, for they will not see at all that Godbole has been bitten, possibly unconsciously, by the worm of evil and has in turn planted his evil into the lives of other people. The whole emphasis of the "Temple" section is not to make Godbole something like a shining knight in armor who has "saved" Mrs. Moore by becoming almost the "immaculate intercessor" between her and the Almighty; nor is it to glorify Hinduism above that of other religions as if E. M. Forster were another Godbole. There is no convincing evidence to show that either before or after the writing of *A Passage to India* Forster had been greatly under the influence of Hinduism, though there can be no doubt that he found its forms interesting, just as an anthropologist will find the culture of a primitive people interesting without ever becoming imbued personally with it. There is plenty of evidence, however, that before and after his writing of the novel Forster was the sceptical, cultured man of the West, inquiring, searching for the philosophy or the creed which a man of his type could believe in, sifting here and there among the world's philosophies and creeds.

The "Temple" section shows the result of Forster's outlook after leaving India; as he said in *The Hill of Devi,* he had to get away from India to be able to look at that great, complex country in an objective manner. In my outlook, then, there is an equation between the first and third sections of the novel: the two leading creeds of India are presented and, for one reason or another, both are found wanting, just as "poor talkative Christianity" is found wanting by Mrs. Moore. The middle section links the two and gives the clue as to their ultimate meanings as the author sees them. Both "Mosque" and "Temple" are like the "Cave": they ultimately come to a curious resounding echo which the finite and limited human ear has not been able to interpret however much it has tried; whether it will ever be able to interpret the strange echo is left to the future. Whether, in other words, the human mind will ever be able to penetrate sufficiently through the illusions of this life to the ultimate realities is anybody's guess, for no one knows. The magnificent ending of the novel, often quoted, in which the earth, the temples (particularly note them), the birds, the horses, and other aspects of Mau, cry out, in their hundred voices, "No, not yet" and the sky says, "No, not there," dovetails completely with the beginning of the last section: all the things mentioned at the conclusion are portions of God's universe, symbolized earlier by the red carpet. And just as Godbole, even with the aid of his Hindu faith, finds himself only on the edge of the carpet, at the opposite end from his God, never able to cross over and become unified with Him, never able to achieve the clarity he desires, so with all these other things at Mau. It is "not there" at Mau, in the temple or anywhere else, as the sky says, that ultimate solution will be found any more than at the Moslem mosque, though one is no less light-giving than the other: it is somewhere else, but exactly where and when the author leaves to our imaginations; he offers no easy solutions. No one is India! Wherever it is, wherever it will be, it is certainly not through the intercession of Godbole or of his religion only. That Professor remains, however, a triumph of art, dancing on the edge of the red carpet, an all-too-human imperfection, a bole in God's universe.

THEMATIC SYMBOL IN *A PASSAGE TO INDIA*

GEORGE H. THOMSON

Like *The Waste Land* (1922), *A Passage to India* (1924) is a study in the spiritual condition of twentieth-century man. To fashion and unfold his theme, Forster employs powerfully ordered symbols that are outwardly in keeping with realistic narrative and inwardly charged with suggestion and meaning. To interpret the theme, then, we must listen to an echo, enter a cave, and participate in a religious festival.

The novel is composed of three sections: "Mosque" serves as prelude, touching lightly upon serious issues; "Caves" represents a physical and spiritual waste-land; "Temple" offers escape from the waste-land and promise of spiritual achievement. This structure may be viewed as symbolic of the three stages of mankind's spiritual history or the three stages of the individual's spiritual development.

The first stage is one of superficial optimism. The shallow arcades of the Mosque, the verbal gymnastics of the ninety-nine names of God, the narrowness of Christianity, and Mrs. Moore's simple-minded belief in oneness with the universe, all these betoken man's immaturity, his blindness to the strenuous realities of the human situation. Our central image is the Mosque, symbolic of the religion that "doesn't carry us far through the complexities of matter and spirit . . . " (p. 276).[1] Our representative human being is Aziz who, through all his experience, remains both young in heart and unenlightened in spirit.

The second stage is one of disillusionment. Earth is a waste-land, God is absent, and every meaning and value is lost in nightmarish mumbo-jumbo. The human waste-land is reflected in the blinding soullessness of the British officials and the debilitating rationalism of Fielding and Adela Quested. Both waste-lands, the human and the physical, are crystallized in the image of the Marabar. Next in importance to the Marabar is Mrs. Moore, whose penetrating awareness of its implications plunges her into a "double" disillusionment.

The third stage is one of qualified spiritual achievement. The physical and human waste-land fades into the background and God is no longer totally absent. Temple as religious image and Godbole as human image indicate a challenging hope for man in his spiritual quest now and in the future.

But if we wish to look at these three stages—represented by Aziz, Mrs. Moore, and Godbole—as phases in the development of one person, it is to Mrs. Moore we must turn for our example. In the beginning she and Aziz are alike in their spiritual naivety and optimism. The great charm of the scene in the Mosque when they first meet is the charm of two children discovering each other in an enchanted place. For Mrs. Moore, the discovery helps confirm her feeling of oneness with the universe. Then the Marabar strikes and hope, human and divine, is shattered. Finally in "Temple" Mrs. Moore attains, in part through the spiritual force of Godbole, triumphant oneness with the universe.

The novel is set in India, a land of immensely varied races, religions, and climatic and geographic conditions, a land reflecting admirably all the world and all its peoples. "Perhaps," says Forster, the word of doubt signifying the uncertain comprehension of Fielding and Adela Quested but not of the author—"Perhaps the hundred Indias which fuss and squabble so tiresomely are one, and the universe they mirror is one" (p. 263). The extraordinary character of this mirrored universe is revealed in the description of the Marabar Hills as "flesh of the sun's flesh," "older than anything in the world," "older than all spirit" (pp. 123-124). Some bits of life—a tank, trees, and plants—appear amid the humps and ravines. But the tank is reduced to a puddle (p. 146), and the little plants are shriveled to ashes by the boiling heat of the sun (p. 151). The Marabar is a universe of physical death.[2]

India, however, has other landscapes. The countryside at Mau offers lush green jungle, an overflowing tank, and radiant skies. Yet in comparison with the religious festival and the little dramas of human interest, this scenery seems oddly unimpressive. The following passage, referring to Aziz, may help us to understand the reason: "the great Mau tank . . . lay exposed beneath him to its remotest curve. Reflecting the evening clouds, it filled the netherworld with an equal splendour, so that earth and sky leant toward one another, about to clash in ecstasy. He spat, cynical again, more cynical than before. For in the centre of the burnished circle a small black blot was advancing—the Guest House boat" (p. 306). In earlier novels the beauty and power of the earth-sky image would not have been canceled out by emotions arising from the human situation. A little later we find an outright statement of Forster's attitude. Aziz has been speaking of the day when India will free herself from the English: "He paused, and the scenery, though it smiled, fell like a gravestone on any human hope" (p. 321). Clearly, man's salvation is not to be found in nature. Indeed, Forster, having once believed in earth's value and its power to support man's spirit (a theme that runs through all his earlier fiction), now seriously accepts the inverse proposition that man must strive to support and give value to earth. The physical universe, the waste-land, becomes part of man's spiritual burden.

The waste-land also invades man's sense of the beautiful, robbing him of the grace and dignity and formality of art. In India one retreats "from the source of life, the treacherous sun, and no poetry adorns it because disillusionment cannot be beautiful. Men yearn for poetry though they may not confess it; they desire that joy shall be graceful and sorrow august and infinity have a form, and India fails to accommodate them" (p. 211). India also fails to accommodate architecture. Fielding, visiting Europe, is overwhelmed by the contrast between Venice and that monstrous and extraordinary land where all is muddle (p. 282). In India even religious ritual—as ritual—fails to achieve beauty. The festival of Gokul Ashtami, this "triumph of India" as Forster calls it, is a muddle as we would call it, "a frustration of reason and form" (p. 285).

Deprived of nature's support and art's solace, the Indian must create in his own person a microcosm of order and beauty: "when the Nawab Bahadur stretched out his hand for food or Nureddin applauded a song, something beautiful had been accomplished which needed no development" (p. 251). In such manner unaccommodated man is driven to rely wholly on his own spiritual resources.

The loss or absence of these resources is the waste-land theme of "Caves." Just as the Marabar Hills signify the material universe void of life, so the Marabar Caves signify the universe of man void of spirit. This significance of the caves can best be approached through the significance of the echo; and the echo can best be approached through Professor Godbole's little lecture on the nature of evil:[3] "Good and evil are different, as their names imply. But . . . they are both of them aspects of my Lord. He is present in the one, absent in the other, and the difference between presence and absence is great, as great as my feeble mind can grasp. Yet absence implies presence, absence is not non-existence, and we are therefore entitled to repeat, 'Come, come, come, come,' " (p. 178). "The original sound may be harmless," thinks Fielding, "but the echo is always evil" (p. 276). The echo, expressing the absence of the original sound and at the same time implying the existence of that sound, symbolizes precisely the situation pertaining in the case of evil in relation to good. And that is why the echo is always evil.[4]

"Everything echoes now," reflects Fielding (p. 276). The reason: "the countryside was too vast to admit of excellence. In vain did each item in it call out, 'Come, come.' There was not enough god to go around" (pp. 87-88). The call of "Come" echoing through India signifies the absence of God in the natural universe, just as in Godbole's religious song it signifies the absence of God in the world of man (p. 80).[5] But these echoes of India, implying by analogy the existence of God, are suggestive of hope, however distant. Not so the echo of the caves, which sounds the negation of every hope.

Since caves, as we shall come to see, are symbolic of man void of spirit, man islolated and turned inward upon himself, a study of characters thus isolated may offer the best approach to the symbol. We can quickly dispose of the British officials, the Turtons and the Burtons, who, having no inner life, are treated simply as pawns in the narrative. If they visited a Marabar Cave they would experience nothing, hence nothing can be said about them. Much more interesting are three characters of intelligence and some insight: Fielding, Adela Quested, and Aziz.

Fielding is a rationalist who believes, not in God, but in fellowship helped on by "good will plus culture and intelligence . . ." (p. 62). Significantly, he omits love. Thus, reflecting on his relations to Aziz, he recognizes that he can not be intimate with anyone (p. 118). His isolation and narrowness of sympathy are exposed in Forster's comment on his (and Aziz's) reaction to the death of Mrs. Moore: "It's only one's own dead who matter. . . . How indeed is it possible for one human being to be sorry for all the sadness that meets him on the face of the earth, for the pain that is endured not only by man, but by animals and plants, and perhaps by the stones?" (pp. 247-248) He is, however, strongly aware of his inadequacy: he "had developed his personality, explored his limitations, controlled his passions," yet in a moment of insight "he felt he ought to have been working at something else the whole time—he didn't know at what, never would know, never could know . . ." (p. 191).

Commenting on the episode in the cave, Adela says to Fielding, "It's as if I ran my finger along that polished wall in the dark, and cannot get further. I am up against something, and so are you." Forster coments: "She was at the end of her spiritual tether, and so was he . . . . Perhaps life is a mystery, not a muddle; they could not tell. . . . They had not the apparatus for judging" (p. 263). Adela is clearly associated with Fielding as a spiritual cripple. Having come to examine the country, and having "no real affection for Aziz, or Indians generally" (p. 259), she sees "India always as a frieze" (p. 47). The frieze reminds us of the mosque, symbol of the religion of Aziz. Like Christianity, Mohammedanism is pathetically deficient. Fielding is not alone in missing the significance of the echo; "the mosque missed it too. Like himself, those shallow arcades provided but a limited asylum" (p. 276). Or as Fielding puts it to Aziz: "You and I and Miss Quested are, roughly speaking, not after anything. We jog on as decently as we can, you a little in front—a laudable little party" (p. 318). Such an understanding is possible only to persons who, having glimpsed a greater reality, are able to "place" themselves. These glimpses on the part of Fielding and Adela offer us a profound insight into the nature of the human spirit in action.

Fielding has a vision of the Marabar Hills expanding till the whole universe is a hill (pp. 191, 250). As he watches, their nasty little cosmos leaps suddenly into beauty, transformed momentarily by the power of his feeling "that we exist not in ourselves, but in terms of each others' minds . . ." (p. 250). Yet the experience has, for Fielding, a kind of unreality, a quality that reminds us of Adela's account of living at half pressure. "Lovely, exquisite moment—but passing the Englishman with averted face and on swift wings. He experienced nothing himself; it was as if someone had told him there was such a moment, and he was obliged to believe" (p. 191). Much the same thing happens to Adela when she contemplates the Hills: "How lovely they suddenly were! But she couldn't touch them. In front, like a shutter, fell a vision of her married life" (p. 50). Spiritual denial or dishonesty—she intends to marry Ronny though she cannot love him—isolates her from the object of vision, the physical universe symbolized by the Marabar. What is important, however, is not the essential failure of these Western rationalists but the character of their limited achievement. The beauty they behold is not the beauty of nature, but nature transformed and rendered beautiful by the human spirit. Through their experience, we are helped to an understanding of the spirit's power.

We are helped even more by Adela's vision at the trial. She relinquishes her presence in the courtroom and, returning to the Marabar Hills, places herself inside and outside the cave. This parallels, in an elementary way, Godbole's religious practice in which he alternately places himself in the position of the supplicant and the position of the God. We are told what Godbole does, but very little of what he experiences. This deliberate gap may be filled in by referring to Adela's expeience. As she turned back to the Marabar and the many events of that fatal day, she experienced an extraordinary detachment, she was both present and absent: "she was of it and not of it at the same time, and this double relation gave it indescribable splendour" (p. 227). This vision, more than any other in the novel, helps define Godbole's experience. It also stands in absolute contrast to Mrs. Moore's "double" vision of the horror and smallness of the universe. To Adela, the universe of the Marabar is "all beautiful and significant" (p. 228).

Fielding, Adela, Aziz—each of these characters is subject to the feeling that he exists in himself. Christians call this the sin of pride. Forster does not give it a name, but its symbol is the cave. The association with the cave is not directly stated. It is hinted at in Mrs. Moore's cynical remark that after she has married off her children she will retire into a cave of her own (p. 200). The following comment on Adela is equally suggestive: "And consequently the echo flourished . . . and the noise in the cave, so unimportant intellectually, was prolonged over the surface of her life" (p. 194). The reader is reminded of the impressive description of the cave's polished surface (p. 125).

When the individual is isolated he finds it impossible to locate himself for he lacks connection with other things. This is Aziz's dilemma when he loses Adela in the caves. "How am I to know which contains my guest? Which is the cave I was in myself?" (p. 154) Later Adela says, "I shouldn't mind if it had happened anywhere else; at least I really don't know where it did happen" (p. 199). What this confused statement means is that the evil event at the cave occurred within herself, that she is not conscious of the fact, and that consequently she does not know where it did happen. The parallel between Adela (the isolated individual) and the cave is decisively confirmed by the echo mentioned immediately after, which, like the echo in the cave, once it has started in her head, goes on reverberating endlessly.

The phenomenon of pride or isolation, symbolized in the cave image, is not restricted to individuals. It is manifest in every human organization. Personal relations, formal religion, government, and race—a series of vast caves—arch ominously over the spirit of man.

Readers of *Howards End* will recall how necessary personal relations were to the Forster of 1910. Now we find them severely questioned (pp. 135, 197) because in any meaningful association between two persons there must be a spiritual bond, "that link outside either participant that is necessary to every relationship" (p. 318). A personl relationship implies exclusion; it is an image in double of the individual in isolaton. But a spiritual relationship reveals what one man has in common with another man (and with all men); it is a mocrocosmic image of the brotherhood of man.

Organized religion, tending always to narrowness and exclusion, is exposed in many ways, in Aziz's religious snobbery, in the fuss over shoe-removal at the mosque, and in the reluctance of the Christian missionaries to extend salvation to all. Though they taught that "In our Father's house are many mansions" (p. 37), they could envisage no mansion for wasps or oranges or clay. Young Mr. Sorley's belief is summed up in a logical illogicality: "We must exclude someone from our gathering, or we shall be left with nothing" (p. 38). Obviously, a religion based on exclusion is a contradiction in terms. Turning inward upon itself, it narrows toward zero and the perfect circle of isolation. The Mau Festival, by contrast, is an example, not of organized religion, but of the religious spirit in action. Here no one and no thing is excluded. Even the representatives of the West, bringing with them unexpected confusion as their boats are swept into the midst of the last act of the ritual, are unhesitatingly included. Nor is their presence an accident. Aziz manoeuvers his boat nearer in response to Ralph Moore's friendship; Fielding, in response to his wife's love. Ralph and Stella are moved by spiritual sympathy with Hinduism; Fielding and Aziz—great though their limitations may be—are moved by love. Hence, the plunge of all four into the ritual close of the Festival is spiritually appropriate.

We turn next to the organized state and to that British colonial government which accords so perfectly with the image of the Indian universe as a waste-land. The India of officialism, materialistic and lifeless, is built on sand and echoes interminably. It is a cave, or perhaps a series of caves. Who can tell? At least, the officials cannot tell, for they have created an India in their own image. And through that image we behold this darker truth: authority inevitably divides the governors and the governed, it moves always towards bureaucratic isolation and spiritual negation. Thus the state stands revealed as a vastly magnified image of man void of spirit.

Racial distinction often allies itself with state authority and the exclusiveness of religion. But in its own right it creates barriers separating man from man and group from group a fact most horrifyingly illustrated by the aftermath of the episode in the caves. To the English, the native appears monstrous, not by reason of religious or national entity, but by reason of his skin coloring. On the other side, the Indian distrusts and hates the white man. At the same time, racial distinctions lead him to distrust his Indian neighbor. Race then is one more instance of man in isolation, man turned inward to behold his own image in those of his own blood. The opposite image, the ideal, is —as usual—envisaged by Godbole. He is an internationalist (p. 293) who believes literally in the obliteration of national and racial barriers.

To sum up in Forster's own words, "where there is officialism every human relationship suffers" (p. 212). For every type of human organization is based on exclusiveness and tends towards spiritual emptiness. Such organizations are magnified images of the novel's negative theme: the nature of individual isolation and soullessness. We should note, however, that spiritual negation, whether individual or organizational, is not absolute. Though there are hints of God's non-existence (to be discussed later), it is his absence that is asserted. Thus, Adela's head, Ronny's footsteps, the Indian earth, the Indian nation, everything, echoes—everything, that is, except the region of the Marabar.

Since echo implies the existence of God, the failure of the Marabar Hills to echo implies the non-existence of God. And the "boum" of perverted reflections of sound in the caves provides ominous confirmation. Echo, like arch, takes on qualities and meanings totally at variance with those it possesses in the world beyond the Marabar. Thus, we know that the echo is always evil, but we also know from Forster's comment on Mrs. Moore's experience that "Nothing evil had been in the cave . . ." (p. 148). The reason is implied in the account of the expedition party as it enters the Marabar: "a new quality occurred, a spiritual silence which invaded more senses than the ear. Life went on as usual, but had no consequences, that is to say, sounds did not echo or thoughts develop. Everything semed cut off at its root, and therefore infected with illusion" (p. 140. We are approaching an unreal world, but one whose implications are felt beyond the Marabar.

Thus, after Fielding's announcement that he feared the dead would not live again and Adela's agreement, "There was a moment's silence, such as often follows the triumph of rationalism" (p. 241). And at the East-West Bridge Party, after Ronnie's condescending talk about the Indians grouped on the other side of the tennis court, "There was a silence . . . at least, more ladies joined the English group, but their words seemed to die as soon as uttered. Some kites hovered overhead, impartial, over the kites passed the mass of a vulture, and with an impartiality exceeding all, the sky, not deeply coloured but translucent, poured light from its whole circumference. It seemed unlikely that the series stopped here. Beyond the sky must not there be something that over-arches all the skies, more impartial even than they? Beyond which again . . ." (pp. 39-40). And a little later we read, with reference to Mrs. Moore's experience: "Outside the arch there seemed always an arch, beyond the remotest echo a silence" (p. 52). The invisible arch, deathlike and appallingly impartial, and the haunting silence beyond the remotest echo are signs or premonitions of the nonexistence of spirit.

This spiritual void in its absolute form is symbolized by the perfectly intact cave, the "bubble-shaped cave that has neither ceiling nor floor, and mirrors its own darkness in every direction infinitely" (p. 125) and knows a silence without end, for it "can hear no sound but its own" (p. 154). But the spiritual void as it arches darkly over the expiring spirit of man is symbolized by the cave with a tunnel. Life is represented by light and sound, though in the first account of the caves at the beginning of Section II only light is introduced—a match is struck:

> Immediately another flame rises in the depths of the rock and moves towards the surface like an imprisoned spirit: the walls of the circular chamber have been most marvellously polished. The two flames approach and strive to unite, but cannot, because one of them breathes air, the other stone. A mirror inlaid with lovely colours divides the lovers, delicate stars of pink and grey interpose, exquisite nebulae, shadings fainter than the tail of a comet or the midday moon, all the evanescent life of the granite, only here visible. Fists and fingers thrust above the advancing soil—here at last is their skin, finer than any covering acquired by the animals, smoother than windless water, more voluptuous than love. The radiance increases, the flames touch one another, kiss, expire. The cave is dark again like all the caves.

Here is the horror and attraction of narcissism: supreme isolation in all its insidious charm and deathlike beauty. The human spirit ravishes the known self, and the lost soul momentarily reflects its own glimmerings—then endlessly reflects its own darkness.

From description, Forster proceeds to drama, showing us the reaction of those characters who enter the caves, that is, who come face to face with the illusory reality of a world without spirit. Fielding, we are told, notices the echo but fails to apprehend its significance. The same is true of Adela until the evil event in the second cave (her evil event) sets the echo going in her own head. She fails to understand the echo because she lacks insight into her spiritual isolation and self-regarding love. Yet her agonizing awareness of the sound indicates some resources of spirit, and prepares us for her moment of insight at the trial.

Mrs. Moore is the one character among the visitors to the Marabar who has the spiritual capacity to grasp the full horror of its meaning. Hence the description we have is essentially an account of her experience. She finds the echo of the cave is not like the other echoes of India: "Whatever is said, the same monotonous noise replies. . . . Hope, politeness, the blowing of a nose, the squeak of a boot, all produce 'boum.' Even the striking of a match starts a little worm coiling, which is too small to complete a circle but is eternally watchful. And if several people talk at once, an overlapping howling noise begins, echoes generate echoes, and the cave is stuffed with a snake composed of small snakes, which writhe independently" (pp. 147-148).

The horror here is not so much in the confusion as in the terrifying revelation that the echoes and the snakes of light are self-perpetuating and take on a violently chaotic and multiple independence. They cease to have reference to any origin, for in a valueless universe no distinction or relationship is meaningful. This vision, suggestve of insanity and nightmare, cannot offer even the empty consolaton of a dark and silent void. Mrs. Moore in her spiritual aliveness must undergo the full horror of perceiving the non-existence of the spirit as a point-by-point negation or perversion of spiritual life.

With Mrs. Moore we approach the thematic centre of the novel. She and Godbole represent the extremes of spiritual apprehension. Mrs. Moore has an overwhelming awareness of the absence of God, an awarenes of evil; Godbole of the presence of God, of good. But the existence of God is as much attested by the one as by the other.

When Mrs. Moore comes to India she believes, as she always has, that God is love. And because she intuitively knows whether she likes a person (p. 23) and whether he is her friend (p. 311), she can love and respond to love instantly, freely, and without calculation. This is the basis of her spiritual strength, her influence, and her final salvation.

When the Marabar strikes, Mrs. Moore comes "to that state where the horror of the universe and its smallness are both visible at the same time—the twilight of the double vision" in which "a spiritual muddledom is set up for which no high-sounding words can be found . . ." (pp. 207-208). The horror is visible in a perception of the universe as void of spirit, as meaningless and death-ridden; the smallness is visible in a perception of the universe as a closed system, as no more extensive than the isolated individual turned inward upon himself (the cave eternally mirroring its own darkness). If Mrs. Moore's vision were complete, both horror and smallness would be obliterated in darkness. Instead they induce a twilight state. Twilight, paralleling echo in structure, is a state in which light is absent but the existence of light is implied. The same principle is at work in the conception of "spiritual muddledom." The meaningless disorder of the caves might be called a muddle. But Forster avoids the word in that context, reserving it for a higher end. Muddledom is a state in which meaning is absent but the existence of meaning is implied. In these ways we know that hope, however distant, is implicit in Mrs. Moore's despair. She may be evil (as she says herself), she may be unable to assert God's presence through love, but at the approach of death she begins to emerge from the twilight of horror and disillustionment. As she leaves India the palm trees of Bombay wave to her, laughing, mocking her thought that an echo—the echo of the Marabar—was India (p. 210).

She becomes herself one of the echoes of India. Absent, her name is chanted at the trial. And, though she is dead, the echoed assurance of her existence and of her love enables Adela to see the caves again and to speak the truth. This same vitality is the source of her final "experience" at the Mau Festival. As the culmination of the ceremony approaches we are told that the singers "loved all men, the whole universe, and scraps of their past, tiny splinters of detail, emerged for a moment to melt into the universal warmth. Thus Godbole, though she was not important to him, remembered an old woman he had met in Chandrapore days. Chance brought her into his mind while it was in this heated state, he did not select her, she happened to occur among the throng of soliciting images, a tiny splinter, and he impelled her by his spiritual force to that place where completeness can be found. Completeness, not reconstruction" (p. 286). In the one word "reconstruction," Forster dismisses Christianity with its notions of redemption and resurrection. In the one word "completeness," he sums up the spiritual aim of Godbole. "That place where completeness can be found" is that which the singers love, it is "all men, the whole universe." Through Godbole's spiritual force, his love (he is imitating God), Mrs. Moore achieves oneness with the universe.

Forster has subtly prepared us for this event. Four passages will serve as demonstration. The first relates to Mrs. Moore's opening days in India: "In England the moon had seemed dead and alien; here she was caught in the shawl of night together with earth and all the other stars. A sudden sense of unity, of kinship with the heavenly bodies, passed into the old woman and out, like water through a tank, leaving a strange freshness behind" (pp. 29-30). As she leaves India, this experience is glanced at: "when she saw the water flowing through the mosque-tank . . . or the moon, caught in the shawl of night with all the other stars, it seemed a beautiful goal and an easy one. To be one with the universe!" (p. 208) After the trial we learn that Mrs. Moore is dead. That evening Aziz and Fielding lie on the roof of the Nawab Bahadur's mansion, "gazing through mosquito nets at the stars. Exactly above their heads hung the constellation of the Lion, the disc of Regulus so large and bright that it resembled a tunnel, and when this fancy was accepted all the other stars seemed tunnels too" (p. 250). We think of the tunnels into the caves, recognizing in the thought a contrast between the universe of life and the universe of death. For the moment, we may miss the oblique introduction of nets.

Up to this moment Aziz has not been told of Mrs. Moore's death. His evening of triumph is to be unmarred by sadness. But suddenly he announces to Fielding that he will consult Mrs. Moore. What is Fielding to answer? The reader knows that he wishes to end the deception. But that is not to be: "Opening his eyes, and beholding thousands of stars, he could not reply, they silenced him" (p. 253). The stars deny that Mrs. Moore is dead; she is one with the universe of which they are the symbol. Fielding experiences the fact without in any way comprehending it. Its importance is twofold. It corroborates the reality of Godbole's religious activity, and it shows that Mrs. Moore's spiritual destiny is not dependent on Godbole alone. It is dependent on all whom she has loved, all who have loved her, and all who have loved their fellow men and the universe in which we dwell. Godbole has his small part.

The larger questions—the nature of God, the nature of love—are clarified in the final section of the novel. But here we must be very careful not to take the Hindu religion of "Temple" too seriously or accept it too literally. Forster in a variety of ways warns against such an error. Thus Stella, the daughter of Mrs. Moore, though she finds "something soothing, some solution to her queer troubles" in the religion of Mau, takes no interest in its form (pp. 319-320). Moreover, its meaning presents problems, for it "is riven into sects and clans" (p. 292); and its ritual is suspect, for it has marked resemblances to vegetation-god and fertility rites. Since nature, as we know, is not one with the spirit of man but must be saved by that spirit, it is apparent that certain phases of the ritual are scarcely more than a parody of the truth. Yet, insofar as these rites renew the life of the spirit they are supremely meaningful and serious. This explains why the tone of the writing—exemplified in the opening paragraph of "Temple"—so often combines the serious and the ironically urbane.

In dealing with the caves we found that Forster presented their essential nature in the abstract and then as it impinged on the individual life. The same procedure is followed in the account of the religious ritual. We may begin with the ultimate spiritual reality. "All spirit as well as all matter must participate in salvation . . ." (p. 289). Thus at midnight, "Infinite Love took upon itself the form of SHRI KRISHNA, and saved the world. All sorrow was annihilated, not only for Indians, but for foreigners, birds, caves, railways, and the stars; all became joy, all laughter; there had never been disease nor doubt, misunderstanding, cruetly, fear" (pp. 287-288). Here is the ideal.

We turn now to Godbole's actual experience. At the height of the religious ceremony he happened to recall an old woman from Chandrapore days; and "It was his duty, as it was his desire, to place himself in the position of the God and to love her, and to place himself in her position and to say to the God, 'Come, come, come, come'" (p. 290). With a love that looks outward always, he is imitating God. And in so doing he impels Mrs. Moore "to that place where completeness can be found. . . . His senses grew thinner, he remembered a wasp seen he forgot where, perhaps on a stone. He loved the wasp equally, he impelled it likewise, he was imitating God. And the stone where the wasp clung—could he . . .no, he could not . . ." (p. 286). The casually remembered old woman, the wasp, and the stone define the goal he aspires to, the goal of salvation for all spirit and all matter. But when we compare the modest achievement of Godbole, who is spiritually the most highly developed character in the novel, with the ideal of universal salvation, we see how wide is the gap between attainment and aspiration.

The same gap is revealed in other phases of the Mau Festival. "When the villagers broke cordon for a glimpse of the silver image, a most beautiful and radiant expression came into their faces, a beauty in which there was nothing personal, for it caused them all to resemble one another during the moment of its indwelling, and only when it was withdrawn did they revert to individual clods" (p. 284). Then the ceremony moves towards its climax. "Mixed and confused in their passage, the rumours of salvation entered the Guest House. . . . The bronze gun up on the fort kept flashing, the town was a blur of light in which the houses seemed dancing, and the palace waving little wings. The water below, the hills and sky above, were not involved as yet; there was still only a little light and song struggling among the shapeless lumps of the universe" (p. 310).

These references to individual clods and shapeless lumps of the universe, by directing attention to that which is as yet unattained, help clarify the final incident of the novel. Fielding and Aziz have ridden out to view the country. As they return, Fielding exclaims:

> "Why can't we be friends now? . . . It's what I want. It's what you want."
>
> But the horses didn't want it—they swerved apart; the earth didn't want it, sending up rocks through which riders must pass single file; the temples, the tank, the jail, the palace, the birds, the carrion, the Guest House, that came into view as they issued from the gap and saw Mau beneath: they didn't want it, they said in their hundred voices, "No, not yet," and the sky said, "No, not there."

The conclusion has been foreshadowed with great care. As characters in the human drama, the two men are incapable of deep spiritual union; symbolically, so little light and song informs the universe that it cannot be expected to do more than struggle with shapeles lumps of clay. Yet the denial of the sky may seem curious. "No, not there" can hardly refer only to Mau; it must refer to earth generally. This conclusion is not, however, as disastrous as it seems. The last act of the Mau ritual suggests that in the unattainable resides man's one indestructible hope:

> Gusts of wind mixed darkness and light, sheets of rain cut from the north, stopped, cut from the south, began rising from below, and across them struggled the singers, sounding every note but terror, and preparing to throw God away, God Himself (not that God can be thrown) into the storm. Thus was He thrown year after year, and were others thrown—little images of Ganpati, baskets of ten-day corn, tiny tazias after Mohurram—scapegoats, h u s k s, emblems of passage; a passage not easy, not now, not here, not to be apprehended except when it is unattainable: the God to be thrown was an emblem of that. (pp. 314-315)

God is the unattainable ideal; he is the universe; he is the spirit of all men united in love and informing all matter with life. As actuality he is inconceivable; but unattainable, he can be apprehended. He is the goal (universal oneness), the spiritual reality (love), towards which man aspires. The goal being unattainable, man is assured of its permanence, of its unalterable power to guide him in his passage towards oneness with the universe. That passage is "not easy, not now, not here." It is attained only in death, and is meaningful only insofar as the spirit of living men informs the universe with life. But man while he exists as an individual may, like Godbole, aspire through love to that which is greater than himself: it will be his duty as it will be his desire to strive towards a passage to the universe —a passage to "India."

Mount Allison University

---

[1]All page references to the novel are incorporated in the text and refer to the 1924 Harcourt, Brace edition.

[2]"The air felt like a warm bath into which hotter water is trickling constantly, the temperature rose and rose, the boulders said, 'I am alive,' the small stones answered, 'I am almost alive.' Between the chinks lay the ashes of little plants" (pp. 150-151). The Marabar Hills, as a dead universe of matter, should not have living boulders. Nor do they. Their livingness is an illusion dependent on heat. The irony is pointed up by the little plants that are dead because the boulders are so scorchingly "alive."

[3]Godbole makes two preliminary observations that help both to develop the theme and to confirm his wisdom. The first is this: "When evil occurs, it expresses the whole of the universe. Similarly when good occurs." Good and evil "are not what we think them, they are what they are, and each of us has contributed to both" (pp. 177-178). These ideas find confirmation in the experience of Fielding and Adela who perceive that evil is loose and has an existence of its own (pp. 187, 194). Next, he distinguishes suffering from evil: "Suffering is merely a matter for the individual." If a young lady with sunstroke "thought her head did not ache, she would not be ill . . ." (p. 178). Near the close of the novel Aziz meets Ralph Moore, who has been stung by bees. When he handles him roughly Ralph says, "Your hands are unkind." Aziz replies that he will not hurt him. And Ralph says, "I don't mind pain, there is no pain. . . . but there is cruetly" (p. 309).

[4]"There are some exquisite echoes in India" (p. 147) is not a contradiction. They are exquisite on account of the faithfulness with which they reproduce the exquisite quality of the original sound, but they are none the less evil. Moreover, Forster's object here is to distinguish emphatically between these echoes and those of the Marabar Caves.

[5]A similar call to God is implied in the Indian's need for kindness. Aziz says: "Kindness, more kindness, and even after that more kindness. I assure you it is the only hope" (pp. 116-117). Later, Forster comments: "Truth is not truth in that exacting land unless there go with it kindness and more kindness and kindness again, unless the Word that was with God also is God" (p. 245). The Word that was with God is truth, the Word that is God is kindness or love. Thus, to ask for kindness is to call to God.

Nirad C. Chaudhuri

Passage To and From India

READING *A Passage to India* some time ago, I was led to think not only of the final collective passage of the British from India but also of Mr. Forster's contribution to that finale. Such an association of ideas between a novel and an event of political history may be objected to, but in this case I think the association is legitimate. For *A Passage to India* has possibly been an even greater influence in British imperial politics than in English literature.

From the first, the more active reaction to it followed the existing lines of political cleavage, its admirers being liberal, radical, or leftist sheep and its detractors conservative, imperialist, and diehard goats. The feud between English liberalism and the British empire in India was as old as the empire itself. Except for a short period of quiescence when Liberal-Imperialism was in vogue, it raged till 1947. Mr. Forster's novel became a powerful weapon in the hands of the anti-imperialists, and was made to contribute its share to the disappearance of British rule in India.

On those, also, who did not follow clear party cues in respect of India, its influence was destructive. It alienated their sympathy from the Indian empire. As it was, the British people taken in the mass were never deeply involved in this empire, emotionally or intellectually. To them it was rather a marginal fact of British history than what it really was—a major phenomenon in the history of world civilisation. Mr. Forster's book not only strengthened the indifference, it also created a positive aversion to the empire by its unattractive picture of India and Anglo-Indian life and its depiction of Indo-British relations as being of a kind that were bound to outrage the English sense of decency and fair play. Thus, the novel helped the growth of that mood which enabled the British people to leave India with an almost Pilate-like gesture of washing their hands of a disagreeable affair.

Even intrinsically, the novel had a political drift. There is of course no necessary connection between a writer's own intentions and the manner in which he is accepted or exploited by his public. It has even been said that it is only when they are debased or deformed that philosophical ideas play a part in history. But in regard to *A Passage to India*, it can be said that the author's purpose and the public response more or less coincided. The novel was quite openly a satire on the British official in India. Perhaps in a veiled form it was also a satire on the Indians who were, or aspired to be, the *clientes* of the foreign patriciate. As such it was, at one remove, a verdict on British rule in India. At the risk of depriving it of its nuances, but perhaps not misrepresenting its general purport, I might sum it up as follows. This rule is the cause of such painful maladjustment in simple human relations that even without going deeply into the rights and wrongs of the case it is desirable to put an end to it. The intention seems to have been to bring even English readers to agree with the last outburst of the hero of the novel, Aziz: "We shall drive every blasted Englishman into the sea, and then you and I shall be friends."

ACCORDINGLY, one is almost forced to appraise the novel as a political essay on Indo-British relations, and as soon as it is considered as such, a striking gap in Mr. Forster's presentation of these relations fixes attention. It is seen that the novel wholly ignores the largest area of Indo-British relations and is taken up with a relatively small sector. The ignored area is the one I watched at first hand from the age of seven to the age of fifty. The other sector, in contrast, was known to me only by hearsay, because I feared its contact almost as much as a Pharisee feared the contact of publicans and sinners.

The Indo-British relations I was familiar with were contained, for the most part, within the conflict between Indian nationalists and the British administration. Here I saw great suffering and distress, but also exultation, a brave acceptance of ill-treatment and conquest of weak tears. The longer the men had been in jail, the more they had been persecuted, the more "sporting" they seemed to be. In the other sector, the conflict was between associates, the British officials and their Indian subordinates or hangers-on, and had all the meanness of a family quarrel. It sizzled without providing any ennobling or even chastening release for passion, only distilling rancour. It contributed much to the pathology of Indo-British relations but virtually nothing to the final parting of ways. If we can at all speak of having driven the "blasted Englishman into the sea," as Aziz puts it, it was not men of his type who accomplished the feat. Those who fought British rule in India did not do so with the object of eventually gaining the Englishman's personal friendship. Just as personal humiliation did not bring them into the conflict, personal friendship did not also lure them as a goal.

But of course there was good reason for Mr. Forster's choice. The reason is not however that the political conflict was impersonal and could not be treated in a novel. It could be, though the result would have been a tragedy of mutual repulsion and not a tragi-comedy of mutual attraction. Mr. Forster chose the sector of which he had personal knowledge. As an Englishman paying a short visit to India, he naturally saw far less of Indians in general than of his own countrymen and of the Indians with whom the latter had official business or perfunctory social relations. Being an Englishman, of humane sensibilities, he was also shocked by the state of these relations, as among others Wilfrid Blunt was before him. On the other hand, he could not observe the larger and the more important area without going considerably out of his way and making a special effort.

There is also another and not less fundamental reason for Mr. Forster's choice. That is the character of his political consciousness. I should really call it humanitarian consciousness. For his is an appeal in a political case to the court of humane feelings to what he himself calls "common humanity" in a later essay. Now, the relationship between common humanity and politics is even more complex than that which exists between morality and politics. I firmly believe that ultimately, politics and morals are inseparable; even so, the most obvious moral judgement on a political situation is not necessarily a right judgement, and for humane feelings to go for a straight tilt at politics is even more quixotic than tilting at windmills.

The consequences of pitting humane feelings against a political phenomenon are well illustrated in *A Passage to India*. One consequence is that it leads to pure negation. In the sphere of Indo-British relations the novel has no solution to offer except a dissolution of the relationship, which is not a solution of the problem but only its elimination. The good feeling that such a dissolution can generate, and has in actual fact generated between Indians and the British after 1947, is the sort of kindly feeling one has for strangers or casual acquaintances. It is of no use whatever for a sane ordering of political relations which one is struggling to raise from an amoral or even immoral level to a moral one.

ANOTHER consequence is that the humanitarian prepossession leads Mr. Forster to waste his politico-ethical emotion on persons who do not deserve it. Both the groups of characters in *A Passage to India* are insignificant and despicable. I have, however, my doubts about Mr. Forster's delineation of his countrymen. I am no authority on the life of White officials in India, for I never cultivated them. Still, observing them in their public capacity, and at times laying incredible stupidities at their door, I did not consider them quite so absurd a class as Mr. Forster shows them to be.

Of one implied charge I will definitely acquit them. Mr. Forster makes the British officials of Chandrapore nervous about the excitement of the Muharram to the extent of making the women and children take shelter in the club, and after the trial of Aziz he makes them reach home along by-ways for fear of being man-handled by a town rabble. Of this kind of cowardice no British official in India was to my mind ever guilty, even in their worst time since the Mutiny, in the years 1930 to 1932, when the Auxiliary Force armoury at Chittagong in Bengal was raided by a band of young revolutionaries, British officials were shot dead in Calcutta and the districts, and attempts were made on the life of the Governor of Bengal and the Police Commissioner of Calcutta. As a class, the British officials kept their head. The courage shown by the District Magistrate of Chittagong on the night of the raid, when an insurrection of unknown magnitude and danger faced him, was admirable. The shortcoming of the British official was not in courage, but in intelligence.

On the other hand, Mr. Forster is too charitable with the Indians. Aziz would not have been allowed to cross my threshold, not to speak of being taken as an equal. Men of his type are a pest even in free India. Some have acquired a crude idea of gracious living or have merely been caught by the lure of snobbism, and are always trying to gain importance by sneaking into the company of those to whom this way of living is natural. Another group of men are more hardboiled. They are always out to put personal friendship to worldly profit, perhaps the most widespread canker in Indian social life even now. Indian ministers and high officials feel this even more strongly than Ronny in Mr. Forster's novel. These attempts at exploitation are making them more outrageously rude than any British official, and all the more so because in India there is no tradition of kindliness among people in power. In British days this bickering gave rise to a corrosive race conflict, now it is fomenting an equally corrosive class conflict. But it is futile to grow censorious over this, no sane or satisfactory human relations can be built up with such material.

Mr. Forster appears to have felt this himself. He is too intelligent to be able to overlook the weak points in the Indian character, and too honest to suppress them in his book. Indeed, he shows himself so acute in seizing them that it is impossible to imagine that he was representing Aziz and his associates as fine fellows who deserved to be treated as equals by the British, and was not conscious of their utter worthlessness. I detect a personal admission in the comment he puts in the mouth of Ronny about the Nawab Bahadur, the "show Indian": "Incredible, aren't they, even the best of them?" So I am not surprised to find a streak of satire even in his presentation of Indians. But such satire not being his aim, he is driven into a corner, from where he can plead for satisfactory Indo-British relations on the only basis which could be proof against disillusionment, the basis of the least respect and the largest charity. Inevitably he has also to make a moralist's impossible demand on human nature.

But even if Mr. Forster's Indians had been good as individuals as they are malodorous, he would not have had a very much stronger case. For he had not chosen his Indian types happily. In regard to the Hindu characters, he relied mostly on the types found in the Princely States. Certainly they were more traditional than those in British India, but they were so traditional that they did not represent modern India at all. For instance, to those of us who are familiar with the teachings of the Hindu reformers of the 19th century, Godbole is not an exponent of Hinduism, he is a clown. Even for us, friendly personal relations with these men became possible only if we assumed we were in an anthropological reserve. Although the States have now been incorporated in India, the unevenness persists, and it presents a serious problem of *Gleichschaltung* for the future.

But Mr. Forster's more serious mistake was in taking Muslims as the principal characters in a novel dealing with Indo-British relations. They should never have been the second party to the relationship in the novel, because ever since the nationalist movement got into its stride the Muslims were playing a curiously equivocal role, realistic and effective politically, but unsatisfying in every other respect. The Muslims hated the British with a hatred even more vitriolic than the Hindu's, because it was they who had been deprived of an empire by the British. Yet they found themselves wooed by the latter as a counterpoise to the Hindu nationalists, and they did not reject these overtures.

They were shrewd in their calculations. They knew that their own battle was being fought by the Hindus and that in an eventual victory their share of the spoils was guaranteed. In the meanwhile, it was profitable to exploit the British, make the best of both worlds. This game, played with boldness and hardheaded realism, succeeded beyond expectation and created an independent state for the Muslims of India.

But a colossal Machiavellian game of politics like this could be played without moral risks only by men of very great strength of character, as indeed all the Muslim leaders, from Sir Sayyid Ahmad Khan to M. A. Jinnah, were. On the rank and file of the Muslims, so far as this policy influenced them, it had a deplorable effect. It left one section unweaned from its barren and rancorous hatred and made another pine for British patronage. Aziz and his friends belong to the servile section and are all inverted toadies. With such material, a searching history of the Muslim destiny in India could have been written, but not a novel on Indo-British relations, for which it was essential to have a Hindu protagonist.

But I think I know why Mr. Forster would not have a Hindu. He shares the liking the British in India had for the Muslim, and the corresponding dislike for the Hindu. This was a curious psychological paradox and in every way unnatural, if not perverse. On the one hand, the Islamic order was the natural enemy of the Christian-European, and the British empire in India was in one sense the product of the secular conflict between the Christian West and the Islamic Middle East, which is still running its course. More than one British Foreign Secretary found the pitch of British policy queered by the incurable phil-Islamic attitude of the British Indian Government, and once Sir Edward Grey expressed frank annoyance at it.

On the other hand, there was between European civilisation and the Hindu in its stricter form a common Indo-European element, which was discovered and described by British Orientalists in the first century or so of British rule, but which came to be forgotten and ignored by Englishmen in later times. Modern Hindu thinkers did not, however, lose sight of the affinity. Swami Vivekananda, speaking at the end of the last century, said that two branches of the same people placed in different surroundings in Greece and India had worked out the problems of life, each in its own particular way, but that through the agency of the British people the ancient Greek was meeting the ancient Hindu on Indian soil, and thus "slowly and silently the leaven has come, the broadening out, the life-giving revivalist movement that we see all around us." The British in India never gave this fruitful idea any encouragement. They were taken in by the deceptive simplicity of the Muslim and repelled by the apparent bizarrerie of Hinduism and its rococo excrescences. I wonder if it was the Hebraic element in the British ethos which was responsible for this.

THIS leads me straight to my objections to the politics of *A Passage to India* and my one positive comment on its central theme. My most serious criticisms are the following. It shows a great imperial system at its worst, not as diabolically evil but as drab and asinine; the rulers and the ruled alike are depicted at their smallest, the snobbery and pettiness of the one matching the imbecility and rancour of the other. Our suffering under British rule, on which a book as noble as Alfred de Vigny's *Servitude et Grandeur militaires* could have been written, is deprived of all dignity. Our mental life as depicted in the book is painfully childish and querulous. Lastly, attention is diverted away from those Indians who stood aloof from the world the book describes and were aristocratic in their way, although possessing no outward attribute of aristocracy. When I consider all this I feel Mr. Forster's literary ability, which has given the book its political importance, as a grievance.

At the root of all this lies the book's tacit but confident assumption that Indo-British relations presented a problem of personal behaviour and could be tackled on the personal plane. They did not and could not. The great Indians who brought about the Westernisation of their country and created its modern culture had none of the characteristic Indian foibles for which Mr. Forster invokes British compassion. They were men of the stature of an Erasmus, Comenius, or Holberg, who could hold their own with the best in Europe. Yet some of them were assaulted, some insulted, and others slighted by the local British. None of them had any intimate personal relations with any member of the British ruling community. There were also thousands of Indians who had adopted Western ideals and were following them to the best of their ability, who were not only not cultivated but shunned with blatant ostentation by the British in India. "What you have got to stamp on is these educated classes," they all said, like the subaltern in the novel. This was due, not to any personal snobbery, but to that massive national snobbery which refused to share British and Western civilisation with Indians.

Those who remember the powerful championship of Westernisation by Macaulay usually forget that his best supporters were Indians and his most determined opponents his own countrymen. In spite of the formal adoption of this policy, the British ruling class in India never felt happy about it and carried it out half-heartedly. Towards the result, the attitude of the thoughtful Englishman was one of regret, while the average Englishman grew maliciously quizzical.

To give only one example, there was hardly one Englishman who had a good word to say about our employment of the English language. I still remember the pleasure I felt when for the first time in my experience, I read praise of our English in Sir Michael Sadler's report on Calcutta University. Normally the better our English the more angry did the Englishman become, and the worse it was the greater was the entertainment of the Memsahib and *ergo* the larger the favours of the Sahib. Even so great a personage as Lady Minto was not above the weakness, and in his kindly manner even Mr. Forster has felt amused by our English.

Of course, I cannot deny that much of our English as indeed much of our Westernisation was quaint. But ours were the shortcomings of self-taught and unguided men everywhere. If, in their days of power, the British had not looked askance at our employment of English, today the battle for English in India would not have been already lost, and we should not have needed the forlorn crusade of the British Council, too late for love, too late for joy, too late, too late!

ONCE the premise of cultural apartheid was admitted, there could be no advance on the personal plane, for men do not treat as equals those who are not of their psychological species. The British in India clinging to the obsolete idea of zoological speciation for mankind, could only cry as the District Collector does in *A Passage to India*: "I have never known anything but disaster result when English people and Indians attempt to be intimate socially. Intercourse, yes. Courtesy by all means. Intimacy—never, never."

A real Englishman, greater than Mr. Forster's Turton, had come to the same conclusion. Sir Edwin Lutyens, the builder of New Delhi, tried friendship with Indians and wrote in disenchantment: "The natives do not improve on acquaintance. Their very low intellects spoil much and I do not think it is possible for the Indians and Whites to mix freely and naturally. They are very different, and even my ultra-wide sympathy with them cannot admit them on the same plane as myself. They may be on a higher plane or a lower one than a White, but the ethics of their planes are different to ours, and for one or the other to leave his plane is unclean and unforgivable."

On the other hand, putting the cultural impact in the foreground, Indians propounded a strikingly contrasted thesis. At that level our personal humiliations ceased to matter and even our great *injuria temporum*, political subjection, presented a second face. Rammohun Roy was grossly insulted by a British baronet and official. He protested against it to the Governor-General but did not allow it to influence his views on Westernisation or even those about British rule in India. He surprised a young French scientist, Victor Jacquemont, who saw him in Calcutta, by an expression of opinion which the Frenchman set down verbatim in his journal: "*La conquête est bien rarement un mal, quand le peuple conquérant est plus civilisé que le peuple conquis, parce qu'elle apporte à celui-ci les biens de la civilisation. Il faut à l'Inde bien des années de domination anglaise pour qu'elle puisse ne pas perdre beaucoup en ressaisissant son indépendance politique.*"

Bankim Chandra Chatterji, the creator of Hindu nationalism, was actually assaulted by a British official though a magistrate himself, but he too, when it came to assessing the larger consequences of British rule in India, argued persuasively that it was in many ways providential. Personal grievance, even when well-founded, did not influence men of this type.

The contrast between the generosity of such Indians and the British narrowness furnishes the key to the real failure of the British in India. It was the failure to see that a nation which was not willing to propagate its civilisation and extend its spiritual citizenship was also incapable of perpetuating, not only an empire, but even friendly political relations with other nations not belonging to its own culture complex. The challenge before the British was to create an open society in the order of the mind. Their opportunity was to make India an extension of the Western world. But they failed as completely in using their opportunity as they did in meeting the challenge. Compared with this failure, which was a betrayal of the West in India, their bad manners were mere peccadillos.

THIS political evaluation of *A Passage to India* has not been attempted for its historical interest, great as that interest is. I believe that the questions which British rule raised in India have only been put aside and not answered by what happened in 1947. I also believe that the British failure to understand the true nature of the Indo-British relationship has a moral, whose application is likely to widen as time passes, for a new set of international relations taking shape today over an area very much larger than India. It is this moral that I have to draw now.

But as a preliminary I should define my position. I represent no school of thought in India, past or present, and there is nothing characteristically Indian in my views except the fact that they are those of an Indian by birth and are based on Indian experience. I differ fundamentally from the nationalistic majority of my countrymen who speak of 19th century imperialism but forget that the century also had its nationalism. I differ no less fundamentally from the influential minority in India who believe in world government, who pin their faith to a world government of the contractual type, carried on by means of a world assembly in which the national representatives will be wise, reasonable, and just. I cannot say, like a Christian, that this conception is bound to be wrecked on the innate sinfulness of man, but I would say that it would hurtle against man's inherent urge to power.

It seems to me that the West is now showing the same incomprehension which destroyed British power in India. The economic and the political impact of the West is being felt. What is absent is that proselytising cultural impact which alone can counteract the mental resistance to the extension of Western culture into the non-Western parts of the world. Instead, there is the same uncritical faith in the promotion of economic prosperity and the converting power of *Pecunia Americana* as there was in the maintenance of law and order and the indispensability of *Pax Britannica*. The West ought to, and in my opinion can, think in terms of something higher than effective diplomacy, higher even than world government, for converting the single zoological species called man into one psychological species. Of course, that might not be possible. But one can never speak of impossibility before an effort has been made.

STRUCTURE, SYMBOL, AND THEME IN E. M. FORSTER'S *A PASSAGE TO INDIA*

By Glen O. Allen

FOR THE THIRTY years since its publication, E. M. Forster's *A Passage to India* has enjoyed the somewhat paradoxical status of being valued without being understood. It is generally recognized as one of the finest literary productions of this century; it is also commonly thought to be one of the most puzzling. No doubt, part of the reason for our difficulty in interpreting it is that the literary problems it raises are continuous with its philosophical problems, or, to put it another way, that the obscurities of the novel duplicate or disappear into the obscurities of life itself. We cannot, of course, expect to explain the latter mystery before attempting to explain the former, nor need it be necessary; yet, if we are to succeed in interpretation, we must guard against that most common critical error of assuming that our own philosophical predilections must apply universally. As Earl R. Wasserman recently observed, "Our failure to grasp as total and integrated experiences such works as . . . E. M. Forster's *A Passage to India* results from our not having succeeded as yet in bringing to these works the proper controlling cosmos, for each cosmos is the creation of the author."[1] Discovering the nature of this "cosmos" and relating it to structure, symbol, and theme of the novel will be the concern of the following pages.

Among the general critical treatments of Forster's novels those of Lionel Trilling, Austin Warren, and Morton D. Zabel[2] deserve special mention for their sensitivity and discernment. All of them, however, suffer the limitation of having comparatively little to say about *A Passage to India*. More recently, three attempts have been made to probe more directly into the meaning of this novel. E. K. Brown[3] has applied one of Forster's own concepts, *rhythm*, in an analysis of his narrative technique, but without any very fruitful results in the interpretation of the book's meaning. Paul Fussell, Jr.[4] has suggested the possibility of the identity of Mrs. Moore and Madame Blavatsky, apparently unaware of Forster's aversion to "psychical research, that dustbin of the spirit."[5] Finally, Gertrude M. White[6] has attempted to embrace the three parts

[1] *The Finer Tone: Keats' Major Poems* (Baltimore, 1953), p. 228.

[2] *E. M. Forster* (New York, 1943), "The Novels of E. M. Forster," *American Review*, IX (Summer 1937), 226–251; "E. M. Forster," *Nation*, CXLVII (22 Oct. 1938), 412–416.

[3] *Rhythm in the Novel* (Toronto, 1950).

[4] "E. M. Forster's Mrs. Moore: Some Suggestions," *PQ*, XXXII (Oct. 1953), 388–396.

[5] *Goldsworthy Lowes Dickinson* (London, 1934), p. 122.

[6] "*A Passage to India*: Analysis and Reevaluation," *PMLA*, LXVIII, iv (Sept. 1953), 641–657.

of the novel in an Hegelian triad. Her recognition that beneath the details of the story runs a philosophical under-current of the broadest dimensions is a valuable contribution; yet I believe her interpretation does violence not only to the meaning of the novel, but to Forster's own philosophical views. The alleged synthesis and the optimism of Hegelian doctrine are quite at odds with Forster's quietism.[7]

One would think that the publication of Forster's Indian correspondence of 1911 and 1921[8] would throw light upon the significance of the novel. The letters do, in fact, contain a number of descriptions of incidents and scenes which appear in the text almost without change. Reported to his mother, or one of his other correspondents, were: an incident in which a wild animal leaped out of a ravine and charged an automobile; an instance in which a small dead tree is mistaken for a snake; a description of an Indian song approximating the strange chant of Professor Godbole; and finally nearly all the details connected with the ceremony of the birth of Shri Krishna. Considering the degree to which Forster has called upon the unembellished incidents of his own experience in the construction of his novel, one is tempted at first to believe that much of the text of the novel might go under the name of "local color," and thus account for the difficulty of synthesizing its many diverse details.

Nothing, however, could be farther from the truth. Few novelists discipline themselves to the omission of extraneous detail more severely than Forster. The following passage from his Clark lectures, delivered three years after the publication of *A Passage to India* and later published as *Aspects of the Novel* (New York, 1927) assures us that a Forster novel should be approached not as a muddle but as a mystery inviting discerning analysis.

The plot-maker expects us to remember, we expect him to leave no loose ends. Every action or word ought to count; it ought to be economical and spare, even when complicated it should be organic and free from dead matter. It may be difficult or easy, it may and should contain mysteries, but it ought not to mislead. And over it, as it unfolds, will hover the memory of the reader (that dull glow of the mind of which intelligence is the bright advancing edge) and will rearrange and reconsider, seeing new clues, new chains of cause and effect, and the final sense (if the plot has been a fine one) will not be of clues or chains, but of something aesthetically compact, something which might have been shown by the novelist straight away, only if he had shown it straight away it would never have become beautiful (p. 133).

[7] In his biography of G. Lowes Dickinson, Forster seems to show no particular interest in his friend's Hegelian studies.

[8] *The Hill of Devi* (New York, 1953).

I

The structure of *A Passage to India* is built around its threefold division into "Mosque," "Caves," and "Temple." Forster, in his notes to the Everyman's edition, tells us that the three parts stand for the three seasons of the Indian year. The action of "Mosque" takes place during the cool spring, that of "Caves" during the hot summer, and of "Temple" during the wet monsoon season of the autumn. But he is not limiting the significance of this division to the times of the year or to the characteristic weather of these seasons, though, to be sure, the weather constitutes an important part of the symbolic structure. In the text itself, the author hints at another meaning of the threefold division. "Ronny's religion was of the sterilized Public School brand, which never goes bad, even in the tropics. Wherever he entered, *mosque, cave,* or *temple,* he retained the spiritual outlook of the Fifth Form, and condemned as 'weakening' any attempt to understand them."[9] Caves, then, like mosques and temples, represent some kind of religion. But by religion Forster means something more than that which attracts the western peoples into church on Sundays and Easter, as one may assume from his indifference to the minutiae of creed and practice. Speaking of the mosque through Aziz, he says, "Here was Islam, his own country, more than a Faith, more than a battle-cry, more, much more . . . Islam, an attitude towards life both exquisite and durable, where his body and his thoughts found their home" (p. 19). Similarly with caves and temples, Forster is endeavoring to represent what is much more than a faith or a battle-cry, much more than orthodox Christianity or the worship of Shri Krishna. These creeds are specifically mentioned, but they are not the basic categories in which Forster conceives "attitudes toward life."

It is easier to understand Forster's treatment of mosque, caves, and temple if we accept as his basic categories the emotional nature, the intellect, and the capacity for love. He has accordingly selected religions to represent his views, each of which offers exercise predominantly to one of these faculties. In Islam, he sees a mode of expression for the emotional nature, an attitude towards life where Aziz's "body and his thoughts found their home." Islam, however, provides no sanctuary for the intellect. "'There is no God but God,' doesn't carry us far through the complexities of matter and spirit; it is only a game with words, really a religious pun, not a religious truth" (p. 276). Nor, indeed, does the worship of Shri Krishna, in which the exercise of the faculty of love predominates, offer satisfaction to intellect or will. Its quietism in the face

[9] Harbrace Modern Classics Ed. (New York: Harcourt, Brace and Co., 1924), p. 257. Italics mine. Quotations will be from this edition.

of the unjust accusation of Aziz is a source of great exasperation to Fielding, while its religious practices are described as a muddle, "a frustration of reason and form" (p. 285). Godbole, the Brahman, charming as he is, remains utterly inscrutable to both Aziz and Fielding, who at the very end of the novel show in one instance continuing indifference and in the other continuing puzzlement over his strange faith. The mysticism underlying devotion to Shri Krishna amounts to an utter renunciation of the intellect, the disintegration of the categories which make distinction—and, therefore, thought—possible. Hence the futility of Fielding's attempt to grasp its meaning.

At the third corner of this triangle of religious attitudes are Fielding and Adela, exemplars of peculiarly western traits. Neither emotional nor strongly endowed with mystical insight, they approach the deeper problems of life and human relationships through the mind and whatever is not reducible to intellectual categories is therefore beyond their grasp. It is this devotion to reason, form, and the sense of purpose as the *sine qua non* of right behavior and attitude that Forster represents as the religion of caves. As Aziz is the principal character in "Mosque" and Godbole in "Temple," so Fielding and Adela dominate the action of "Caves."

Mrs. Moore, the other major character of the western group, bears a strong though subtle resemblance to Fielding and Adela. Though endowed with some of the emotional spontaneity of an Aziz and the mystical sensitivity of a Godbole, her strongest moorings are of ultimate intellectual origin. Though not doctrinaire in her beliefs, she is nevertheless a practising Christian, and so deeply embedded are the roots of Christianity in the traditions of western thought that Mrs. Moore, without being intellectually disposed, is intellectually committed; without having the capacity for thought, she is nevertheless a victim of her intellectual heritage. Because of her widely diverging traits, Mrs. Moore appropriately exercises an influence in all three parts of the novel: in "Mosque," as an active character spanning the gulf between Fielding and Adela and the volatile Aziz; in "Caves," as the pettish old woman disappointed by her vision of the mystical realm beyond the limits of the intellectual categories; and, in "Temple," both as a spiritual residue and as the progenitor of the mystically inclined Ralph and Stella.

It is not surprising that India, which, according to Forster, "mirrors the universe" and likewise has no unity itself, should in the history of its religious philosophy have embraced an approximation of each one of these "attitudes towards life" as a way of salvation. The historians of Hindu philosophy provide ample documentation for this trichotymous division;[10] however, for its succinctness of expression, I have chosen the statement of E. W. F. Tomlin.

Indian philosophical tradition has fully recognized the different degrees in wisdom to which the three great elements of Hindu scripture approximate. In the first place there is the so-called Path of Activity, or *Karmamarga*. To this path belong the Vedas, songs to be chanted in public as a stimulus to effort: the anthems of a people engaged in a communal exploit needing for its accomplishment a burning faith in its mission. In the second place there is the so-called Path of Knowledge, or *Inanamarga*. To this path belong the *Upanishads*, explorations by the mind in secret conclave of that which is permanently knowable behind the world of appearances and illusion. In the third place there is the so-called Path of Devotion, or *Bhaktimarga*. To this path belongs the *Bhagavad-Gita*.[11]

The principal function of the threefold division of the novel, then, is to represent these three "attitudes toward life" both as they partake of regularized religious views and as they are expressions of varying types of culture and of individual character.[12]

Within this embracing architectural structure, Forster has spun a web of marvelously rich and complex detail. Characteristic of his technique is the repetition of detail in different contexts and with slight variations, and to this method Forster has applied the term, "rhythm." The effect of this rhythm is not only to knit together aesthetically the detail of the novel; it also contributes very considerably to the meaning of it.

The wasp, for instance, is mentioned in three different contexts—first, when Mrs. Moore finds it on a coat-peg; second, when the missionaries consider the possibility of admitting wasps to heaven; and third, when Godbole is described as impelling the wasp to completeness of union in God. In all of these instances the wasp retains its identity as a

[10] See, e.g., S. Radhakrishnan, *Indian Philosophy* (London, 1929), pp. 552–574. Also Heinrich Zimmer, *Philosophies of India*, ed. Joseph Campbell (New York, 1951), pp. 403–409 et passim.

[11] *The Great Philosophers: The Eastern World* (London, 1952), pp. 158–159. Historically, these attitudes developed in the order in which Tomlin presents them, the *Karmamarga* belonging to the earliest recorded history of Indian culture. The *Inanamarga* represents a somewhat more sophisticated culture of a later date, while the *Bhaktimarga* is estimated as the development of a period preceding the birth of Christ by some 600 or 800 years. It is significant that the *Bhagavad-Gita*, the most highly admired of Hindu scriptures, which provides the authority for the *Bhaktimarga*, does not do so to the exclusion of the other two doctrines. Most scholars accept the point of view that the *Gita* is an eclectic document which attempts the harmonious reconciliation of all three ways of salvation.

[12] Another purely formal function of the threefold division should be noted in passing. Forster's deep interest in musical form and its relation to fiction offers support to the view that the three parts of the novel correspond to the three divisions of the sonata form in which themes of East and West are stated, developed, dexterously interwoven, and finally brought to a harmonious conclusion in the coda of the final pages of the book.

pretty creature but somewhat undesirable because of its sting, as "good-and-evil," to use a term of Forster's coinage, but it functions differently according to each context in which it appears. It is not, that is to say, a full-fledged symbol, but rather an instance of repetition for the sake of its unifying effect. Our first acquaintance with the wasp comes directly after Ronny has demonstrated to his mother the "official" way of penetrating the subterfuges of the Indian character, and his mother cannot deny that his accusation of Aziz "sounds very sensible," though she thinks to herself, "how false a summary of the man." Similarly, there are two ways of looking at a wasp, as a creature possessing a stinger and capable of inflicting great pain, or, as Mrs. Moore did: "'Pretty dear,' said Mrs. Moore to the wasp" (p. 35).

When the wasp next appears in the remarks of the missionaries, its function is quite subservient to the function of the whole parable. It remains a pretty but dangerous creature which even the advanced Mr. Sorley can not readily find room for in the house of many mansions. The whole parable exists to comment on the inclusions and exclusions involved in the invitations to the bridge party at the club, a British-style heaven. But the ultimate significance of the parable reaches out to one of the basic ideas of the novel, the necessity of exclusion to make inclusion meaningful, or, in the most general terms, the necessity of distinction to intellectual processes and hence the basic repugnance of the western mind to mysticism.

The last mention of the wasp illustrates the consequences of the complete indifference to distinction which results in "the frustration of reason and form." Had he been a Christian missionary, Godbole might have concentrated on Mrs. Moore and then, as a second choice, perhaps Fielding. But no, for the Hindu no such distinctions exist. God is equally immanent, though perhaps not equally evident, in man, wasp, and stone, and no one is to be preferred above another. "Thus, Godbole, though she was not important to him, remembered an old woman he had met in Chandrapore days. Chance brought her into his mind while it was in this heated state, he did not select her, she happened to occur among the throng of soliciting images, a tiny splinter, and he impelled her by his spiritual force to that place where completeness can be found. Completeness, not reconstruction. His senses grew thinner, he remembered a wasp seen he forgot where, perhaps on a stone. He loved the wasp equally, he impelled it likewise, he was imitating God" (p. 286).

The effect of rhythm is achieved in the case of the wasp by virtue of the material similarity of wasp in one instance with wasp in another. In passing I noted also the parable of the missionaries, another example of rhythm, but in this case repetition occurs not in the material but in the formal similarities existing between invitations to the club and admission to heaven. A more complex and significant instance of this sort of rhythm lies in the similarities between the accident involving "the savage pig" and Adela's entrance into the cave. The essential features of the accident are the approach to the scene durmg which Adela is concerned with the problem of marriage, the collision with the animal, the confused attempt at identifying the animal, and the return in Miss Derek's car. These features are reproduced in the incident of the cave. "As she toiled over a rock that resembled an inverted saucer, she thought, 'What about love?' The rock was nicked by a double row of footholds, and somehow the question was suggested by them. Where had she seen footholds before? Oh yes, they were the pattern traced in the dust by the wheels of the Nawab Bahadur's car. She and Ronny—no, they did not love each other" (p. 152). Thereafter, Adela asks Aziz her offensive question, enters the cave, believes herself attacked, and descends wildly from the summit of Kawa Dol to return to Chandrapore in Miss Derek's automobile. The incidents are basically similar in form, and the reference to the earlier accident is an invitation to us to infer further similarities. The obvious inference to make is that just as the accident is not to be unilaterally explained by appeal to a naturalistic cause, so too the incident of the cave is not to be accounted for by blaming Aziz or the guide. In both cases Adela's wish for explanation at all cost is the source of her error.[13]

II

I have avoided using the word symbol in referring to those repeated items composing the rhythm of the novel in order to preserve its significance for reference to the major symbolic structure of the book—the Marabar Hills, the caves, the sun, echoes, serpents, snakes, and worms. A distinction between the two can be made on this basis: the former, to which I have referred as instances of rhythm, take their meaning from their context; they have no stable meaning but grow and wane in significance according to the way in which they are used.[14] The wasp, the circumstances of the accident and the affairs of the cave, the speculations of the missionaries, Godbole's song, the Tank of the Dagger, and

[13] This effort to identify, to label the cause of the accident, Forster had prepared for earlier in the scene at the polo field where Ronny and Adela had pointlessly attempted to name the green bird (p. 85). Both of these events are, of course, closely related to their plans for sanctifying a shaky and uncertain affection for each other by the label of marriage. And if we carry the significance of this pattern of images to its extreme, we see that it symbolizes the attempt to wed Britain and India, East and West, without the sanction of mutual affection, nor the hope of anything more than the label of marriage to result from it.

[14] For Forster's grounds for distinction, see *Aspects of the Novel*, p. 239.

a host of others fall under the head of rhythm because their meaning is not stable but varies according to context.

The Marabar Hills and related symbols, on the other hand, while they are certainly not unconnected with the other details of the novel, derive their essential meaning from sources outside the novel itself. This no doubt accounts for the silence in some critical quarters and the puzzlement in others when the inevitable question of the caves arises. Mostly, the practice has been to look the other way; however, Austin Warren sees the caves as something "bare, dark, echoing," echoing "eternity, infinity, the Absolute" (p. 246). Gertrude White declares that they are "the very voice of that union which is the opposite of divine; the voice of evil and negation" (p. 647). Virginia Woolf suggests hesitantly that "the Marabar Caves should appear to us not real caves but, it may be, the soul of India,"[15] while Lionel Trilling, after observing the radical alterations undergone in their depths by Mrs. Moore and Adela, offers to call them "wombs."

Of the Marabar Hills and Caves, the most important characteristics are that they are "flesh of the sun's flesh" (p. 123); that "nothing, nothing attaches to them" (p. 124), that is, that they are without attributes; that they reflect, either as a mirror or as an echo, all the light and sound which touches their surface; and that that echo is spoken of sometimes in the image of a serpent, sometimes as a snake, and sometimes as an "undying worm."

"Nothing, nothing attaches to them." We remember that Godbole attempted to describe the caves at Fielding's tea-party but discovered that he could predicate no attributes of them. "Neti, neti," the Hindus say of their conception of deity, "I know not, I know not," for to predicate attributes of deity is to limit him and the Hindu deity extends universally comprehending all that exists.[16] "All that exists" is embraced in the terms of Indian philosophy by Atman and Brahman, the Self and the Not-Self. But Atman and Brahman are not truly distinct; rather they are parted by Maya, the veil of illusion, and when the mystical release comes, whether from the discipline of sacrifice or knowledge or love, Maya is dissipated and Atman and Brahman, the Self and the Not-Self, are seen to be one. With the release, all distinction, all individuation ceases to exist. Thus Mrs. Moore, dejected by her experience in the cave,

[15] "The Novels of E. M. Forster," *The Death of the Moth* (New York, 1942), p. 168.

[16] Hindu philosophy, it should be understood, is not all of one piece. Though not quite so diversified as Western philosophy, it comprehends at least six distinct interpretations of its ancient Vedic writings. When I speak in general terms of Hindu philosophy, as indeed I must, I shall intend what is common to all the Brahmanical systems; or, where that is impossible, I shall follow Shankara, the most widely admired of the interpreters.

could reflect: "Pathos, piety, courage—they exist, but are identical, and so is filth. Everything exists, nothing has value" (p. 149).

The *Upanishads*, which are the sacred philosophical scriptures of Hinduism, contain the basic revelations of this doctrine. In them we find fairly frequent reference to Brahman and Atman as "in the cave." In the *Katha-Upanishad*, for instance, Yama, the teacher, says to his pupil, Nakiketas: "The wise who, by means of meditation on his Self, recognizes the Ancient, who is difficult to be seen, who has entered into the dark, who is hidden in the cave, who dwells in the abyss, as God, he indeed leaves joy and sorrow far behind."[17] Again, in the same Upanishad, the teacher says: "There are the two, drinking their reward in the world of their own works, entered into the cave . . . dwelling on the highest summit. Those who know Brahman call them shade and light." Atman and Brahman, the Self and the Not-Self, which are truly identical, dwell in the cave on the highest summit.

The relation between Atman and Brahman is ultimately a mystical one, not truly to be understood except intuitively on the occasion of release. However, one of the imaged relationships specified in the *Vedanta-Sutras* which approximates that relationship is that of the snake to its coils. As it is explained by Shankara in his commentary: "We therefore look on the relation of the highest Self and the soul as analogous to that of the snake and its coils. Viewed as a whole the snake is one, non-different, while an element of difference appears if we view it with regard to its coils, hood, erect posture, and so on" (*SBE*, XXXVIII, 174). The import of the snake symbol, then, is the equivalent of the cave symbol itself—the ultimate identity of Brahman and Atman.

The echo which assaulted the ears of Adela and Mrs. Moore also has its counterpart in Hindu scriptures and religious practice. Forster writes the echo as "Boum" or "ou-boum," but there is little phonetic difference between it and the mystic syllable, *Om*. The pronunciation of and meditation upon this syllable is a very important part of the discipline of those seeking Brahman.[18] In the *Prasna-Upanishad*, we find this discipline prescribed for meditation upon the syllable *Om:* "The syllable Om (AUM) is the highest and also the other Brahman; therefore he who knows it arrives by the same means at one of the two. . . . He who meditates with this syllable AUM of three Matras, on the Highest Person, he comes to light and to the sun. And as a snake is freed from its

[17] *Sacred Books of the East*, ed. F. Max Müller (Oxford, 1900), xv, 10.

[18] Although it is spelled "Om," the syllable stands for the letters A,U,M which in turn stand for the threefold manifestation of the godhead: Brahma, the creator; Vishnu, the preserver; and Siva, the destroyer. It must be remembered, of course, that deity remains one in spite of its manifold emanations.

skin, so is he freed from evil. . . . He learns to see the all-pervading, the Highest Person" (*SBE*, xv, 281–282).

These few passages from Hindu scriptures will suggest what Forster has in mind in the symbols of cave, echo, and snake. What of light, the match struck within the cave?

> The visitor arrives for his five minutes and strikes a match. Immediately another flame rises in the depths of the rock and moves towards the surface like an imprisoned spirit: the walls of the circular chamber have been most marvelously polished. The two flames approach and strive to unite, but cannot, because one of them breathes air, the other stone. A mirror inlaid with lovely colours divides the lovers, delicate stars of pink and grey interpose, exquisite nebulae, shadings fainter than the tail of a comet or the midday moon, all the evanescent life of the granite, only here visible. . . . The radiance increases, the flames touch one another, kiss, expire. The cave is dark again, like all other caves.

Surely this is one of the most exquisite images ever put into words. It is even more remarkable for the abstruse thought it expresses. The light and sun imagery in Hindu philosophy is associated with intelligence even as it is in the West. Forster here is pointing to the inadequacy of intelligence or reason in its effort to discover within the limits of its categories the ultimate nature of the universe. The concept of time implies the irrational idea of eternity; the concept of space implies the irrational idea of infinity of space; the concept of causality implies an infinite regress in the concatenation of causes and their effects. The flames touch, kiss, expire, and light is followed by darkness. Elsewhere, Forster uses again the image of the match to illustrate a philosophical subtlety. "Even the striking of a match starts a little worm coiling, which is too small to complete a circle but is eternally watchful" (p. 147). His purpose here is similar to that which I have explained above: Even the smallest glimmer of intelligence implies a total conception of the universe. The coil of the serpent implies the whole serpent; the concept of time implies the irrational concept of eternity. It is these limitations of reason which support the monistic idealism characteristic of Hindu philosophy and which lead its interpreters to the point of view that all philosophy is ultimately a critique of mind.

In addition to Hindu scriptures, Forster's symbolism has still another source of significance in the work of the western philosopher, Schopenhauer. Though greatly separated in time and in cultural background, the system of Schopenhauer has a great deal in common with the philosophic teachings of the *Upanishads*.[19] Thus, though these sources may at first

[19] Schopenhauer himself readily avows this connection in his preface to the first edition of *The World as Will and Idea.*

seem widely disparate, they are in fact almost of one piece and one moves readily from one source to the other in interpretation. The principal difference between the metaphysics of Schopenhauer and Shankara, the great Hindu enlightener, is that the ultimate monism of the former lies in that single substance, the blindly striving will, while that of the latter is a monism in which no qualities can be attributed to ultimate being. On the other hand, Schopenhauer specifically states that an equation exists between his *principium individuationis* and the Hindu Veil of Maya such that the categories of space, time, cause and the like occupy the same position in his thought as in the thought of Shankara.[20]

A Passage to India contains one direct allusion to Schopenhauer in the mention of "the world of dreams—that world in which a third of each man's life is spent, and *which is thought by some pessimists to be a premonition of eternity*" (p. 238, italics mine).[21] Indirect allusions are frequent: Schopenhauer's work provides the explanatory context for Mrs. Moore's game of Patience;[22] for the mirror-like quality of the interior of the caves and such phrases as "the mirror of the scenery was shattered" (p. 320);[23] and the frequently echoed phrase, "Before time, it was before space also" (p. 208), which may be regarded as referring to the will as a thing-in-itself logically prior to the *principium individuationis*. The phrase, "undying worm," though taken from the New Testament,[24] nonetheless alludes indirectly to Schopenhauer's blindly striving will.

More important, however, than these occasional allusions is the light that Schopenhauer's work throws on the meaning of the major symbols—the Marabar Hills, the caves, and the sun. On at least three occasions Forster speaks of the "fists and fingers" of the Marabar Hills. According to Schopenhauer, "The parts of the body . . . completely correspond to the principal desires through which the will manifests itself; they must be the visible expression of these desires. Teeth, throat, and bowels are

[20] *The World as Will and Idea*, trans. R. B. Haldane and J. Kemp, 7th ed. (London, n.d.), I, 454.

[21] Compare Schopenhauer: "This is nature's great doctrine of immortality, which seeks to teach us that there is no radical difference between sleep and death, but the one endangers existence just as little as the other" (III, 267 and I, 364).

[22] Cf. "This need for excitement of the will manifests itself very specially in the discovery and support of card-playing, which is quite peculiarly the expression of the miserable side of humanity" (I, 406). That the game should be Patience is appropriate in view of the philosophical context.

[23] Cf. "Life, the visible world, the phenomenon, is only the mirror of the will" (I, 354).

[24] Mark IX.41 ff. "And if thy hand offend thee cut it off: it is better for thee to enter into life maimed, than having two hands to go into hell, into the fire that never shall be quenched: Where their worm dieth not, and the fire is not quenched."

objectified hunger; the organs of generation are objectified sexual desire; the grasping hand, the hurrying feet, correspond to the more indirect desires of the will which they express" (I, 141). There is perhaps an intended phallus in the Marabar symbol, but surely Forster, in speaking of the "fists and fingers" of the Marabar Hills, is representing the intellect as under the service of the will—knowledge as power and power expressed as the desire to possess.[25] The symbol of the sun bears out this contention. It is represented to us in two aspects—as the source of light and as the source of heat. In the former aspect, it has its usual identification with intelligence; in the latter, it is represented as will and power. "Strength comes from the sun" (p. 9), we learn at the opening of the book, and "Caves," which is concerned principally with the western attitude, the way of knowledge, shows us a malignant sun, "with power but without beauty . . . through excess of light" (p. 115) failing to triumph, a "treacherous sun" (p. 211), "insanely ugly" (p. 235). According to Schopenhauer, "As man is at once impetuous and blind striving of will (whose pole or focus lies in the genital organs), and eternal, free, serene subject of pure knowing (whose pole is the brain); so, corresponding to this antithesis, the sun is both a source of *light*, the condition of the most perfect kind of knowledge, and therefore of the most delightful of things—and the source of *warmth*, the first condition of life, i.e., of all phenomena of will in its higher grades. Therefore, what warmth is for the will, light is for knowledge" (I, 262–263).

Like Schopenhauer, Forster, too, is forever reminding us of the insignificance of human endeavor. His reminders take the form of an observation on the vastness of the universe which stretches arch beyond arch into the blue infinity of space; or he observes how tenuously held is the human empire against the burgeoning nature which surrounds it. Again, he sees his characters from a gigantic perspective as "dwarfs shaking hands" (p. 264), or he shows their trivial bickerings in contrast to the supreme indifference of the beautiful punkah wallah who has not been touched by moral or intellectual enlightenment. But what if man, by some desperate contortion of mind, should reduce the universe to the scale of his own thoughts? The world might indeed be his idea, but the consequence of this effort would remain the same; the Marabar "robbed infinity and eternity of their vastness, the only quality that accommo-

[25] This interpretation of the Marabar symbol is also supported by Forster's description and name of the highest summit, Kawa Dol. "The boulder because of its hollowness sways in the wind, and even moves when a crow perches upon it: hence its name and the name of its stupendous pedestal: the Kawa Dol" (pp. 125-126). In Hindustani, the phrase, Kawa Dol, means the crow's swing. However, if Kawa Dol were taken to be a transliteration of Sanskrit, it would approximate a meaning of vacillating, uncertain or limited knowledge.

dates them to mankind" (p. 150). The universe, so reduced, would no longer eclipse the human being; but the human being, in turn, for being everything, would, as a result, be nothing. This is "the twilight of the double vision," a "state where the horror of the universe and its smallness are both visible at the same time" (p. 207).

With this introduction to the significance of the Marabar Hills and related symbols, we are prepared to study the events which took place there and discover their meaning. Mrs. Moore and Adela both wished to "see India"; their efforts to do so had their first promise of success at Fielding's tea party, but the intimation that it would be strange and unpleasant came at the same time in Professor Godbole's song. Both Adela and Mrs. Moore traced their uneasiness to this beginning. Godbole had called upon Krishna to come to him, but in spite of the ardor of his prayer, he "neglects to come" (p. 80). Mrs. Moore suggested hopefully that he "comes in some other song," but is assured that he does not. This song and its token, "come, come, come," runs like a thread through the entire novel; it is connected, on the one hand, with the formlessness, the muddle of India, the India which is "not a promise, only an appeal" (p. 36), and, on the other, with the natural repugnance of western intellectuality toward what is formless, what is not infused with order and purpose.

Although Adela and Mrs. Moore are very different in temperament, they are both expressions of western intellectuality in that they both demand that orderly and purposeful conception of the universe. [Mrs. Moore, a Christian, demands a universe supported and justified by a divine being who is the promise of righteousness and of ultimate reward for good works.] It is in this respect that Mrs. Moore shares with the others of the western group a commitment to the way of knowledge. Adela, like the liberal, Fielding, is skeptical, agnostic in her religious views, but, though she does not affirm or deny deity, she nevertheless refuses to believe that the categories in which she conceives of the spatio-temporal world are not sufficient to her needs. Every problem for Adela is "something more to think out." Whether the western attitude is shown through the temperament of a Mrs. Moore or an Adela, it is in either case distinctly at odds with that of the Orient which accepts from the beginning the inadequacy of the intellect, under what Schopenhauer would call the principles of sufficient reason, to approach a conception of deity. The mind, in order to perform its functions, must necessarily identify, individuate, and force into a causal pattern all the events which come before it, but the mystical conception of deity occurs only with the disintegration of these categories. The experience of the caves thrusts upon these western women the inadequacy of the Christian and the intellectual points of view.

What did in fact happen in the caves?[26] In treating this question we must recognize that there are two answers—one natural, and one supernatural—just as there are two answers to the question of what caused the strange automobile accident. It is characteristic of Forster to portray incidents from two points of view and it is this double perspective (or, as he refers to this trait in Mrs. Moore, "double vision") which has been the source of a great deal of confusion in the interpretation of his novel. When we ask the question, "What did in fact happen in the caves?" we are asking for a naturalistic explanation, because we are puzzled that a nice girl like Adela could so malign a decent fellow like Aziz. Forster does give us such a naturalistic explanation, though he deliberately subordinates it in two dependent clauses. Mrs. Moore and Adela, prior to the visit to the caves, have had somewhat similar experiences and have reacted similarly. They both wished to see India, though they have gone about it in their different ways. They both attended Fielding's party, and both were subtly affected by Godbole's song. At the Marabar, both were strangely stricken by their experiences in caves. Even as Adela is approaching the cave in which the assault is alleged to have occurred, Mrs. Moore is at the base of the summit meditating peevishly on her experience. "She tried to go on with her letter, reminding herself that she was only an elderly woman who had got up too early in the morning and journeyed too far, that the despair creeping over her was only her despair, her personal weakness, and that *even if she got a sunstroke and went mad*, the rest of the world would go on" (p. 150, italics mine). In the next paragraph, we pick up Adela and Aziz ascending the summit of Kawa Dol and are reminded that "the sun was getting high. The air felt like a warm bath into which hotter water is trickling constantly, the temperature rose and rose, the boulders said, 'I am alive,' and small stones answered, 'I am almost alive.' Between the chinks lay the ashes of little plants" (p. 151). And in the following paragraph we learn that Adela's mind was "blurred by the heat" (p. 151). Surely, if we demand a naturalistic explanation, we may accept this invitation to infer that Adela, upon entering the close confines of that last cave, "got a sunstroke and went mad," and that her impression that someone had attacked her was hallucinatory. Later on we find a confirmation of this hypothesis coming from the disinterested Professor Godbole. "Suffering," he points out to Fielding with meticulous care, "is merely a matter for the individual. *If a young lady has sunstroke*, that is a matter of no significance to the universe" (p. 178, italics mine).

On the other hand is the supernatural explanation of the incident partaking of the symbolical significance of the caves. Adela enters her

[26] Austin Warren reports that "Dickinson, as well as others, asked Forster, What really happened in the caves?" then declares, "the author does not say" (p. 246).

cave with the problem of love and marriage on her mind. Love is for her "something to think out" and the declaration of having discovered an answer is marriage. What assails her in the cave, however, is beyond thinking out, and her false charge against Aziz is witness to the inadequacy of her means to do so. She had a terrifying experience, hallucinatory to be sure, but nevertheless terrifying. Her only recourse, within the limitations of her mode of behavior, was to eliminate the terror by trying to understand. The intellect took over; the causal pattern was imposed; and Aziz was arrested and brought to trial. Adela was some time recovering. There was the sunstroke, the shock, the cactus needles she had picked up in her precipitous descent of Kawa Dol: "She lay passive beneath their fingers, which developed the shock that had begun in the cave. Hitherto she had not much minded whether she was touched or not: her senses were abnormally inert and *the only contact she anticipated was that of mind*. . . . 'In space things touch, in time things part,' she repeated to herself while the thorns were being extracted—her brain was so weak that she could not decide whether the phrase was a philosophy or a pun" (p. 193, italics mine). Adela was awakening from her experience of contact with an immaterial world and convincing herself of the consequences of living in a world of space and time.

Although she manages the physical recovery, Adela retains ringing in her ears the echo of the caves, and she will not be rid of it until she has withdrawn her charge against Aziz. We see this foreshadowed in Professor Godbole's parable of the Tank of the Dagger. Just as the rajah cannot rid himself of the dagger with which he had murdered his nephew until he has offered water to the cow, so Adela cannot rid herself of the echo until she recognizes the common being of humanity by defaulting on her accusation. However, her own reason and the evidence of the prosecution have justified the false accusation, and thus, in order to make her default honest, she must transcend the sphere of reason. She does so in a vision in which she is released from the limitations of the self, the principle of individuation: "She didn't think what had happened or even remember in the ordinary way of memory, but she returned to the Marabar Hills, and spoke from them across a sort of darkness to Mr. McBride. The fatal day recurred in every detail, but now she was of it and not of it at the same time, and this double relation gave it indescribable splendour" (p. 227). That evening Adela could report to Fielding, "My echo has gone" (p. 239). But neither she nor Fielding was ever able to understand what had really happened at the Marabar. Such things transcend rational explanation, and rational explanation was all that she and Fielding could accept.

Although Adela's experience in the cave carries the story, that of Mrs.

Moore is more complex and more important. Her heightened sensitivity allowed her to grasp what was denied to Adela, and though her vision was not a total one, she captured the essential meaning of the caves. She was not able to explain that meaning to Adela any more than Professor Godbole could describe the caves for Aziz, for the meaning of such an experience transcends the principle of individuation and hence defies all attempts to conceptualize it. Moreover, Mrs. Moore was not the kind to fret over explanations; the experience did not touch her intellect, but her soul, her sense of values. "Suddenly at the edge of her mind, Religion appeared, poor little talkative Christianity, and she knew that all its divine words from 'Let there be light' to 'It is finished' only amounted to 'boum'. Then she was terrified over an area larger than usual; the universe, never comprehensible to her intellect, offered no repose to her soul, the mood of the last two months took definite form at last" (p. 150). Mrs. Moore, on her arrival, had been immediately attracted to India "with its cool nights and acceptable hints of infinity" (p. 158). "To be one with the universe. So dignified and simple" (p. 208). She had not calculated the costs of this union. For her India was a mystery, inscrutable perhaps, but certainly not confused, disorderly, purposeless. And Mrs. Moore liked mysteries; in this she differed from the clear-headed Fielding and Adela. "I do so hate mysteries," said Adela, and Mrs. Moore replied, "I like mysteries, but I rather dislike muddles." "A mystery is only a high-sounding term for a muddle," Fielding declared. "India's a muddle." And Mrs. Moore, unsettled by Fielding's statement, expressed her uneasiness: "India's—Oh, what an alarming idea!" (p. 69). Fielding's statement was shortly thereafter borne in upon her by Godbole's song. To her plaintive question, Godbole replied assuredly that Krishna never does come, and to Mrs. Moore this meant that that state of perfection called Heaven which Christianity shrouds in mystery and promises as a reward for good works is always becoming, never being. In this sense, India is an appeal, not a promise. At once, the justification of moral purpose was undermined. Mrs. Moore grew peevish; her duties became onerous. She had hoped for a glorious union of mankind through love, and her contribution to that endeavor, she felt, lay in assisting the marriage of her children. But Godbole had suggested to her what she was to find confirmed in her experience in the caves—that the costs of being "one with the universe" are the loss of a transcendent sanction for values, the loss of absolute distinctions between good and evil, the loss of that ultimate reward for good works which made her accept duties as bearable, and, finally, the loss of that sublime emotion which comes from contemplating God in the infinitudes.

Such costs were too great. In the cave, the echo spoke out to her of the oneness of all things; it revealed itself to her as a serpent, the universal will, composed (under the principle of individuation) of a manifold of wills, writhing independently, struggling against each other. From that moment forward, she lost all desire for ultimate union; she lost interest in her "duties" to her children; she conceived of life as a game of Patience, always another card to turn, another duty to be done, with no final consummation. The individual will had reasserted itself in her. "What had spoken to her in that scoured-out cavity of the granite? What dwelt in the first of the caves? Something very old and small. Before time, it was before space also. Something snub-nosed, incapable of generosity—the undying worm itself" (p. 208).

But Mrs. Moore's vision, Forster suggests, was not a complete one. As she left Central India on the way to Bombay, there passed before her eyes the fortress at Asirgarh which ten minutes later reappeared seeming to say, "I do not vanish" (p. 209). Here is a kind of permanence not touched by the vision of the caves. And when she set sail "thousands of coconut palms appeared all round the anchorage and climbed the hills to wave her farewell. 'So you thought an echo was India; you took the Marabar caves as final?' they laughed. 'What have we in common with them, or they with Asirgarh? Good-bye!' " (p. 210).

III

Forster's handling of Mrs. Moore is characteristic. As with Adela, with Fielding, with Aziz and Godbole, there is something in her nature which he affirms; but in none of these instances does he affirm without qualification. Thus, if *A Passage to India* may be said to have a theme, may be said to express symbolically some predication about the way life is or ought to be, we cannot expect to find that expression in the person of any of his characters. Nor may we expect to find it by generalizing the outcome of action in the story, for nothing is so apparent as the absence of complete resolution of dramatic conflict. We must, in fact, look beyond the single character and beyond the story itself for the theme, for neither Forster's conception of the form of the novel nor his view of the human predicament allows him to permit a single character or a single element of the novel to pronounce the whole of his theme. Life and the novel are more complex than that, and the novel as a representation of life must speak through all its parts. "Expansion," Forster says of the form of the novel, "that is the idea the novelist must cling to. Not completion. Not rounding off but opening out."[27] Nor is the complete resolution of the conflicts which comprise the plot consistent with his view of life. "The

[27] *Aspects of the Novel*, p. 242.

business man who assumes that this life is everything, and the mystic who asserts that it is nothing, fail, on this side and on that, to hit the truth.... Truth being alive [is] not halfway between anything. It [is] only to be found by continuous excursions into either realm, and though proportion is the final secret, to espouse it at the outset is to insure sterility."[28]

Critics writing on *A Passage to India* have unconsciously deferred to Forster's philosophy of the novel by failing to show anything like unanimity of opinion on its theme. Gertrude M. White would seem to imply that the novel is an espousal of the Hindu religion. Peter Burra declares that "the real theme of the book" is the "friendship of Fielding and Aziz."[29] Rose Macaulay finds the "moral" of the book in the criticism of "the legions of ought and ought not."[30] Some critics find a multiplicity of themes. E. B. C. Jones discovers three, while Lionel Trilling mentions at least half a dozen, perhaps eight. Strangely, in spite of the lack of agreement, none of these conclusions is wholly insupportable. They fail for not being sufficiently comprehensive. It is owing to its comprehensiveness that the statement of Morton D. Zabel, though it was made of Forster's novels in general, seems the most applicable of them all to *A Passage to India*. Forster, he says, "made his object the search for the wholeness of truth; the synthesis of matter and essence, of civilization with its inhibitions and nature with its blind energy, of the fragments and denials on which life is commonly founded and the total vision of reality that man's sloth or cowardice forbids him to unveil" (p. 413). But we must particularize this statement somewhat before it will become significant with respect to *A Passage to India*.

In "Temple" as in "Caves" the dominant symbolism is drawn from the landscape. On the hill overlooking the tank at Mau stands a fortress from which centuries earlier a Mohammedan saint had released prisoners, but, in doing so, had lost his own head. As Forster reports the legend, his head had been severed at the top of the hill, but, disregarding its absence, he had fought his way back to the bottom to report his feat to his mother. This heroic fight had necessitated the erection of two shrines—the Shrine of the Head and the Shrine of the Body. This divided shrine and consequent divided allegiance, Forster implies, is the awkward dichotomy with which the varying plans of salvation by religion have left us—the mutual exclusion of mind and body, spirit and flesh. In effect this description of the physical scene is a restatement of the conflict which has evolved in "Mosque" and "Caves." The Way of Works which we have identified with "Mosque" and its principal character,

[28] *Howards End* (New York, 1948), p. 223.
[29] "The Novels of E. M. Forster," *Nineteenth Century and After* (Nov. 1934), p. 589.
[30] *The Writings of E. M. Forster* (New York, 1938), p. 203.

Aziz, is associated with the Shrine of the Body which stands in Aziz's garden. The Way of Knowledge, which we have identified with "Caves" and the western protagonists, is associated with the Shrine of the Head and its infestation of bees which attack Fielding and Ralph. At the foot of the hill lies the third element of symbolism—the tank at Mau where the ceremony connected with the birth of Krishna is to take place. Needless to say, we have here represented the Hindu factor and the Way of Love, associated throughout the novel with Godbole and, by implication, with his western counterpart, Mrs. Moore.

Over this scene hang the heavy clouds of the monsoon, intermittently wetting the earth, but through them, occasionally, "the friendly sun of the monsoons shone forth and flooded the world with color" (p. 305). These are the symbols of life and fertility, and it is under their influence that the reunion of Aziz and Fielding will take place. The principal event of the long ceremony, the event to which all of the characters will be drawn, is the drowning of the village of Gokul, birthplace of Shri Krishna. Here in the midst of wind and rain, the confusion of crowds, the trumpeting of elephants, the sounding of artillery, thunder and lightning, the boats containing Aziz and Ralph, Fielding and Stella, will collide, upset, dumping them ignominiously into the tank. "That was the Climax," Forster observes, "as far as India admits of one" (p. 315). The fusion of the three ways of life—mosque, caves, and temple—comes to pass in the tank at Mau. Fielding and Aziz, British and Indian, are brought together (though not completely united) under the influence of the Hindu Way of Love.

As Forster moves from mosque to cave and from cave to temple, from the Way of Works to the Way of Knowledge and the Way of Love, his acquiescence is always tentative. We hear the judgment—made quietly and more in the comic spirit than with compassion—"yes, but. . . ." Each of these ways of salvation has something to offer to the whole life, but each also contains the defects of its qualities. Aziz, whom we have taken as representative of the Way of Works, is made charming by his volatile affections, but he is also victimized by the very emotional traits which we find most winning. We see also, and even more distinctly, the limitations of the purely intellectual attitude, the Way of Knowledge, as it is represented, for instance, in Fielding. For all of his well-meaning liberalism, there is something lacking in his nature, something the intelligence cannot supply. "After forty years' experience, he had learnt to manage his life and make the most of it on advanced European lines, had developed his personality, explored his limitations, controlled his passions—and he had done it all without becoming either pedantic or worldly. A creditable achievement, but as the moment passed, he felt he ought to have been working at something else the whole time—he didn't know at what, never would know, never could know, and that was why he felt sad" (p. 191). The moment referred to was the advance of the Marabar Hills moving "graciously towards him like a queen" (p. 191) in the evening sky. This was Fielding's opportunity for mystic vision, missed on this occasion and again thereafter when "he lost his usual sane view of human intercourse, and felt that we exist not in ourselves, but in terms of each others' minds—a notion for which logic offers no support and which had attacked him only once before, the evening after the catastrophe, when from the verandah of the club he saw the fists and fingers of the Marabar swell until they included the whole night sky" (p. 250). "Clarity," we are told, "prevented him from experiencing something else" (p. 118).

Unlike Fielding and Adela, who were blinded by their own clarity of thought, Mrs. Moore achieved full recognition of her failure. "I think everyone fails," she said early in the novel, "but there are so many kinds of failure" (p. 52). And having undergone her experience in the caves, she concluded, "There are different ways of evil and I prefer mine to yours" (p. 205). In short, the Way of Knowledge, whether it be of the sort belonging to Fielding and Adela or that belonging to Mrs. Moore, is not enough: "Though the intellect is our best friend," Forster wrote in his biography of G. Lowes Dickinson, "there are regions whither it cannot guide us" (p. 118).

In the Way of Love, represented in Hindu ceremonies attending the birth of Shri Krishna, Forster again finds inadequacies. Here is no beauty, no taste, no sense of the appropriate; the entire ceremony is a muddle, a frustration of reason and form. Love is a good, Forster seems to say, but not in its extreme nor to the exclusion of all other goods.[31] The final friendship of the protagonists, like "the God to be thrown," is but an emblem of passage, "*a passage not easy, not now, not here, not to be apprehended* except when it is unattainable" (pp. 314–315, italics mine). Passage is the mystical return which can occur only with complete renunciation of the will and utter loss of individuality in union with the whole. Such renunciation and loss is the equivalent of death. Forster does not propose this unhappy extreme: "There was death in the air, but not sadness; a compromise had been made between destiny and desire, and even the heart of man acquiesced" (p. 307). Intimations of passage had occurred to Adela, to Mrs. Moore, to Aziz, and to Fielding himself, but in each instance the experience was momentary, and, to all, ultimately uncongenial. Like the Way of Works and the Way of Knowl-

[31] Cf. *The Hill of Devi*, p. 176.

edge, the Way of Love has its repugnant extreme. And thus, as the novel ends, Fielding and Aziz, whose friendship had been reborn in the tank at Mau, are preserved from consummate union as the hundred voices of the earth speak out and say, "No, not yet" (not in time), and the sky says, "No, not here" (not in space).

Does the novel contain a statement of theme? With all its negations, does it yet affirm some unequivocal truth about the way life is or ought to be? Indeed it does. "Proportion is the final secret," Forster had observed in *Howards End*. Works, knowledge, love—these are the ingredients of the good life, but no one of them is to be affirmed to the exclusion of the others. Nor can that proportion be realized except as the product of vital activity. "Truth being alive [is] not half way between anything." Thus it is only when Fielding is passing through "that exquisite lake" between the extremes of India and England that we learn that "the Mediterranean is the human norm," for here is exemplified "the harmony between the works of man and the earth that upholds them, the civilization that has escaped muddle, the spirit in reasonable form, with flesh and blood subsisting" (p. 282).

IDAHO STATE COLLEGE
Pocatello

Symbolism in *A Passage to India*: 'Temple'

V. A. SHAHANE

This reassessment of E. M. Forster's *A Passage to India*, 1924, while laying stress on the unexplored elements of Forster's symbolism, aims at expounding the significance of the third section of the novel, 'Temple', in a new way. Lionel Trilling, the most brilliant of Forster's critics, says:

> It is not easy to know what to make of the dominant Hinduism of the third section of the novel.[1]

Rose Macaulay offers no analysis in her monograph[2] of this significant aspect of *A Passage to India*. Though it has been suggested that the single theme of *A Passage to India* is 'the chasm between the world of actions and the world of being',[3] or the antithesis 'between Real and not-Real, true and false, being and not-being' or 'the harmonising of the tragic antithesis of mankind' or the artistic exposition of the three well-known Hindu philosophical 'doctrines of Knowledge, Work and Love',[4] I think the problem of the wholeness of truth in relation to *A Passage to India* is not yet fully explored.

A Passage to India is, among other things, a symbolic novel. Of all the critics R. A. Brower[5] has done the greatest justice to this aspect of Forster with special reference to *A Passage to India*. Other critics have merely hinted at the fruitful possibilities of this kind of study. Rex Warner remarks:

> Forster's symbols do deserve study. It is they which make his writings poetical and which give to his later work its peculiar distinction.[6]

Brower's idea of interpreting the novel as symbolic seems to have been, partly, encouraged by Forster himself, though Brower's line of interpretation is different from Forster's suggestion. Forster writes in the 'Author's Notes'[7] to the Everyman edition: 'The three sections — Mosque, Caves, Temple — represent the three seasons' of the Indian Year. R. A. Brower dwells on 'the central design' of Forster's novel, which is 'composed of a group of symbolic metaphors'. Mosque is associated with

---

[1] Lionel Trilling, *E. M. Forster: A Study*, 1944, p. 136.
[2] Rose Macaulay, *The Writings of E. M. Forster*, 1938.
[3] E. K. Brown, 'E. M. Forster and the Contemplative Novel', *University of Toronto Quarterly* III (April, 1934), 349-361.
[4] Glen O. Allen, 'Structure, Symbol and Theme in *A Passage to India*', *PMLA*, Dec. 1955 Vol. LXX.
[5] R. A. Brower, *The Fields of Light: An Experiment in Critical Reading* (New York, 1952), p. 182.
[6] Rex Warner, *E. M. Forster* (London, 1950), p. 18.
[7] E. M. Forster, *A Passage to India* (Everyman, London, 1942), p. ix.

ENGLISH STUDIES, XLIV, December 1963.

Arch, Caves with Echo, Temple with Sky. These symbols have a positive as well as a negative meaning. The positive meaning of the Mosque symbol consists in the possibilities of friendly intercourse between Aziz and Mrs. Moore; Aziz and Fielding. The Mosque episode brings people together, but also alienates them from each other. Adela Quested fails to develop a real, intimate feeling for Ronny Heaslop. Nor does she succeed in coming close to Mrs. Moore. She fails to come to terms with life under the tropical sky. Her failure coincides with the failure of a wider social circle — of the 'Bridge' party. This is the negative aspect of the Mosque symbol.

The symbolic meaning of the Marabar Caves or the echo is complex. It may mean collapse of will and human relationship or it may hint at the idea of nothingness. It implies that ideas of 'mystery' are encountered by those of 'muddle'. The symbol of 'Temple' or sky, in my view, signifies reconciliation and harmony. The 'Mosque' suggests an attempted getting together; the 'caves' indicate frustration and alienation; the 'Temple' signifies reconciliation. In one of the last scenes in 'Temple' Forster alludes to this cycle. Aziz calls Ralph Moore an Oriental:

> Those words — he had said them to Mrs. Moore in the mosque in the beginning of the cycle, from which after so much suffering, he had got free. Never be friends with the English! Mosque, caves, mosque, caves ....[8]

I suggest that in the very first chapter Forster's use of these words is significantly revealed. A pointed reference to the 'fists and fingers' of the Marabar Hills is followed up by alluding to the sky as 'strong and enormous', which 'settles everything'. The sky thus becomes the symbol of 'the universe and of infinity'. This symbol seems to recur in the last scene of the novel and Forster appears to complete the circle. Fielding desires to cement his bond of friendship with Aziz, but the novel ends on a rather sceptical note:

> 'No, not yet', and the sky said, 'No, not there.'[9]

Brower does not investigate why Forster associates the three sections with the three seasons. Forster identifies Mosque with the Indian winter which is a very pleasant season. Against this happy climatic background, Cyril Fielding, the cultured, intelligent, liberal humanist is drawn towards the human and affable Aiziz. The Marabar, which is a very unhappy episode, is associated with the Indian 'Hot Weather'. The earth, scorched by the cruel sun, devoid of all spiritual vegetation cries for water — the life-giving nectar which will restore her to her past glory. Forster associates 'Temple' with 'the Rains'. It means that the spiritual and human waste land will be green again and 'the Marabar will be wiped

---

[8] E. M. Forster, *A Passage to India* (Everyman, London) 1950, p. 272.
[9] *Ibid.*, p. 282.

out.' Forster's own allusions and implicit and explicit references to objects of nature bear testimony to this symbolic interpretation.

A Passage to India has a well-marked-out structure, the three divergent currents 'Mosque', 'Caves', 'Temple', in their symbolic and dramatic import converging on the central stream and giving the novel an organic unity. Forster appears to express his dramatic design, symbolic meaning and ironic attitudes through the medium of social comedy. *A Passage to India* reveals Forster's philosophical attitudes, yet the endeavour to fit it into a philosophical formula, e.g., of the 'Hegelian thesis — antithesis — synthesis', seems to me to be wide of the mark.

A particular aspect of Forster's method in relation to the import of scene-making needs to be clarified. He manipulates scenes and situations and endows them with dramatic or ironic or symbolic significance. There seems to be a curious admixture of the symbolic and the comic. The Herritons go to see an Italian Opera; Lucy Honeychurch visits Santa Croce in Florence; Aziz embarks upon an expedition to the Marabar. The God Pan creates panic in the minds of the phlegmatic, stoical English middle class tourists. The situations are comic in a way, yet they reveal Forster's aim of making 'a poetic communication about life'.[10] Scenes of Godbole's Temple ceremony seem farcical in one way, yet in my view, they have a deep symbolic meaning.[11] This is why David Cecil finds the 'flavour' of a Forster novel 'eminently complex'. I. A. Richards finds something 'odd' about Forster's methods as a novelist which makes him 'on the whole the most puzzling figure in contemporary English letters'.[12]

One may trace a continual development of Forster's symbolic pattern in the short stories and four novels. Though in *A Passage to India*, the conflicts of the inner life are extended to the outer life, yet the old themes continue to nourish the narrative. The third section 'Temple' forms part of the symbolic pattern in Forster.

My main objective is to demonstrate with evidence from the text that R. A. Brower's ideas with reference to 'Temple' are not acceptable. 'Of all the symbols', he writes, 'the Temple seems to me most crudely ironic.'[13] In fact, the opposite is true. The symbol of the 'echo' or the 'Marabar' is surely more crude than that of 'Temple' or 'sky' or 'rain'.

Forster himself has narrated in *The Hill of Devi* the story of Krishna's birth in the *Bhagwad-Purana* which needs no repetition. Forster writes about the Lord's birth in the novel: 'He is, was not, is not, was ...'

---

[10] F. R. Leavis, *The Common Pursuit* (London, 1952), p. 261.

[11] I met Mr. E. M. Forster at King's College, Cambridge on November 17, 1957. The discussion was very pleasant and instructive. Mr. Forster fully agreed with me that the symbolic interpretation of 'Temple' held good. The third section was written with all artistic earnestness and not intended to convey purely comic impressions of the episodes.

[12] I. A. Richards, *'Passage to Forster', The Forum*, December 1927, p. 915.

[13] R. A. Brower, *Ibid.*, p. 195.

Does the Lord Krishna transcend the processes of birth and existence? The Lord is a silver image beside the clay models of Gokul — Krishna's Bethlehem — and the images of His parents on the tray. Kansa (Herod) is the killer of children. Music, cymbals, dancing, continue endlessly. Merriment is obtained at the cost of good taste because 'all spirit as well as all matter must participate in salvation'.

Clashing the cymbals Godbole sings:

> Tukaram, Tukaram
> Thou art my father and mother and everybody.
> Tukaram, Tukaram,
> Thou art my father and mother and everybody.
> Tukaram, Tukaram. . .[14]

He offers obeisance not to God but to Tukaram, the greatest mystic saint of Maharashtra. Tukaram is the exponent of the Bhakti cult, man's union with God through love, which is the central issue in Hindu mysticism. The idea of love as the pathway to God is common to Hinduism and Christianity.

What must be said here is that the whole Hindu festival of the Lord's Birthday is symbolic of love and harmony. It is intended to convey and transmit a note of reconciliation to the sorely distracted characters in the novel. It is not functionless. It brings to bear upon Aziz, Fielding, Adela, Ronny, Stella, Ralph, a feeling of reconciliation, however momentary this might be. This assertion will be supported with evidence from the text. The evidence cited is not merely circumstantial, it has deeper roots.

'Temple' as a symbol of harmony is related in the novel to the Marabar echo as a symbol of evil. We hear the afflicted Adela complaining of the echo. It was the utterance of Mrs. Moore's name which silenced the painful echo.

The relevance of Godbole's worship to the situation at the end of the novel has been hinted by Forster himself. Brower and all other critics have missed this completely:

> *Infinite Love* took upon itself the form of *Shri Krishna,* and saved the world. All sorrow was annihilated, not only for Indians, but for foreigners. . .[15]

Godbole's chanting 'Radhakrishna, Radhakhrishna' and clanging of

---

[14] *A Passage to India,* p. 148.
The original of this song may be found in the *Marathi* language, which is the mother-tongue of Godbole and the Maharajah of Dewas. Forster, though he knew Sir Tukoji and his family intimately, does not probably know Marathi. The original Marathi song is given below:

[15] *A Passage to India,* p. 251.

> Tukaram, Tukaram,
> Tunchi maza bāp, tunchi mazi maya, tunchi sarwȧswȧ maze
> Tukaram, Tukaram,

cymbals might seem amusing to foreigners, though, on another level, they are expressions of a very genuine religious faith intuitively held.

At this stage Forster depicts scenes which are apparently comic on one level, and symbolic on another. The juxtaposition of scenes must be carefully looked into to understand the levels on which Forster's strategy works.

The whole idea of reconciliation and harmony is revealed in stages. The actual events and the places where they occur are equally important since 'all matter' partakes of the process of creating harmony.

The situation at the opening of the section 'Temple' is that Aziz has developed a deep prejudice against Fielding on false presumptions mostly manipulated by Mahmoud Ali. Aziz is not pleased by Godbole's cryptic information regarding Fielding's expected arrival. He thinks Fielding has married Adela and robbed him of the compensation he would have otherwise received from Adela. Fielding's note to Godbole expressing a desire to see the procession kindles in Aziz's mind bitter memories of the past. To escape from this unwelcome situation, Aziz goes with his children for a stroll in the precincts of 'The Shrine of the Head'. 'Author's Notes' say that the Shrines are situated at Dhar.

The whole story of the Muslim saint who sacrificed his body and head for the liberation of prisoners is highly suggestive. He obeyed his mother's words: 'Free prisoners.' We find Aziz imprisoned by his own prejudices against Fielding. Sometimes the fences that surround us are of our own making. Fielding too, in a way, suffers from it. His relations with Stella illustrate it. If the fences are merely racial, they may seem external to the mind. In some cases, they may be more inward and reveal an aspect of the problem of the harmony between body and mind. At least, Fielding is 'up against' some elements in Stella's character. He has grown cold towards Aziz.

Perhaps Godbole has realised this estrangement, though he does not say so explicitly. Yet his action in asking Aziz to guide Fielding (on the pretext that he is busy himself) is secretly animated by the desire to remove the misunderstandings between them.

Quite significantly Forster has brought in Ralph Moore in this episode of the Shrine's Head and the boating scene. Ralph and Stella, as children of Mrs. Moore, have a specified symbolic relevance to the ideas in Aziz's mind.

The scene has a comic level which is observed in the description of Fielding and Ralph pursued by the bees :

> The two visitors entered the octagon, but rushed out at once pursued by some bees. Hither and thither they ran, beating their heads, . . . and out of heaven, as if a plug had been pulled, fell a jolly dollop of rain.[16]

---

[16] *A Passage to India,* p. 261.

Even Aziz's remarks are great fun :

> ... I cannot control them, they are State bees; complain to His Highness of their behaviour.[17]

The symbolic undercurrent is illustrated by the drops of rain. Rain, water, tank, sky are symbols of harmony and quite relevant to Forster's own description of the division of *A Passage to India* into three seasons.

When the holy procession reaches the Mau tank, a prisoner is released. This event is symbolic, and in a way related to the story of *The Shrine of the Head* and emphasises the idea of release from personal and racial bonds. Places and events are equally important.

One must consider the background of the boating scene carefully. At first, Aziz is unsympathetic to Fielding's brother-in-law. He also discourages Fielding from boating in the tank and watching the procession. In fact the oars are missing. But soon Aziz learns that Fielding's brother-in-law is indeed Ralph, Mrs. Moore's son. His mind is released from the prison of prejudices and he offers to go to the Guest House. He calls at the Guest House and secretly reads the letters of Adela, Ronny and Stella. He comes to know that they are getting reconciled and forgetting the past. He gives an embrocation to Ralph. First, Ralph complains that Aziz's hands are 'unkind'. Later Ralph's words, 'Dr. Aziz, we have done you no harm',[18] win him over.

This reconciliation between Ralph and Aziz takes place exactly at the time of the release of the prisoner and the marching of the Lord's procession. Forster's remarks are full of meaning :

> God has *extended* His temple ... Mixed and confused in their passage, the rumours of salvation entered the Guest House ...[19]

Aziz became amiable and 'one kind action was with him always a channel for another'. He told Ralph :

> This is our monsoon — the best weather ... the tanks are full; so they dance; and this is India.[20]

Aziz took Ralph boating in the Mau tank to 'do this one act of homage to Mrs. Moore's son'. The Fieldings had already taken a boat earlier.

Aziz was charmed by the atmosphere and suddenly in the chants of 'Radhakrishna, Radhakrishna' he heard

> almost certainly, the syllables of salvation that had sounded during his trial at Chandrapore.[21]

---

17 *Ibid.*, p. 261.
18 *A Passage to India*, p. 271.
19 *Ibid.*, p. 282.
20 *Ibid.*, p. 273.
21 *Ibid.*, p. 274.

The boating scene can be comic on one level, yet on another level it is deeply symbolic. The collision itself is comic. The situation in which two boats of the two groups collide is entertaining especially so because Stella's 'motions capsized them'. Mrs. Moore's daughtter is instrumental in bringing them together.

The background of the collision and its effect on the minds of those plunged in water are points which lend weight to its symbolic interpretation.

First, the tank of Mau, quite significantly, is the scene of reconciliation. The situation of the tank itself is suggestive. It is spread over an area which seems a sort of link between the place of procession and the Guest House. The sacred images are committed to the deep, thereby giving the tank almost a religious sanctity. It suggests a parallel to the water used for Baptism. At this stage

> The boats had collided with each other. The four outsiders flung out their arms and grappled, with oars and poles sticking out, revolved like a mythical monster in the whirlwind . . .[22]

The effect of the collision is very significant. For some time psychological and racial differences are forgotten and Aziz and Ralph, Fielding and Stella, partake of the joyous experience of harmony:

> The shock was minute, but Stella, nearest to it, shrank into her husband's arms, then reached forward, then flung herself against Aziz, and her motions capsized them.[23]

Forster makes his characters relate their experiences of this boating episode. He himself says:

> This reconciliation was a success, anyhow. After the funny shipwreck there had been no more nonsense or bitterness, and they went back laughingly to their old relationship, as if nothing had happened.[24]

Aziz is reconciled with Adela and writes her a charming letter. His words are significant:

> As I fell into our largest Mau tank under circumstances our other friends will relate, I thought how brave Miss Quested was, and decided to tell her so, despite my imperfect English.[25]

Fielding, the agnostic, is also conscious of the effect of this experience on his wife, Stella. Aziz and Stella believe that 'the Marabar is wiped out'. Fielding speaks to Aziz about Stella:

---

[22] *Ibid.*, p. 275.
[23] *Ibid.*, p. 275.
[24] *A Passage to India*, p. 277.
[25] *Ibid.*, p. 278.

She has ideas I don't share ...
My wife's after something.
I can't explain ... why do my wife and her brother like Hinduism, though they take no interest in its forms ? ...[26]

The boating experience has brought about a sense of intimate companionship between Fielding and Stella. Fielding says:

From her point of view, Mau has been a success. It calmed her — both of them suffered from restlessness. She found something soothing, *some solution of her queer troubles here.*[27]

What was the dissonance? Fielding has become 'physically passionate' and thought that 'his wife did not love him as much as he loved her'. Forster's own comments are significant:

But during the visit to Mau the situation had improved. There seemed a link between them at last ... *In the language of theology, their union had been blessed.*[26]

But the effect of this or other episodes in 'Temple' is not everlasting. It is a procession which must pass. Other elements of actualities of existence intervene — social, racial, political, personal. Aziz and Fielding find themselves unable to cement their bonds of friendship and the novel ends on a sceptical note. Forster's comment is significant:

The divisions of daily life were returning, the shrine had almost shut.[29]

This means that in sounding a sceptical note regarding the Aziz-Fielding relationship, Forster has taken care to explain why the effect of the Temple ceremony is short-lived.

This 'end' of the novel is not 'defeatist' since it shows Forster, not as a moral tutor, but a moral realist. His key symbols visualise what life ought to be, his social comedy modifies the conceptual vision and shows what life really is. Forster visualises that floods of love should 'fructify every hour of life'. He, as a moral realist, also realises that barriers do not get broken easily and the flood of friendship — in the case of Aziz and Fielding — do not fructify 'every hour' of their lives. The values of the inner life are revealed against the background of the impediments of the outer life.

To sum up, the three episodes in 'Temple', (a) Godbole's participation in the Krishna festival, (b) the meeting of Aziz and Ralph in the precincts of the Shrine of the Head, and (c) the boating scene in the Mau tank offer substantial evidence in support of the idea that *A Passage to India*, among other things, is a symbolic novel.

Osmania University,
Hyderabad (India).

V. A. SHAHANE.

---

26 *Ibid.*, pp. 278-9.
27 *Ibid.*, p. 279.
26 *Ibid.*, p. 278.
29 *Ibid.*, p. 281.

Passage To More Than India

by Benita Parry

The aspiration of man to understand himself and his universe has resulted in various systems of belief and codes of behaviour—but also in alienation from his fellow-men within other cultures, and therefore in a more complex bewilderment about his social and spiritual identity. This is the paradox explored in *A Passage to India,* explored by examining the areas of relationship and dissonance between the ancient and enduring patterns of Indian civilization and the more "advanced" patterns of the West. Forster avoids the familiar contrast of the materialist West and the contemplative East, so often the subject of this type of international fiction. He does concern himself with questions about which society more effectively satisfies man's quest for certainty and revelation, but his answers are neither confident, nor entirely spiritual. The book has a deep social and historical sense; the clash of cultures is firmly placed, in the historical situation of a British Raj ruling a subject people at a particular point in time; cultural and political as well as spiritual matters are fully explored by the action; and if East and West are in any way to meet, then Forster considers a change in the external relations between them to be quite as necessary as a revolution in man's restricted spiritual and human responses.

"India's a muddle," says Fielding; and while Forster understands this bewilderment, his own perplexity is more complex than his character's.[1] By Western standards, India is indeed equivocal, intricate, and strange; nothing is identifiable, nothing quite fits, and seen with eyes that take their human norm from the Mediterranean and that conceive of proportion as the ideal of beauty, moderation as the standard of deportment,

[1] In his essay "Syed Ross Masood" (1937), reprinted in *Two Cheers for Democracy* (New York: Harcourt, Brace, and World, Inc., 1951), Forster observes that Syed Ross Masood (the Indian to whom *A Passage to India* is dedicated, and on whom Aziz is modelled) "showed me new horizons and a new civilization and helped me towards the understanding of a continent. Until I met him, India was a vague jumble of rajahs, sahibs, babus, and elephants, and I was not interested in such a jumble: who could be?" If Forster is compared with the tradition of Anglo-Indian fiction, and with a sizable proportion of the memoirs that were produced in the late nineteenth and early twentieth centuries, it is striking how far he gets beyond the amazed evocations of the dark, unknowable, menacing East and of its "colourful" atmosphere.

the excesses of India and Indians must seem grotesque. Reason and form are frustrated; yet India "could it be viewed from the moon" might acquire a "definite outline," and Forster's detached, and sympathetic, perceptions about this ambiguous country bring suggestions of shape to it. Even so, because his is a view from a distance, the obscurities of India remain even while the meanings of its various civilizations are brought into focus.

One particular area of difficulty is the implacable and malignant quality of nature in India, which hardly encourages the Western view that man is in harmony with the earth.[2] Here, man is subject to weather and landscape. The Hot Weather dictates how he shall regard himself and others; people entering the valley by the Marabar Hills seem to have attempted a "feeble invasion of it," just as a train in its vicinity is a "coffin from the scientific north which troubled the scenery four times a day". Significantly, the scenic beauty of India is seldom mentioned in the novel, though we know that Forster was very much aware of it; the hopeless and melancholy plains and a treacherous sun without splendour dominate. The depiction of man in nature's grip is sharpened by the use of natural imagery for social facts and tensions: the unease at the leave-taking after Fielding's tea-party is likened to irritation exuding "from the very soil. Could one have been so petty on a Scotch moor or an Italian alp?" In the opening pages, man is shown as imprisoned in a divided town precariously maintaining itself against the encroachments of nature; ultimately it is the earth and sky which intrude to separate Aziz and Fielding.

The Indian landscape is an essential force in the novel. It seems to confuse distinctions: an elephant looks like a hill, a train like an insect, a patch of field jumps as if it were being fried, a snake is a stick or perhaps a stick is a snake; if the boulders in the heat seem alive, why should a stone not feel? This abolition of barriers between animate and inanimate, and the listing of layers from man through animals to insects, plants and stones, and from birds to the sky and beyond, make meaningful the Hindu view of man as just another creature in the chain of creation, and suggest the possibility that equal value attaches to all things. How are men to accommodate to the indifference of nature, which mocks at their categories and derides their aspirations?[3] Hinduism imitates the

[2] James McConkey, in *The Novels of E.M. Forster* (Ithaca, N.Y.: Cornell University Press, 1957), regards man's alienation from the earth "and hence from ultimate reality" as a fundamental modern dilemma, and so finds Forster's India "the contemporary condition, the separation between all mankind and all earth." But Forster does not see India so abstractly, and recognises the way in which pre-industrial civilizations of the Indian type must have a special relationship with the earth.

[3] Cf. Rabindranath Tagore, *Glimpses of Bengal Selected from the Letters of Rabindranath Tagore: 1885 to 1895* (London: Macmillan and Co., Ltd., 1921). Tagore speaks of the Indian sense of nature belittling man and creating a distinctive passiveness before it.

appearance of the physical world in India, overriding barriers between man and the inarticulate world; and while this allows for subtle speculation on the nature of creation and the transcendental, it short-circuits a scientific understanding of the universe. Hinduism in this sense both matches and perpetuates an undynamic society. Because *A Passage to India* is informed by Forster's Western concern with rootlessness, and the need for harmony and stability, there is conjecture on the value of accommodation—perhaps unchanging India, its material growth stunted by the predominance of a malevolent nature, nurtures modes of thought and feeling which make for greater personal harmony, a more integrated social and spiritual life.

By shifting focus from the mud-like monotony of Chandrapore, where the soaring vegetation is terrifyingly stronger than man or his works, to hints of value in the very immobility and passivity, Forster gives tension to this possibility. Two world views are suggested in a significant passage where the boundaries of a well-ordered mind, Adela Quested's, are identified with the limitations of Western consciousness and priorities. Adela's thoughts about her future in India are accompanied by the rhythm of the train:

> . . . the train half asleep, going nowhere in particular and with no passenger of importance in any of its carriages, the branch-line train, lost on a low embankment between dull fields. Its message—for it had one—avoided her well-equipped mind. Far away behind her, with a shriek that meant business, rushed the Mail, connecting up important towns such as Calcutta and Lahore, where interesting events occur and personalities are developed. She understood that. Unfortunately, India has few important towns. India is the country, fields, fields, then hills, jungle, hills, and more fields. The branch line stops, the road is only practicable for cars to a point, the bullock-carts lumber down the side tracks, paths fray out into the cultivation, and disappear near a splash of red paint. How can the mind take hold of such a country? Generations of invaders have tried, but they remain in exile. The important towns they build are only retreats, their quarrels the malaise of men who cannot find their way home. (p. 136) [4]

An India indifferent to the intentions of the technically advanced intruders, an India with a past remote from anything in recorded history, still evident in a red splash signifying perhaps a god, perhaps a sati, is measured against the "important," the "interesting," the world of "shriek" and "rush." The contrast satirises Western pretensions and bustle; but the scales do not easily reach equilibrium. The sense of the continuity, cohesion, and stability of village life at Mau is balanced by the glimpse of the mild-featured ryots "for whom anything outside their village passed in a dream"; perhaps they have harmonious relationships with each other and their environment, but does not their circumscribed

[4] All page-references are to the American edition of *A Passage to India* published by Harcourt Brace and Co. in 1924.

stagnation diminish them as human beings?[5] The sight of the god-like untouchable punkah-wallah, aloof from and unconscious of his surroundings, seated opposite the westernized assistant-magistrate, Mr. Das, who is "cultivated, self-conscious, and conscientious," jolts Adela Quested into reappraising her assumptions: "Her particular brand of opinions, and the suburban Jehovah who sanctified them—by what right did they claim so much importance in the world, and assume the title of civilization?" (p. 218) This juxtaposition of alternatives is shown without sentimentality: the "god's" blankness is a reduction of his humanity; thrown out by nature in defiance of society's categories, he had been nourished by the city's garbage and "would end on its rubbish heaps." Caste-ridden, poverty-stricken India is not screened from sight; these are the accompaniments of that India where men are not divorced from the earth and have not refashioned their surroundings.

The close relationship between the Indian mind and the Indian landscape throws the weight of the challenge onto the Westerners. Natural disasters, religious injunctions and invasions are accepted by the Hindus; passivity towards conditions imposed by nature or thrust upon them by men provides the strength to resist the punishments of both. So the invaders remain in exile, while the Hindus, here identified with India, are peculiarly victorious:

> The triumphant machine of civilization may suddenly hitch and be immobilized into a car of stone, and at such moments the destiny of the English seems to resemble their predecessors', who also entered the country with intent to refashion it, but were in the end worked into its pattern and covered with its dust. (p. 211)

India's passivity, then, is not absolute; the apparent flabbiness of the Hindus contains their unique activity of passive resistance. Forster presents this, yet equally affirms man's insistence on activity and creation as a true assertion of his humanity; and the images of bowed acquiescence are balanced by those of liberation from the chains of circumstances. It is man's "itch for the seemly" which has transformed the shapeless universe, still potent in the Marabar Hills—which "rise abruptly, insanely, without the proportion that is kept by the wildest hills elsewhere." The emptiness and denial of meaning in the Caves—"Pathos, piety, courage—they exist, but are identical, and so is filth" (p. 149)—are counteracted by the works of man. The abased Indian section of Chandrapore which persists "like some low but indestructible form of life," or "the indestructible life of man and his changing faces, and the houses he has built for

[5] In "Art for Art's Sake" (1949), reprinted in *Two Cheers . . .* , Forster touches again on this problem, which has long interested him: "How can man get into harmony with his surroundings when he is constantly altering them? The future of our race is, in this direction, more unpleasant than we care to admit, and it has sometimes seemed to me that the best chance lies through apathy, uninventiveness, and inertia."

himself and God," which revive Mrs. Moore on her journey to Bombay, are victories against meaninglessness. The use of "indestructible" conveys the toughness and durability of man's triumphs and gives the physical world reality and importance, just as Mrs. Moore's thoughts of the Indian cities she had never seen, and of "the obscurer marvels that had sometimes shone through men's speech: the bilingual rock of Girnar, the statue of Shri Belgola, the ruins of Mandu and Hampi, temples of Khajraha, gardens of Shalimar" (p. 210) are a tribute to human imagination and creative genius.[6] Though the Indian masses appear at first to be without identity, to be inseparable from the natural scene—the inhabitants of Chandrapore seem to be moving mud, the villagers collected round the elephant's feet are the scurf of life—they gradually reveal their potential. During Aziz' trial the moving mud is stirred to anger; the sweepers strike, leaving the commodes of Chandrapore unattended; a new spirit is abroad which the Anglo-Indians, whose official boast it is that they know the "real Indians," cannot understand.

I

Hinduism takes its place at the core of the novel just as it lies at the heart of India. It succeeds and survives because it is relevant to the lives of the people.[7] In the state of Mau, where Western influence is waning, the cultivators, officials, tradesmen, courtiers, and nobles are united in common worship which for them expresses a total outlook and way of life, and which entails a complete, if temporary, spiritual involvement. Their religion is for them a living force, embracing as it does all spirit and all matter and intertwining the secular with the divine—God is apprehended in so many ways that there are gods who own cows and the betal leaf industry and are shareholders in the Asirgarh motor omnibus. Its "myriad of merging gods" (Forster in the essay "The Emperor Babur," 1921, reprinted in *Abinger Harvest*) reflects nature's energies and, unlike the symmetrical injunctions of Islam suitable "to pilgrimages and universities," it is a faith constant with feudalism and agriculture. Like India, which embraces a hundred Indias, Hinduism has grown through assimilating the customs and beliefs of the indigenous peoples and cushioning

[6] Critics like Glen O. Allen, McConkey, and Frederick C. Crews have perhaps overestimated the degree to which Forster stresses the insignificance of human endeavour; he also puts much stress on man's indestructibility and creativity.

[7] Even incidental comments draw on Hindu concepts. Thus, after Aziz' trial the victorious Indians "suffered from the usual disillusionment that attends warfare. The aims of battle and the fruits of conquest are never the same." This is a reference to Arjuna's encounter with Krishna in the *Bhagavad-Gita* (Forster comments on it in his essay "Hymn Before Action" (1912), reprinted in *Abinger Harvest*). Clearly, too, Forster grasped the depth of popular involvement with Hinduism before the great political upsurge of the later twenties; historians have pointed out that the Indian masses only moved decisively when Gandhi appealed to them through Hinduism.

the onslaught of invaders' ideas by partial absorption; and this syncretistic impulse of Indian religious faith is woven into the novel's fabric. In Mau, the Moslem Aziz finds that a Moslem saint is worshipped by Hindus after their fashion and that under their influence the Moslems of the area had grown idolatrous. He is at first scornful and, like Alamgir, longs to purify the place: "But soon he didn't mind, like Akbar." (p. 296) India has tamed the proselytizing zeal of Islam; it triumphs against all comers simply by being; and Hinduism, mirroring India, survives, grows, and influences by undogmatic integration. Mrs. Moore is transformed into "Esmiss Esmoor," a Hindu goddess, just as a century earlier Europeans who had settled in the country occasionally became local deities after death, "not a whole god, perhaps, but part of one, adding an epithet or gesture to what already existed, just as the gods contribute to the great gods, and they to the philosophic Brahm." (p. 257)

India is the nullity of the Caves, and the obscure marvels fashioned by men; the hopeless plains, and the cities of Kashmir and Delhi. Its infinite variety is echoed in the diversity of Hinduism: the incarnation of God as a monkey, God conceived as Krishna sporting with the milkmaids, ascetics who suppress the senses, saddhus who satiate them, the creed of harmlessness to all living things, violent sacrificial rites—all have their place. Hinduism's all-inclusiveness contains a profound apprehension of a world in which good and evil, the ridiculous and the august, cruelty and pacifism coexist. In her moment of anti-vision Mrs. Moore, nurtured in concepts of exclusive truths ("God is Love"), understands the message of the Caves and of India to be: "Everything exists, nothing has value." Hinduism has nothing in common with this nihilism, and the novel moves away from it. Godbole distinguishes between good and evil and defines their nature, and his concepts are played back through the thoughts and reactions of the other characters. He tells Fielding: "All perform a good action, when one is performed, and when an evil action is performed, all perform it. . . . When evil occurs, it expresses the whole of the universe. Similarly when good occurs." (pp. 177, 178) Both Adela and Fielding, as they see evil loose, entering and infecting the lives of all around, as if it had an existence of its own, reach this awareness. No one character in the book is good or evil, and Mrs. Moore and Adela come to realise that they contain these opposites within themselves, just as Hinduism embraces the contest. The eclecticism of Hinduism is all-important; because truth is not conceived as monolithic, varied beliefs are accepted as revealing different aspects of truth; thus contradictions do not exclude a fruitful coexistence. The Caves reconcile ideas both of pacifism and violence. Forster, in his *Paris Review* interview, has called the scene in the Caves a "good substitute for violence" (certainly its impact on Mrs. Moore and Adela *is* violent) but during the trial we learn that the Caves are Jain—the most pacific sect within Hinduism, to whose creed respect for all forms of life is cardinal. Hinduism can accommodate the mystic and the sceptic, the free-thinker and the believer, the ascetic and the hedonist, and perhaps this is its lesson to the world, just as perhaps "the hundred Indias which fuss and squabble so tiresomely are one, and the universe they mirror is one." (p. 263) Yet Forster, who in his essay "Mohammed Iqbal" (1949, reprinted in *Two Cheers For Democracy*) has expressed preference for pantheism rather than the orderliness of Islam, surely fears that the breadth and tolerance of Hinduism (which in *A Passage to India* he imaginatively reconstructs) inevitably carries within itself the seeds of muddle and chaos. This seems evident in his description of the Gokal Ashtami Festival; although the mess is divine and the confusion benign, the great blur lacks an emotional center. "God si Love"—the precise Christian definition is incorporated into the worship to indicate God's universality, but in the process has become muddled. Perhaps exclusion and exclusiveness is the price of accuracy in meaning; perhaps, as the timid missionaries nervously insist, "We must exclude someone from our gathering, or we shall be left with nothing." (p. 38)

Forster, aware of the "conventional conclusion" that India is the home of religion (in *Goldsworthy Lowes Dickinson,* Harcourt, Brace, & World, Inc., New York, 1934), and therefore that India constitutes a special test of man's capacity to respond to the infinite,[8] handles this theme with great complexity. Fielding comments that there is "something in religion that may not be true, but has not yet been sung. . . . Something that the Hindus have perhaps found," (p. 277) and this points to Forster's interest. In the Indian landscape Eternity ceases to be an abstraction and becomes reality, dwarfing man. The Marabar Hills and Caves contain visible remnants of the aeons preceding man's evolution; and this gives a perspective, largely obscured in the West, of the infinitesimal area within which man exists, and of the immensity of ages to come. In the landscape near the hills, "a new quality occurred, a spiritual silence which invaded more senses than the ear. Life went on as usual, but had no consequences, that is to say, sounds did not echo or thoughts develop. . . . Nothing was explained, and yet there was no romance." It is an atmosphere which necessarily impels men to psychic exploration. Lionel Trilling, in his book on Forster, makes the point that Forster has a tenderness for religion because "it expresses, though it does not solve, the human mystery." This mystery is identified with India; and this, together with the variety and many-textured quality of Hinduism, is expressed in Godbole. In part, he is a comic figure, the opaque word-spinner possessed of an inexplicable prescience, a sort of wise fool. But he is also an expression of

[8] This view was held by Whitman, whose poem "Passage to India" (1871) gave Forster his title. Hugh MacLean, in "The Structure of *A Passage to India,*" *The University of Toronto Quarterly,* XXII (January 1953), 151-71, makes much of the connection between Forster and Whitman.

Hinduism, embodying passive resistance, harmonious contradictions. He is a series of characteristics rather than an individual, fulfilling Forster's observation that "there is scarcely anything in that tormented land which fills up the gulf between the illimitable and the inane." ("Pan," 1922, reprinted in *Abinger Harvest.*) His appearance suggests harmony, "as if he had reconciled the products of East and West, mental as well as physical, and could never be discomposed." (pp. 72-73) Yet from the West he has taken only the externals, the English language and socks with clocks. Aloof and tranquil, he embodies an India which tolerated the invaders but submitted only physically to them. The thoughts and motives of the enigmatic Deccani Brahman remain obscure, and the presentation of these is prefaced by "as if" and "perhaps." That Godbole is saturated with the traditions and concepts of the continent is made vivid by the reference to him as "Ancient Night," with its implication of a mind which has inherited and contains the memory of an India interminably old. Godbole's energies are directed towards developing the life of the spirit, and this philosophy makes him ill-equipped for practical tasks; he can neither catch a train nor establish the King Emperor George V High School at Mau. He epitomises an abstract stance: he who must eat apart from the outcastes and eliminate their touch by bathing, who lives within "the sects and clans" of Hinduism, responds warmly to Aziz' enlightened poem acclaiming internationalism: "Ah, that is bhakti; ah, my young friend, that is different and very good. Ah, India, who seems not to move, will go straight there while the other nations waste their time." (p. 293) Godbole accommodates both a speculative, flexible, and tolerant philosophy and acceptance of its earthly expression in a caste-divided social sytem; he accepts internationalism in his head just as Hinduism obliterates identities, eliminates suffering, and loves all things in the abstract. Hinduism contains within itself both the recognition and acceptance of divisions as well as the impulse to eliminate barriers and embrace all; the religious injunctions commit men to untouchability, and the holy festival includes in its ritual "the moment of the Despised and the Rejected." (p. 305)

Hinduism is the central factor in India; but the Moslems too have been integrated into a communal Oriental civilization in which all Indians share and from which the West is excluded. While Godbole and Aziz personify the divisions within India, they also represent its unity. Both want the pre-British past back; Aziz dreams of the vanished Moghul Empire, Godbole's heritage is the great days of the Mahrattas. Both are poets and can be transported from the confines of the immediate, and there is a striking similarity in the descriptions of these flights and their disruption. In the heated state of his religious ecstasy, Godbole strives to impel towards completeness the images which come unsolicited to his mind, but he fails with the stone: "logic and conscious effort had seduced, he came back to the strip of red carpet and discovered that he was dancing upon it." (p. 286) Similarly, across the surface of Aziz' mind, always responsive to the unseen, flit thoughts of Mecca, the Friend, his wife, "and then the whole semi-mystic, semi-sensuous overturn, so characteristic of his spiritual life, came to end like a landslip and rested in its due place, and he found himself riding in the jungle with his dear Cyril." (p. 320) While Forster persuades us to accept that Mrs. Moore and Ralph Moore are Orientals, he *shows* that Aziz, the Moslem, and Godbole, the Hindu, are. Godbole's invocations to the God Krishna, who neglects to Come, is akin to Aziz' recital of poetry which voices "our loneliness . . . , our isolation, our need for the Friend [the Persian expression for God] who never comes yet is not entirely disproved." (p. 106) There are recurring references to the difficulties of entente between Hindus and Moslems; yet it is clear that they share more with each other than with the West–the Moslem "restfulness of gesture—it is the Peace that passeth Understanding, after all, it is the social equivalent of Yoga. When the whirring of action ceases, it becomes visible, and reveals a civilization which the West can disturb but will never acquire." (pp. 251-52) Aziz' experiences at the hands of the Anglo-Indians drive him towards a conscious identification with his common civilization; he expresses his nationalism in an illogical, unstable and contradictory way which, because it is in character, is wholly convincing. He comes to have a genuine, if abstract, hatred for the English—"I am an Indian at last," he thinks, (p. 293) and to the British he says: "I do not want you, I do not want one of you in my private life, with my dying breath I say it." (p. 302) But this does not prevent him from responding again to Fielding and to Mrs. Moore's children. Though he continues to write poems with bulbuls and roses, lamenting the decay of Islam, he longs to compose a song of the future which would transcend creed and be acclaimed by the multitudes. He moves "towards the vague and bulky figure of a mother-land. He was without natural affection for the land of his birth, but the Marabar Hills drove him to it. Half closing his eyes, he attempted to love India." (p. 268) While retaining his bored cynicism at their religion, and while still finding it difficult to like them, Aziz determines to move closer to Hindus, and becomes aware that Hinduism is, in a fundamental sense, India. His explanations to Ralph Moore during the Krishna festival suggest the flux of his responses—in his use of "our" or "my" and "they" or "their" is revealed both the need and desire to identify himself with a motherland, and his continuing sense of estrangement from Hindus:

> This is our monsoon, the best weather. . . . How I wish she [Mrs. Moore] could have seen them, our rains. Now is the time when all things are happy, young and old. They are happy out there with their savage noise, though we cannot follow them; the tanks are all full so they dance, and this is India. I wish you were not with officials, then I would show you my country. (p. 312)

Aziz of course continues to love Islam but he gains insight into its equivocal role in India:

> Of what help, in this latitude and hour, are the glories of Cordova and Samarcand? They have gone, and while we lament them the English occupy Delhi and exclude us from East Africa. Islam itself, though true, throws cross-lights over the path to freedom." (p. 268)

II

In blind arrogance towards the Oriental civilizations stand the Anglo-Indians, their attitudes epitomizing the hostility which a self-contained group can display towards alien concepts and customs. Any real intercourse with India is to them unthinkable, and despite their cry of bringing "civilization," their purpose is not to share their ideas and techniques with Indians, but to administer a subject people. Official relationships take the place of human ones, social intimacy is taboo; those Indians who are dependent on the good will of the Raj must fawn and be patronized by the British officials and humiliated by their wives. In a land where excessive heat is part of the seasons' cycle, the British "circulate like an ice-stream," and talking of them brings a "wintry surface" to the conversation of the Moslems. The Anglo-Indian divorcement from the land and its peoples is one of the cliches of the Indian services; its members live amidst scenery they do not understand, in a country they see as poisonous and intending evil against them. Lacking in intellectual curiosity, their range of responses corsetted, they have little insight into their motives and are unaware of the gap between the pretentious myth they have evolved about themselves and the smallness of their stale and ungenerous views. Themselves caught in the net which Britain has thrown over India, they give vent to the frustrated bewilderment lying behind official boasts of their indispensability in emotional brutality towards Indians and nonconformists in their own ranks. The presence of erotic obsessions in their image of Indians is made explicit; furtive fantasies about the prowess and perversions which they believe are part of Indians' sexual habits lie in the undergrowth of their attitudes—consider the remarks of Major Callendar and McBryde, and the expression of Adela's hallucination,[9] at a point when she is bending towards accepting Anglo-India. Behind their calculated alienation from the land lies a fear that India will discompose

[9] Following a review of the novel in the *New Statesman and Nation* (August 16, 1924) a correspondent, E. A. Horne of Patna, offered this ingenious explanation of what had happened in the Caves: because of his sexual vanity and physical obsessions, Aziz, thrown off balance by Adela's question about the number of his wives, suffers the hallucination and communicates it to Adela. As Hamidullah ironically says when he hears Adela and Fielding conjecturing on her experience, 'There are one hundred and seventy million Indians in this notable peninsula, and of course one or other of them entered the cave. Of course some Indian is the culprit, we must never doubt that.' Adela's fears closely resemble those expressed by Anglo-Indian lady-novelists writing in the early decades of the century.

their codes and values. India does destroy Mrs. Moore's tidy view of the world, and it unbalances Adela; she who refuses to believe in the Hot Weather is defeated by the Indian sun, and she comes to realise that she must return to an environment in which her mould of responses is relevant: "I am not astray in England. I fit in there—no, don't think I shall do harm in England," (p. 262) she tells Fielding.

The social and political elements of *A Passage to India* are important, though they have been somewhat overstressed in much of the early criticism. To read the book as a social document about the British in India, and the Indians in British India, does stunt an appraisal of its complexities of meaning; but the political insights should not be ignored,[10] for the pressures of imperialism are very much involved in the development of characters and relationships and in the shaping of the area and nature of contact between the civilizations represented. It is not only the dissimilarities of the cultures which inhibit understanding and interflow, but a particular insensitivity in the English, which generates unease, mistrust, and a sense of inferiority in the Indians. In the relationship so spontaneously and effortlessly established between Aziz and Mrs. Moore, more is stated than explored, and we do not here see an effective contact between the cultures. Far more satisfying in this respect is the friendship between Fielding and Aziz. The ebb and flow of their relationship is disturbed by differences of background and values and by the clash of standards on beauty, propriety, and emotional expression—"A pause in the wrong place, an intonation misunderstood, and a whole conversation went awry." (p. 274) But the primary barrier to their communication is that Fielding is one of the British in India and Aziz a member of a subject people.[11] Yet they do have an interlude of friendship before India intervenes to separate them, and both, having previously shied away from politics, now assume firmer positions within the divisions, Fielding with Anglo-India, Aziz with Indian nationalism. This divisive tendency in the book is very evident, and it creates difficulties for those critics who suggest that the novel is an affirmation of proportion, as the truth about the

[10] In *E.M. Forster: A Tribute* (New York: Harcourt, Brace, & World, Inc., 1964), edited by K. Natwar Singh, Forster is reported as saying of the political impact of the novel: "It had some political influence—it caused people to think of the link between India and Britain and to doubt if that link was altogether of a healthy nature. The influence was not intended; I was interested in the story of the characters. But I welcomed it." And Forster's understanding of the political forces playing upon his characters is deep—particularly in his understanding of the political role of the Moslems, sadly placed between a potentially powerful Hindu majority and the British Raj. However, for a dissenting view see Nirad C. Chaudhuri, "Passage to and from India," *Encounter,* II (June 1954), 19-24.

[11] Though it is true that there are much more fundamental differences than political ones between East and West, there are quite evidently political pressures distorting the relationship between Aziz and Fielding, as Arnold Kettle points out in his essay on the novel in his *An Introduction to the English Novel* (Volume 2). (London: Hutchinson University Library, 1953).

way life is or ought to be.[12] John Beer argues, more aptly, that the point of the novel lies "not in an assertion of normality but in an exploration of extremes. And this exploration is not simply social or political. Further issues are involved, which reflect Forster's basic preoccupation as a thinker, and his own experience in India." [13]

This is surely true. Fielding, who epitomizes normality and proportion (his discontent appears to be a temporary aberration), emerges as spiritually incomplete and ready to compromise with a milieu he had formerly despised. The letter to him from Heaslop indicates this retreat: "I'm relieved you feel able to come into line with the Oppressors of India to some extent." (p. 307) If proportion is, as Allen suggests, "the final secret," then how poor final secrets are, and perhaps this is the implication Forster intends. Despite Fielding's belief that the world "is a globe of men who are trying to reach one another and can best do so by the help of good will plus culture and intelligence," (p. 62) he prefers to "slink" through India and regrets having to take sides against the Anglo-Indians, whose very presence is a violation of his creed. The accusation against Aziz and its aftermath does lead him to take a stand and does involve him in doubts and dissatisfaction, but he returns to normality and ultimately his past heroism over Aziz seems "a momento, a trophy." The inconsistency and extravagances of Aziz, his need for friendship, affection, sensuality, and spiritual experiences, make him the most complete character in the novel. His volatile lack of proportion—"Is emotion a sack of potatoes, so much the pound, to be measured out? Am I a machine?"—is more attractive than Fielding's prim reprimand, "Your emotions never seem in proportion to their objects." (p. 254) Forster is aware, it seems, both of the serenity of moderation and of its incompleteness.

The same sense of incompleteness, of personal limitation seen both in national and in general human terms, is surely present in the treatment of the spiritual theme. Trilling tells us that it is not easy to know what to make of the dominant Hinduism in the third section of the novel; and answers to the problem have come to assume a central place in critical interpretations. Gertrude M. White follows Trilling in suggesting that the major theme is that of "fission and fusion; of separateness and desired union," but goes beyond his cautious recognition of Hinduism as "the vision in which the arbitrary human barriers sink before the extinction of all things," to an affirmation of it as "a prophetic vision, for what happens in 'Temple' is reconciliation on the human level." [14] Glen O.

[12] See for instance Glen O. Allen's argument, in "Structure, Symbol, and Theme in E.M. Forster's *A Passage to India*," *PMLA*, LXX, December 1955, 934-54.

[13] In *The Achievement of E.M. Forster* (London: Chatto & Windus, Ltd., 1962).

[14] Gertrude M. White, "*A Passage to India:* Analysis and Revaluation," *PMLA*, LXVIII, September 1953, 652, where she holds that Godbole stands for "the union in reality of all men, whether they will or no." And V.A. Shanane, in his *E.M. Forster: A Reassessment* (Delhi: Kitab Mahal, 1963), goes one stage further and claims Forster for

Allen and James M. McConkey have subjected the words describing the atmosphere in the caves to semantic analysis, finding parallels between the text and Hindu Scriptures.[15] While McConkey points out that Forster is not a mystic, and warns against overemphasising the importance of Hinduism in the book, observing, like Trilling, that Forster does not so much accept Hinduism as select those aspects which have the greatest affinity to his own attitudes, he does give prominence to the metaphysical strain, finding in Godbole the true prophetic character and the character-equivalent of the Forsterian voice. Yet the tone of the transcendental allusions is tentative and undefined, moving between uncertainty and whimsicality. Forster's hesitant suggestions should not be read as affirmations, and the irony in his voice should be considered. A squirrel with a mangy tail whose squeals "were in tune with the infinite, no doubt, but not attractive except to other squirrels," (p. 114) undermines the portent of absolutes. Godbole's significant and poignant invocation to Krishna is reduced to bathos by its application to the inferior countryside—"In vain did each item in it call out, 'Come, come.' There was not enough god to go round." (pp. 87-88)

That which lies beyond man's vision and understanding is conveyed as without attributes: the farther distance beyond the blue sky is "beyond colour," beyond the remotest echo in the vistas which evade Mrs. Moore's understanding is silence. "Beyond the sky must not there be something that overarches all the skies, more impartial even than they? Beyond which again. . . ." (p. 40) This suggests the vastness of what is still unknown, and perhaps unknowable, to man, rather than, as McConkey maintains, the order and harmony of unifying reality. When hints of the transcendental serve to indicate man's dissatisfaction with the limits of his knowledge and understanding, and to affirm his need to push back the boundaries of his perceptions by science, art, and philosophy, these merge with related themes of human insistence on inventing meanings in the universe. Man's capacity for curiosity and the boundless possibilities of his imagination must lead him to assume that there are always further realms to be penetrated, that there are systems and laws governing the universe and society which he has not yet discerned. It is the incompleteness in man's comprehension which makes it impossible for him to accept death and drives him to seek some form of immortality; Aziz, whose belief in the life to come is infirm, is solaced by the knowledge that

---

Brahman mysticism, seeing the "Temple" section as a final solution to the problem presented.

[15] Glen O. Allen observes that there are, in the Hindu scriptures, references to Atman and Brahman, the Self and the Not-Self, dwelling "in the cave"; he also sees the similarity between Forster's "Boum" and the mystical symbol "Om," the pronunciation of and meditation on which is part of the discipline of this seeking Brahman. McConkey acknowledges this argument and sees Forster as intending the emptiness of the caves to represent the absolute Brahman . . . while the echo represents Mrs. Moore's incomplete awareness of that absolute.

he will live on in his children, while Fielding, an atheist, aspires to leave a thought behind.

The portrayal of Fielding and Adela as persons confronted with the awareness of their own limitations is fully realised: "Were there worlds beyond which they could never touch, or did all that is possible enter their consciousness? They could not tell. . . . They had not the apparatus for judging." (p. 263) But does anyone possess the apparatus? Herein lies a central difficulty of the novel, one which has created much critical discussion and has led to enormous variations of reading, frequently tempting critics to see Forster as *almost* a Christian, *almost* a Catholic, *almost* a Hindu. For though Mrs. Moore does not attain the desired oneness with the universe, and Professor Godbole's spiritual aspirations to reach unity with God are frustrated, both of these failures are converted by sleight of hand to imply triumphs. The evil released by the Marabar is driven back by Godbole's cult of love, and Mrs. Moore reemerges after her death as a benign influence, guiding Adela to retract her wrongful accusation and Aziz to forgive his persecution. And in the scene of meeting between Mrs. Moore's son Ralph and Aziz there are intimations of her mysterious continuation. Ernest Beaumont has called Mrs. Moore a "strange mystic" and has commented that her intercessory role is a disquieting aspect of her portrayal; she represents a "somewhat dubious supernatural." [16] To critics who do not see the strong visionary concern of the novel, this scene can be especially puzzling; to those who do, it still presents a problem. F.R. Leavis points out that in the first part of the book Mrs. Moore is an ordinary character, but she becomes after her death "a vague pervasive suggestion of mystery." His objection is that it is "all too easy. It amounts to little more than saying, 'There may be something in it,' but has the effect of taking itself for a good deal more." [17] Forster has always been interested in the question of human continuity; it is within the pattern of his figurative writing that he should be so now. What, I think, worries us is that Forster asks us to suspend disbelief in the operation of mysteries without quite trusting in them himself.

Because of such difficulties, because *A Passage to India* is so difficult and intricate a book, critics will continue to debate its meaning. But it does seem important to single out, as I have tried to, one important feature—that the book is an interpretation of India, traditionally a land of mysteries and muddles, and an interpretation of its impact on those who live in it and on the aliens who come to it. Forster—working in what is in fact a traditional genre, the Anglo-Indian novel—advances it as a form far beyond a simple interpretation. He shows the land as challeng-

[16] Ernest Beaumont, "Mr. E.M. Forster's Strange Mystics," *The Dublin Review*, 453 (Third Quarter 1951), 41-51.

[17] F.R. Leavis, "E.M. Forster" in *The Common Pursuit* (London: Chatto & Windus, Ltd., 1952), pp. 261-77.

ing to the stranger—a land threatening what is hollow in his beliefs and incomplete in his outlook—and makes the experience a severe moral test, a test in encountering transcendence. It is an international novel which, like many such novels, challenges the characters with larger views than they have known. And Forster's judgment seems to be that, if East and West cannot meet, this is evidence of the limitations of man. Yet it would seem that he does not regard them as immutable; his hope, the hope of the novel, is surely that the final "No, not yet" can be transcended.

The Last Movement of the Symphony

K. W. Gransden

The final section begins: the theme of the last movement of the symphony is stated:

> Some hundreds of miles westward of the Marabar caves, and two years later in time, Professor Narayan Godbole stands in the presence of God. God is not born yet—that will occur at midnight—but He has also been born centuries ago, nor can He ever be born, because He is the Lord of the Universe, who transcends human processes.

In the superb description of the Krishna festival which follows, there are still occasional tones of light-heartedness, even ludicrousness, reminiscent of the corresponding description in *The Hill of Devi* where the central figure is Forster himself—a sceptical though sympathetic Western liberal enjoying an impressive spectacle and a not-too-serious religious romp: and it is right that such elements should be retained here, for they are part of Hindu inclusiveness, which does not mind a joke: "by sacrificing good taste this worship achieves what Christianity has shirked: the inclusion of merriment." Thus the spectacle may be amusing, and may even be seen through Western eyes to be amusing, as when we are told that the local draughtsman's spelling of the English slogan contained "an unfortunate slip":

God si love.

But power is lent to the description through the presence of Godbole, the Hindu believer.

At the festival only Hindus matter: Moslems and English are equally unimportant, equally outsiders. The festival is a muddle in their eyes, just as the caves were a muddle: yet the festival is also "the triumph of India";

if understanding is to be sought, it must be sought here; if the caves raised questions, only the temple can answer them: neither the mosque nor the church, with their personal, romantic creeds, are adequate. At Gokal Ashtami form and reason are outraged—the band plays selections from English musical comedy; "God si love." "Is this," asks the author, "the final message of India?" Mrs Moore's tentative words, spoken to her son two years before, have been deformed but they have not been lost. Details may be absurd, personalities warped, but the Hindu worshippers, when they see the image of God, take on

> a beauty in which there was nothing personal, for it caused them all to resemble each other during the moment of its indwelling.[19]

The divine removes differences, annihilates distinctions: Mrs Moore's vision, the echo in the cave, was true: at the moment of the birth "infinite love saved the world" and sorrow was ended, not just for Indians, but for "foreigners, birds, caves, railways, and the stars." Godbole's religion is absolutely inclusive; all creation is one, and shares in joy. During this, his spiritual climax, Godbole again has a vision of Mrs Moore "and round her faintly clinging forms of trouble." "It made no difference whether she was a trick of his memory or a telepathic appeal."[20] She is a part of infinite love; human and divine are interchangeable; no one and nothing is rejected. Godbole's humility is contrasted with the pride of the active characters; the only other character in the book who wants nothing for herself is Mrs Moore. In the pouring rain—for the rainy season has come—the fragments float together, and the rain washes over the world, recreates and unifies it, bringing refreshment, and the semblance at least of a new start: it is the happy time of the Indian year, the time of reconciliation and relaxation.

Godbole connects everything, though not as the West

connects. Only Hinduism, indiscriminating in its hocus-pocus and butter-smearing horse-play, its joyful belief in the universal, can comprehend and assimilate the wisp of hay, the echo in the cave. If you widen the context sufficiently, you will embrace the whole of creation, not just the "civilised" Western minority. Aziz and Fielding have taken their stand on enlightenment; when it fails, the part, defeated. Both are vigorous passionate men who pay, at best, lip-service to an imported, alien religion. But Hinduism, an ancient religion flourishing in an ancient part of the earth, implies that the transient emotions which beset us are in the long run unimportant. The influence of Mrs Moore, the wisdom of Godbole, become more important than the passions they have witnessed and ultimately disclaimed.

As a character-creation, the enigmatic Godbole seems to have a different kind of life from that of Aziz: but Forster has Hindu as well as Moslem friends, and Godbole is probably, like Aziz, a composite portrait. He is certainly assimilable in the context of Forster's total work, and much more convincing in his setting than that earlier saint and guardian, Mr Emerson, had been in his. Godbole is the mouthpiece of the contemplative life; he practises universal love, and to love everything is in a sense to love nothing; he surrenders his own identity to that of love, which he sees as the right use of the self. To him love is not romance but ritual, not self-expression but self-effacement, not desire but service.

While the festival is deploying its esemplastic power, we return to the unbelievers, the active characters, Aziz and Fielding, still muddled and suffering. Aziz has come to Mau to escape the English and is now doctor to the Ruler. He has ceased to open Fielding's letters since he received one beginning " 'I am to marry someone whom you know'," and read no further, assuming this to be Miss Quested. But Fielding arrives at Mau on a visit—Godbole knew, but had said nothing, just as he had known the identity of Fielding's wife and said nothing. She is Stella, Mrs Moore's daughter; and with Fielding now is Ralph Moore, who brings Aziz and Fielding together for the last time, and to whom Aziz says:

'Can you always tell when a stranger is your friend?'
'Yes.'
'Then you are an Oriental.'[21]

The words of the mosque are repeated, the cycle is closed. Despite his suffering, Aziz, understanding now and forgiving, cannot resist a fresh act of love, towards the old woman who has in some strange way stolen his heart and who has now sent her son to speak for her once more. The final message of India and the final message of Mrs Moore are the same: God is love, God si love; mosque, cave, temple, romantic, appalling, or divine, it all amounts to the same, for in all the heart and the spirit speak, not the mind.

The book ends with a last ride together by Aziz and Fielding. The festival is over, "the divisions of daily life are returning." Religion has brought Fielding and Aziz together again: not theirs, but India's, Godbole's, Mrs Moore's; but with the withdrawal of its beneficent influence facts and differences assert themselves again.

'Why can't we be friends now? . . . It's what I want. It's what you want.'

But the horses didn't want it—they swerved apart; the earth didn't want it, sending up rocks through which riders must pass single file; the temples, the tank, the jail, the palace, the birds, the carrion, the Guest House, that came into view as they issued from the gap and saw Mau beneath; they didn't want it, they said in their hundred voices: 'No, not yet,' and the sky said: 'No, not there.'

With these words the novel ends, under the same hostile sky which had looked down on Chandrapore and the Marabar at the beginning. What had been unified by the spirit of Hinduism, in whose vocabulary "nothing" and "everything" are interchangeable and God is praised without attributes, suffers fragmentation again. What seems to be proposed in this beautiful, meticulously constructed pattern, is an endless process of sundering and reconciliation; the eternal need of the practical, the romantic, the individual, to submit itself to the collective, the inclusive, the self-transcending. And fragmentation, collapse, may destroy the one, but the fragments of that one can in some mystical way be reassembled; Mrs Moore's collapse at the caves, her vision of the hollowness of things, was something she personally could not survive; yet her influence survives the collapse, her perception of the collapse is accompanied by a realisation that collapse does not exclude renewal: in Hinduism the creator and the destroyer are two aspects of the divine.

A Passage to India seems to say the last word (not technically as Joyce seemed to) but spiritually, emotionally, morally: it drained a whole tradition to the dregs, and we are left with the alternative of contemplating an empty cup or refilling it again from the past. The novel poses infinite speculations. How far is Forster offering—and not just within the Indian framework of the story—the vague mysticism of Hinduism as a possible general corrective to the limitations of individualism, an all-inclusive salvation for a world doomed to fragmentation by its own ignorance and selfishness? How far is his final message a despairing judgment on the thrust and assertiveness of Western man since the Renaissance? The terrifying insights of the caves, the joyous ones of the temple, seem to be put forward as not only morally better but as more sensible than the constantly failing simplifications, the crude techniques of the will to power.

It is as if Forster finally assumes the role of one of his own guardians—Emerson, Ruth, Mrs Moore, Godbole—all of them elderly, their *mana* remaining though their vitality is spent, all of them slipping away from the struggle. Forster had written four of his five novels in about six years, an extraordinary concentration of creative energy in a time of hope, the swimmer on the crest of the wave. Suddenly the swimmer, who had seemed to have everything—style, poise, staying-power, knowledge of the currents and love of the sea—found himself out of his depths, and turned to the shore. He was not the only one. "When the crash comes nothing is any good. After it—if there is any after—the task of civilisation will be carried on by people whose training has been different from my own."[22] These words were written at the end of the nineteen-thirties, but might be as true of the nineteen-twenties, when the world Forster had interpreted and criticised with such sympathy had already crashed. He tried other novels but set them aside; I quoted from one earlier in this chapter, and part of another, *Arctic Summer*, was read by the author at the Aldeborough Festival of 1951. Of this fragment, which has never been printed, Forster has said:

> I got my antithesis all right, the antithesis between the civilised man who hopes for an arctic summer in which there is time to get things done, and the heroic man. But I had not settled what is going to happen. . . .[23]

Forster's novels have all been contrived, constructed: the moralist has always put down the required antithesis and then summoned the narrative artist to give them life. It was not the moralist in Forster who failed, but the narrative artist, without whom the creative processes could not take place. The artist retired, the moralist went on alone, the player became a commentator. The novelist may have been worried and pessimistic about making further sense of life, but the critic by definition remains an optimist and goes on searching for order however chaotic and unintelligible things have become outside.

Notes on Contributors

GLEN O. ALLEN, American critic. Professor of English, Idaho State College, Pocatello, Idaho.

TED E. BOYLE, American critic. Associate Professor of English, Southern Illinois University, Carbondale, Illinois. Author of *Symbol and Meaning in the Fiction of Joseph Conrad.*

NIRAD C. CHAUDHURI, Indian literary and social critic. Author of *The Autobiography of an Unknown Indian* and *Passage to England.*

LOUISE DAUNER, American critic. Associate Professor of English, Indiana University, Indianapolis, Indiana.

K. W. GRANSDEN, English critic, poet, and editor. Deputy Editor of *The Listener.* Author of *Any Day* (collected poems) and *E. M. Forster.*

KEITH HOLLINGSWORTH, American critic. Professor of English, Wayne State University, Detroit, Michigan. Author of *The Newgate Novel, 1830–1847: Bulwer, Ainsworth, Dickens and Thackeray* and "Freud and the Riddle of *Mrs. Dalloway*" in *Studies in Honor of John Wilcox.*

HUGH N. MACLEAN, American critic. Professor of English, State University of New York at Albany, Albany, New York.

JAMES McCONKEY, American critic. Professor of English, Cornell University, Ithaca, New York. Author of *The Novels of E. M. Forster.*

EDWIN NIERENBERG, American critic and short story writer. Associate Professor of English, San Francisco State College, San Francisco, California.

BENITA PARRY, English critic and historian. Research Fellow (British Writings on India), Department of History, The University of Birmingham, Birmingham, England.

V. A. SHAHANE, Indian critic and short story writer. Professor of English, Osmania University, Hyderabad, India; Visiting Professor, Wisconsin State University, La Crosse, Wisconsin. Author of "E. M. Forster's Place in the Novel Tradition" (Doctoral dissertation, 1957, University of Leeds) and *E. M. Forster—A Reassessment.*

DAVID SHUSTERMAN, American critic. Associate Professor of English, Indiana University, The Southeastern Campus, Jeffersonville, Indiana. Author of *The Quest for Certitude in E. M. Forster's Fiction.*

GEORGE H. THOMSON, American critic. Professor of English, Mount Allison University, New Brunswick, Canada; Visiting Professor, Wayne State University, Detroit, Michigan. Author of *The Fiction of E. M. Forster*.

GERTRUDE M. WHITE, American critic. Professor of English Literature, University of Oakland, Rochester, Michigan.